William Carew Hazlitt

Shakespeare Jest-Books

Reprints of the early and rare jest-books supposed to have been used by Shakespeare

William Carew Hazlitt

Shakespeare Jest-Books
Reprints of the early and rare jest-books supposed to have been used by Shakespeare

ISBN/EAN: 9783744748414

Printed in Europe, USA, Canada, Australia, Japan

Cover: Foto ©Thomas Meinert / pixelio.de

More available books at **www.hansebooks.com**

Shakespeare Jest-Books;

REPRINTS OF THE EARLY
AND VERY RARE JEST-BOOKS SUPPOSED TO
HAVE BEEN USED BY SHAKESPEARE.

[Vol. 1]

I.

A Hundred Mery Talys,

FROM THE ONLY KNOWN COPY.

II.

Mery Tales and Quicke Answeres,

FROM THE RARE EDITION OF 1567.

Edited, with Introduction and Notes,
BY
W. CAREW HAZLITT,
OF THE INNER TEMPLE, BARRISTER-AT-LAW.

—— *That I was disdainful,—and that
I had my good wit out of the Hundred Merry Tales.*
BEATRICE, in Much Ado about Nothing.

LONDON:
WILLIS & SOTHERAN, 136, STRAND.
MDCCCLXIV.

¶ A C, mery
Talys.

The Table.

	PAGE
¶ Of him that said there were but two commandementes. i.	11
¶ Of the wyfe who lay with her prentys and caused him to beate her husbande disguised in her rayment. ii.	12
¶ Of John Adroyns in the dyuyls apparell. iii.	14
¶ Of the Ryche man and his two sonnes. iv.	18
¶ Of the Cockolde who gained a Ring by his iudgment. v.	19
¶ Of the scoler that gave his shoes to cloute. vi.	20
¶ Of him that said that a womans tongue was lightest of digestion. vii.	ib.
¶ Of the Woman that followed her fourth husbands bere and wept. viii.	21
¶ Of the Woman that sayd her woer came to late. ix.	22
¶ Of the Mylner with the golden thombe. x.	23
¶ Of the horseman of Irelande that prayde Oconer for to hange up the frere. xi.	ib.
¶ Of the preest that sayd nother Corpus meus nor Corpum meum. xii.	26

	PAGE
¶ Of the two freres whereof the one loued nat the ele heed nor the other the tayle. xiii.	27
¶ Of the welche man that shroue hym for brekynge of hys faste on the fryday. xiv.	28
¶ Of the merchaunte of London that dyd put nobles in his mouthe in hys dethe bedde. xv.	30
¶ Of the mylner that stale the nuttes of the tayler that stale a shepe. xvi.	31
¶ Of the foure elementes where they should sone be founde. xvii.	36
¶ Of the woman that poured the potage in the iudges male. xviii.	37
¶ Of the wedded men that came to heuen to clayme theyr herytage. xix.	39
¶ Of the merchaunte that charged his sonne to fynde one to synge for hys soule. xx.	40
¶ Of the mayde wasshynge clothes that answered the frere. xxi.	42
¶ Of the thre wyse men of Gotam. xxii.	ib.
¶ Of the graye frere that answered his penytente. xxiii.	43
¶ Of the gentylmen that bare the sege borde on hys necke. xxiv.	44
¶ Of the merchantes wyfe that sayd she wolde take a nap at a sermon. xxv.	47
¶ Of the woman that said and she lyued another yere she wolde haue a cockoldes hatte of her owne. xxvi.	48
¶ Of the gentylman that wysshed his tothe in the gentylwomans tayle. xxvii.	ib.
¶ Of the Welcheman that confessyd hym howe he had slayne a frere. xxviii.	49
¶ Of the Welcheman that coude nat gette but a lytell male. xxix.	50

The Table.

¶ Of the gentyll woman that sayde to a gentyll man ye haue a berde aboue and none benethe. xxx.	51
¶ Of the frere that sayde our Lorde fed fyue M. people with iii fysshys. xxxi.	52
¶ Of the frankelyn that wold haue had the frere gone. xxxii.	53
¶ Of the prest that sayd Our Lady was not so curyous a woman. xxxiii.	54
¶ Of the good man that sayde to his wyfe he had euyll fare. xxxiv.	55
¶ Of the frere that bad his childe make a laten. xxxv.	ib.
¶ Of the gentylman that asked the frere for his beuer. xxxvi.	56
¶ Of the thre men that chose the woman. xxxvii.	ib.
¶ Of the gentylman that taught his cooke the medycyne for the tothake. xxxviii.	58
¶ Of the gentylman that promysed the scoler of Oxford a sarcenet typet. xxxix.	60
¶ Of mayster Skelton that broughte the bysshop of Norwiche ii fesauntys. xl.	62
¶ Of the yeman of garde that sayd he wolde bete the carter. xli.	65
¶ Of the fole that saide he had leuer go to hell than to heuen. xlii.	66
¶ Of the plowmannys sonne that sayde he sawe one to make a gose to creke swetely. xliii.	67
¶ Of the maydes answere that was wyth chylde. xliv.	ib.
¶ Of the seruaunt that rymyd with hys mayster. xlv.	68
¶ Of the Welcheman that delyuered the letter to the ape. xlvi.	60

¶ Of hym that solde ryght nought. xlvii.	71
¶ Of the frere that tolde the thre chyldres fortunes. xlviii.	72
¶ Of the boy that bare the frere his masters money. xlix.	74
¶ Of Phylyp Spencer the bochers man. l.	75
¶ Of the courtear and the carter. li.	76
¶ Of the yong man that prayd his felow to teche hym hys paternoster. lii.	77
¶ Of the frere that prechyd in ryme expownynge the ave maria. liii.	78
¶ Of the curat that prechyd the Artycles of the Crede. liv.	80
¶ Of the frere that prechyd the x commaundementis. lv.	82
¶ Of the wyfe that bad her husbande ete the candell fyrste. lvi.	84
¶ Of the man of lawes sonnes answer. lvii.	ib.
¶ Of the frere in the pulpet that bad the woman leue her babelynge. lviii.	85
¶ Of the Welcheman that cast the Scotte into the see. lix.	86
¶ Of the man that had the dome wyfe. lx.	87
¶ Of the Proctour of Arches that had the lytel wyfe. lxi.	89
¶ Of ii nonnes that were shryuen of one preste. lxii.	ib.
¶ Of the esquyer that sholde haue ben made knyght. lxiii.	91
¶ Of hym that wolde gette the maystrye of his wyfe. lxiv.	92
¶ Of the penytent that sayd the shepe of God haue mercy vpon me. lxv.	93

The Table.

	PAGE
¶ Of the husbande that sayd he was John daw. lxvi.	94
¶ Of the scoler of oxforde that proued by souestry ii chykens iii. lxvii.	95
¶ Of the frere that stale the podynge. lxviii.	97
¶ Of the frankelyns sonne that cam to take ordres. lxix.	98
¶ Of the husbandman that lodgyd the frere in his owne bed. lxx.	99
¶ Of the preste that wolde say two gospels for a grote. lxxi.	100
¶ Of the coutear that dyd cast the frere ouer the bote. lxxii.	101
¶ Of the frere that prechyd what mennys sowles were. lxxiii.	ib.
¶ Of the husbande that cryed ble vnder the bed. lxxiv.	102
¶ Of the shomaker that asked the colyer what tydynges in hell. lxxv.	103
¶ Of Seynt Peter that cryed cause bobe. lxxvi.	104
¶ Of hym that aduenturyd body and soule for hys prynce. lxxvii.	105
¶ Of the parson that stale the mylner's elys. lxxviii.	106
¶ Of the Welchman that saw one xl s. better than God. lxxix.	ib.
¶ Of the frere that said dyryge for the hoggys soule. lxxx.	ib.
¶ Of the parson that sayde masse of requiem for Crystes soule. lxxxi.	108
¶ Of the herdeman that sayde: ryde apace ye shall haue rayn. lxxxii.	109
¶ Of hym that sayde: I shall haue neuer a peny. lxxxiii.	110

The Table.

	PAGE
¶ Of the husbande that sayde his wyfe and he agreed well. lxxxiv	111
¶ Of the prest that sayde Comede episcope. lxxxv.	ib.
¶ Of the woman that stale the pot. lxxxvi. . . .	112
¶ Of mayster Whyttyntons dreme. lxxxvii. . . .	113
¶ Of the prest that killed his horse called modicus. lxxxviii.	114
¶ Of the Welcheman that stale the Englysshmans cocke. lxxxix.	115
¶ Of hym that brought a botell to a preste. xc.	ib.
¶ Of the endytement of Jesu of Nazareth. xci.	116
¶ Of the frere that preched agaynst them that rode on the Sondaye. xcii.	117
¶ Of the one broder that founde a purs. xciii. .	118
¶ Of the answere of the mastres to the mayde. xciv.	119
¶ Of the northern man that was all harte. xcv.	ib.
¶ Of the burnynge of olde John. xcvi. . . .	ib.
¶ Of the courtear that ete the hot custarde. xcvii.	121
¶ Of the thre pointes belonging to a shrewd wyfe. xcix.	122
¶ Of the man that paynted the lamb upon his wyfes bely. c.	123

INTRODUCTION.

WHEN a small impression of these quaint old books issued from the Chiswick Press, many years ago, under the auspices of the late Mr. S. W. Singer, that gentleman merely designed the copies struck off for presentation to a select circle of literary friends who, like himself, felt a warm interest in every relic of the past which helped to illustrate Shakespeare and ancient English manners. He did not consequently feel under the necessity of furnishing notes, and he preserved not only the old orthography, but the old punctuation, and the most palpable errors of the press. His edition unfortunately laboured under one disadvantage: when he printed, in 1814, the *Mery Tales and Quick Answers* from Berthelet's edition, he imagined that this was the book to which Beatrice is made to allude in *Much Ado About Nothing*, and under this idea he christened the volume *Shakespeare's Jest Book*. He also thought he was safe in assuming that the edition by Berthelet was the only one extant. But Mr. Singer discovered, before his undertaking was a year old, that he had come to an erroneous conclusion on both these points: for an impression of the *Mery Tales, &c.* printed by Henry Wykes in 1567, and containing, with all the old matter, twenty-six additional stories, was brought under his notice, and about the same time a totally unknown work, bearing the very title mentioned by Beatrice, was accidentally rescued from oblivion by the Rev. J. J. Conybeare, who, it is said by Dunlop, picked up the treasure at a bookstall. This was no other than A C. MERY TALYS.

The copy of *C. Mery Talys* thus casually brought to light, had been used by a binder of or about the time of its appearance as pasteboard to another book, and it was in this state when it fell in the way of Mr. Conybeare. As might have been expected, many of the leaves were damaged and mutilated; but (which rendered the matter still more curious) it happily chanced that *more than one copy* had been employed by the aforesaid binder in fashioning the aforesaid pasteboard, and the consequence was that a much larger fragment than would have been otherwise saved was formed by means of duplicate leaves. Still several gaps in the text remained, which it was found impossible to fill up, and as no other copy has since occurred, no better means exist now than existed fifty years ago of supplying the deficiencies. Where the hiatus consisted of a word or two only, and the missing portion could be furnished by conjecture, Mr. Singer took the liberty of adding what seemed to be wanting, in italics; his interpolations have been left as they stood. The old orthography and language, besides the charm of quaintness, appeared to the editor to possess a certain philological value, and he has rigidly adhered to it. In respect to the punctuation, the case was different; there were no reasons of any kind for its retention; it was very imperfect and capricious; and it has therefore been modernized throughout.

The *C. Mery Talys*, of which the copy above described has a fair pretension to the distinction of uniqueness, were first printed by John Rastell, without date but circa 1525, in folio, 24 leaves. Whether Rastell printed more than one edition is an open question. The book was not reprinted, so far as we know at present, till 1558, when John Walley or Waley paid two shillings to the Stationers' Company for his licence to produce this and other iv *Introduction.*

pieces. Walley reprinted a great number of books which had originally come from the press of Wynkyn de Worde and other early masters of the art, but it is not very likely that the *C. Mery Talys* made their appearance prior to 1525, and there is room to doubt whether even then the severe reflections on the scandalous lives of the Roman Catholic priesthood were not slightly premature. The almost total destruction of copies may be, after all, due, not to the excessive popularity of the publication, but to its early suppression by authority or otherwise. After the triumph of the Reformation, and until the death of Edward VI. however, although these tales still remained as unpalatable as ever to a certain party, there was nothing to hinder their circulation, and that there were intermediate impressions between that from Rastell's press, and the one licensed to Walley,[1] if not printed by him, is not at all improbable. The *C. Mery Talys* were subsequently and successively the property of Sampson Awdley and John Charlwood, to the latter of whom they were licensed on the 15th January, 1582. All trace of editions by

(1) Walley obtained his licence for the *C. Mery Talys* in 1557-8, during the reign of Mary, perhaps in anticipation of a change in the government, and in order to forestall other stationers. If Walley printed the Tales, it is most likely that he waited, till Elizabeth came to the throne.

Walley, Awdley, or Charlwood, has disappeared, although doubtless all three printed the work.

Of the MERY TALES AND QUICKE ANSWERES, which forms the second portion of the present volume, only two impressions are known. One of these, supposed to be the original, was printed by Thomas Berthelet, without date (about 1535), in 4to.; it contains 114 anecdotes. The other, from the press of Henry Wykes, bears the date 1567, and is in the duodecimo form; it reproduces with tolerable exactness the text of Berthelet, and has twenty-six new stories. Besides these, at least one other impression formerly existed: for, in 1576-7, Henry Bynneman paid to the Stationers' Company fourpence "and a copie" for "a booke entituled mery tales, wittye questions, and quycke answers."[1] No copy of Bynneman's edition has hitherto been discovered; a copy of that of 1567 was in the Harleian library. At the sale of the White-Knights collection in 1819, Mr. George Daniel of Canonbury gave nineteen guineas for the exemplar of Berthelet's undated 4to, which had previously been in the Roxburghe library, and which, at the dispersion of the latter in 1812, had fetched the moderate sum of 5*l*. 15*s*. 6*d*.

The reader who is conversant with this class of

---

[1] Collier's Extracts from the Reg. Stat. Co. ii. 25.

literature will easily recognise in the following pages many stories familiar to him either in the same, or in very slightly different, shapes; a few, which form part of the *Mery Tales and Quick Answers*, were included in a collection published many years since under the title of *Tales of the Minstrels*. No. 42 of the *Mery Tales and Quick Answers* was perhaps at one time rather popular as a theme for a joke. There is an Elizabethan ballad commencing, "ty the mare, tom-boy, ty the mare," by William Keth, which the editor thought, before he had had an opportunity of examining it, might be on the same subject; but he finds that it has nothing whatever to do with the matter.[1] It may also be noticed that the story related of the king who, to revenge himself on God, forbad His name to be mentioned, or His worship to be celebrated throughout his dominions, is said by Montaigne, in one of his essays, to have been current in his part of France, when he was a boy. The king was Alfonso xi of Castile. No. 68 of *A C. Mery Talys*, "Of the Friar that stole the Pudding," is merely an abridgment of the same story, which occurs in *Tarltons Newes out of*

---

(1) An abridgment of this ballad was published in Ritson's *Ancient Songs and Ballads*, 1829, ii. 31. But see the *Townley Catalogue*, No. 358.

Purgatorie, where it is told of the "Vickar of Bergamo." Many of the jests in these two pamphlets are also to be found in *Scoggins Jests*, licensed in 1565; a few occur in the *Philosopher's Banquet*, 1614; and one—that where the lady ties a string to her toe as a signal to her lover—is repeated at greater length in the "Cobler of Canterbury," edit. 1608, where it is called "the old wives' tale." It would be a curious point to ascertain whether the anecdotes common to these collections and to "Scoggin's Jests," do not refer to the same person; and whether Scoggin is not in fact the hero of many of the pranks attributed to the "Scholar of Oxford," the "Youngman," the "Gentleman," &c. in the following pages, which were in existence many years before the first publication of *Scoggins Jests*. It will hardly be contested at the present day, that "books of the people,"[1] like these now reprinted, with all their occasional coarseness and frequent dulness, are of extreme and peculiar value, as illustrations of early manners and habits of thought.

The editor has ventured to make certain emendations of the text, where they were absolutely necessary to make it intelligible; but these are always carefully noted at the foot of the page

(1) The elder Disraeli has a chapter on this subject in his *Amenities of Literature*.

where they occur. A word or two, here and there, has been introduced between brackets to complete the sense; and a few notes have been given, since it was thought desirable to point out where a tale was common to several collections in various shapes or in the same shape, to indicate the source from which it was derived, and to elucidate obscure phrases or passages. But he has refrained from overloading the book with comment, from a feeling that, in the majority of cases, the class of readers, to which a publication such as this addresses itself, are fully as competent to clear up any apparent difficulties which may fall in their way, as himself.

The allusions to the *C. Mery Talys* and to its companion in old writers are sufficiently numerous.[1]

Bathe, in his *Introduction to the Art of Musick*, 1584, says: "But for the worthiness I thought it not to be doubted, seeing here are set forth a booke of a hundred mery tales, another of the bataile between the spider and the flie, &c." A few years later, Sir John Harington, in his *Apologie* (for the *Metamorphosis of Ajax*) 1596, writes: "Ralph Horsey, Knight, the best housekeeper in Dorset-

---

[1] For some of these notices I am indebted to Mr. Singer; others I have added myself from the various sources.

shire, a good freeholder, a deputie Lieutenant. Oh, sir, you keep hauks and houndes, and hunting-horses: it may be som madde fellowe will say, you must stand up to the chinne, for spending five hundred poundes, to catch hares, and Partridges, that might be taken for five poundes." Then comes this note in the margin: "according to the tale in the hundred Mery Tales." It is No. 57. In the Epilogue to the play of *Wily Beguild*, printed in 1606, but written during the reign of Elizabeth, there is a passage in which the *C. Mery Talys* are coupled with *Scoggins Jests*, and in his *Wonderful yeare*, 1603, Decker says: " I could fill a large volume, and call it the second part of the *Hundred Merry Tales*, only with such ridiculous stuff as this of the justice." From this extract, first quoted by Mr. Collier in his valuable History of the Drama, and from the manner in which Shakespeare, through the mouth of Beatrice, speaks of the *Mery Talys*, it is to be gathered that neither writer held this book of jests in very high estimation ; and, as no vestiges are traceable of an edition of the work subsequent to 1582, it is possible that about that time the title had grown too stale to please the less educated reader, and the work had fallen into disrepute in higher quarters. The stories themselves, in some shape

x   *Introduction.*

or other, however, have been reproduced in every jest-book from the reign of Elizabeth to the Restoration, while many of them multiply themselves even to the present day in the form of chap books.

A C. Mery Talys was one of the popular tracts described by the pedantic Laneham, in his *Letter from Kenilworth*, 1575, as being in the Library of Captain Cox, of Coventry.[1]

---

(1) In Act v. Sc. iii. of Fletcher's *Nice Valour* (Dyce's B. & F. x. 361) there is mention of the *Hundred Novels*, alluding, not to the *C. Mery Talys*, but to the *Decameron* of Boccaccio, of which an English translation appeared in 1620-5.

A C.
MERY TALYS.

¶ *Of hym that said there were but two commande-mentes.* i.

¶ A CERTAYNE Curate in the contrey there was that *preched* in the pulpet of the ten comaundementys, saye*ng that* there were ten commaundementes that euery man *should* kepe, and he that brake any of them commytt*ed* syn, howbeit he sayd, that somtyme it was *dedely and* somtyme venyal. But when it was dedely syn and whan venyall there were many doutes therin. ¶ And a mylner, a yong man, a mad felow that cam seldom to chyrch and had ben at very few sermons or none in all his lyfe, answered hym than shortely this wyse : I meruayl, master person, that ye say there be so many commaundementes and so many doutes: for I neuer hard tell but of two commaundementes, that is to saye, commaunde me to you and commaunde me fro you. Nor I neuer harde tell of more doutes but twayn, that ys to say, dout the candell and dout the fyre.[1] At which answere all the people fell a laughynge.

By this tale a man may well perceyue that they, that be brought vp withoute lernynge or good maner, shall neuer be but rude and bestely, all thoughe they haue good naturall wyttes.

¶ *Of the wyfe who lay with her prentys and caused him to beate her husbande disguised in her rayment.* ii.

¶ A WYFE there was, which had apoynted her prentys to com to her bed in the nyght, which seruaunt had long woed her to haue his plesure; which acordyng to the apoyntement cam to her bed syde in the night, her husbande lyenge by her. And whan she perceyuyd him there, she caught hym by the hande and helde hym fast, and incontynent wakened her husbande, and sayde: syr, it is so ye haue a fals and an vntrue seruant, which is Wylliam your prentys, and hath longe woyd me to haue his pleasure; and because I coulde not auoyde

---

(1) *i.e.* do out. It is, perhaps, scarcely necessary to mention that in French, the term *commander* has a double signification, *to command* and *to commend*. In our language, the two words are of course distinct; hence the jest.

his importunate request, I haue apoynted hym this nyght to mete me in the gardeyne in the herber; and yf ye wyll aray your selfe in myn aray and go theder, ye shall see the profe therof; and than ye may rebuke hym as ye thynk best by your dyscrecyon. This husbande, thus aduertysed by hys wyfe, put upon him his wyue's rayment and went to the herber; and whan he was gone thyder the prentys cam in to bed to his mastres; where for a season they were bothe content and plesyd ech other by the space of an hour or ii; but whan she thoughte tyme conuenient, she said to the prentyse: now go thy way into the herber, and mete hym and tak a good waster[1] in thy hand, and say thou dyd it but to proue whether I wold be a good woman or no; and reward him as thou thinkyst best This prentys doyng after his mastres councell went in to the herber, where he found his master in his mastres' apparell and sayd: A! thou harlot, art thou comen hether? now I se well, if I wod be fals to my master, thou woldest be a strong hore; but I had leuer thou were hangid than I wold do him so trayterous a ded: therefor I shall gyve the som punyshment as thou lyke an hore hast deseruyd; and therewith lapt him well about the sholders and back, and gaue him a dosen or ii. good stripes.

(1) Cudgel.

The master, felyng him selfe somwhat to smarte, sayde: peace, Willyam, myn own trew good seruant; for Goddis sake, *holde thy* handes: for I am thy mayster and not thy maystres. Nay, hore, quod *he, thou know*est thou art but an harlot, and I dyd but to proue the; and smote him agayn. *Hold! Hold!* quod the mayster, I beseech the, no more: for I am not she: for I am thy *mayster*, for I haue a berde; and therwith he sparyd hys hand and felt his berd. Good mayster, quod the prentyse, I crye you mercy; and then the mayster went unto hys wyfe; and she askyd hym how he had sped. And he answeryd: I wys, wyfe, I haue been shrewdly betyn; howbeit I haue cause to be glad: for I thank God I haue as trew a wyfe and as trew a seruant as any man hath in Englonde.[1]

By thys tale ye may se that yt ys not wysdome for a man to be rulyd alway after his wyuys councell.

¶ *Of John Adroyns in the dyuyls apparell.* iii.

¶ It fortunyd that in a market towne in the counte of Suffolke there was a stage play, in the which play one, callyd John Adroyns which dwellyd in a

---

[1] This story is merely the latter portion of the seventh novel of the Seventh Day of the Decameron; but Boccaccio tells it somewhat differently. It may also be found in the *Pecorone* of Ser. Giovanni Fiorentino, and in *A Sackful of Newes*, 1673 (a reprint of a much older edition). In the latter there are one or two trifling particulars not found here.

nother vyllage ii. myle from thens, playde the dyuyll. And when the play was done, thys John Adroyns in the euynyng departyd fro the sayde market towne to go home to hys own house. Because he had there no change of clothying, he went forth in hys dyuylls apparell, whych in the way comyng homeward cam thorow a waren of conys[1] belongyng to a gentylman of the vyllage, wher he him self dwelt. At which tyme it fortunyd a preste, a vycar of a churche therby, with ii or iii other vnthrifty felows, had brought with them a hors, a hey[2] and a feret to th'entent there to get conys; and when the feret was in the yerth, and the hey set ouer the pathway where thys John Adroyns shuld come, thys prest and hys other felows saw hym come in the dyuyls rayment. Consideryng that they were in the dyuyls seruyce and stelyng of conys and supposyng it had ben the deuyll in dede,[they] for fere,ran away. Thys John Adroyns in the dyuyls rayment, an' because[3] it was somewhat dark, saw not the hay, but went forth in hast and stomblid therat and fell doun, that with the fal he had almost broken his nek. But whan he was a lytyll reuyuyd, he lookyd up and spyed it was a hay to catch conys, and [he] lokyd further and saw that they ran away for fere of him, and saw a horse tyed to a bush laden wyth conys whych

(1) A rabbit-warren.   (2) Net, Fr. *haie*.   (3) In orig. *and because*.

they had taken; and he toke the horse and the haye and lept upon the horse and rode to the gentylmannys place that was lorde of the waren to the entente to haue thank for takynge suche a pray. And whan he came, [he] knokyd at the gatys, to whome anone one of the gentylmanny's seruauntys askyd who was there and sodeinly openyd the gate; and assone as he percyuyd hym in the deuyls rayment, [he] was sodenly abashyd and sparryd the dore agayn, and went in to his mayster and sayd and sware to his mayster, that the dyuell was at the gate and wolde come in. The gentylman, heryng him say so, callyd another of his seruauntys and bad him go to the gate to knowe who was there. Thys seconde seruant [that] came to the gate durst not open it but askyd wyth lowd voyce who was there. Thys John Adroyns in the dyuyls aparell answeryd wyth a hye voyce and sayd: tell thy mayster I must nedys speke with hym or[1] I go. Thys seconde seruaunt heryng * * *

8 *lines of the original are wanting.*

the deuyll in dede that is at the gate syttynge vpon an *horse laden with* soules; and be lykelyhode he

(1) *i.e.* ere, before.

is come for your soule. Purpos *ye* to *let him have your* soule and if he had your soule I wene he shulde be *gon*. The *genty*lman, than, meruaylously abasshed, called his chaplayne *and sayd: let a ca*ndell be light, and gette holy water ; and [he] wente to the gate *with* as *manye ser*uantes as durste go with him ; where the chaplayne with *muche con*iuracyon sayd : in the name of the father, sonne and holy *ghost, I commaunde* and charge the in the holy name of God to tell me *wherefore thou* comeste hyther. ¶ This John Adroynes in the deuylls *apparell, seying* them begynne to coniure after such maner, sayd : nay, *feare not* me ; for I am a good deuyll ; I am John Adroynes your neyghboure in this towne and he that playde the deuyll to day in the playe. I *bryng* my mayster a dosen or two of his owne conyes that were stolen in *dede* and theyr horse and theyr haye, and [I] made them for feare to ronne *awaye.* Whanne they harde hym thus speke by his voyce, [they] knewe him well, and opened the gate and lette hym come in. And so all the foresayd feare was turned to myrthe and disporte.

By this tale ye may se that men feare many tymes more than they nede, whiche hathe caused men to beleue that sperytes and deuyls haue ben sene in dyuers places, whan it hathe ben nothynge so.

¶ *Of the ryche man and his two sonnes.* iv.

¶ THERE was a ryche man whiche lay sore sycke in his bedde to *deth*. Therefore his eldest sonne came to hym, and besechyd him to gyue *him hys* blessyng, to whome the father sayde: sonne, thou shalt haue Goddes blessyng and myne; and because thou hast ben euer good of condicyons, I *giue and* bequethe the all my lande. To whome he answered and sayd: nay father, I truste you shall lyue and occupy them your selfe full well by Goddes grace. Sone after came another sonne to him lyke wyse and desyred his blessyng, to whome the father said: my sonne, thou hast ben euer kynde and gentyll; I gyue the Goddes blessyng and myne; and I bequethe the all my mouable goodes. To whome he answered and said: nay father, I trust you shall lyue and do well and spende and vse your goodes *yourself* * * * *

8 *Lines wanting.*

—*By this tale* men may well perceyue that yonge people that * * * * * * * theyr frendes counsell in youthe in tymes * * * * full ende.

A C. Mery Talys. 19

¶ *Of the cockolde who gained a ring by his iudgment.* v.

¶ *Two gentylmen* of acquoyntaunce were apoynted to lye with a gentylwoman both in one nyght, the one nat knowynge of the other, at *dyuers houres.* ¶ Thys fyrste at hys houre apoynted came, and in the *bedde chanced* to lese a rynge. The seconde gentylman, whanne he *came to bedde*, fortuned to fynde the same rynge, and whan he hadde *stayde som tyme* departed. And two or thre dayes after, the fyrste gentylmanne *saw hys* rynge on the others fynger, and chalenged it of hym and he *refused it,* and badde hym tell where he had loste it: and he sayd: in suche a *gentylwo*mans bedde. Than quod the other: and there founde I it. And the *one gentylman* wolde haue it and the other said he shulde nat. Than they agreed *to be decyded* by the nexte man that they dyd mete. And it fortuned them to *mete* the husbande of the said gentyll woman and desyred hym of his *iudg*ment, shewynge hym all the hole mater. Than quod he: by my iud*gmente, he t*hat ought[1] the shetes shulde haue the rynge. Than quod they: and *for your* good iudgement you shall haue the rynge.

(1) Owned. In *Northward Hoe*, 1607, by Decker and Webster, act i. scene i., the writers have made use of this story. See Webster's Works, edit. Hazlitt, i. 178-9.

¶ *Of the scoler that gave his shoes to cloute.* vi.

¶ IN the Uniuersyte of Oxeforde there was a scoler that delyted moche to speke eloquente englyssshe and curious termes, and came to the cobler with his shoes whyche were pyked before (as they used that tyme), to have them clouted, and sayde this wyse: Cobler, I praye the sette *two tryangyls* and two semycercles vpon my subpedytales, and I shall *paye* the for thy laboure. The cobeler, because he vnderstoode hym nat halfe, answered shortely and sayd: syr, your eloquence passeth myne intelly*gence*. But I promyse you, yf he meddyll with me the clowtynge of youre *shoon* shall cost you thre pens.

By this tale men may lerne, that it is foly to study to speke eloquently before them, that be rude and vnlerned.

¶ *Of hym that said that a womans tongue was lightest of digestion.* vii.

¶ A CERTAYN artificer in London there was, whyche was sore *seke and* coulde not well dysgest his meat. To whom a physicyon ca*m to give* hym councell, and sayd that he must vse to ete metis that be light *of di*gestyon and small byrdys, as sparowes, swalowes, and specyally that byrd *which is* called a wagtayle, whose flessh is meruelouse lyght of dygestyon, *bycause that* byrd is euer mouying and styryng. The sekeman, herynge the phesicion *say so*, answered hym and seyd : sir, yf that be the cause that those byrdes be lyght of dygestyon, than I know a mete moch lyghter of dygestyon than other[1] sparow swallow or wagtaile, and that is my wyues tong, for it is neuer in rest but euer meuying[2] and sterryng.

By this tale ye may lerne a good generall rule of physyke.

¶ *Of the woman that followed her fourth husbands bere and wept.* viii.

¶ A WOMAN there was which had had iiii husbandys. It fourtuned also that this fourth husbande dyed and was brought to chyrche vpon the bere ; whom this woman folowed and made great mone, and waxed very sory, in so moche that her neyghbours thought she wolde swown and dye for sorow. Wherfore one of her gosseps cam to her, and spake to her in her ere, and bad her, for Godds sake, comfort her self and refrayne that lamentacion, or ellys it wold hurt her and perauenture put her in ieopardy of her life. To whom this

(1) either.   (2) moving.

woman answeryd and sayd : I wys, good gosyp, I haue grete cause to morne, if ye knew all. For I haue beryed iii husbandes besyde this man ; but I was neuer in the case that I am now. For there was not one of them but when that I folowed the corse to chyrch, yet I was sure of an nother husband, before the corse cam out of my house, and now I am sure of no nother husband ; and therfore ye may be sure I haue great cause to be sad and heuy.

By thys tale ye may se that the olde prouerbe ys trew, that it is as great pyte to se a woman wepe as a gose to go barefote.

¶ *Of the woman that sayd her woer came too late.* ix.

¶ ANOTHER woman there was that knelyd at the mas of requiem, whyle the corse of her husbande lay on the bere in the chyrche. To whome a yonge man cam and spake wyth her in her ere, as thoughe it had ben for som mater concernyng the funerallys ; howe be it he spake of no suche matter, but onely wowyd her that he myght be her husbande to whom she answered and sayde thus : syr, by my trouthe I am sory that ye come so late, for I am sped all redy. For I was made sure yesterday to another man.

By thys tale ye maye perceyue that women ofte tymes be wyse and lothe to lose any tyme.

¶ *Of the mylner with the golden thombe.*[1]   x.

¶ A MARCHAUNT that thought to deride a mylner seyd vnto the mylner syttynge amonge company: sir, I haue harde say that euery trew mylner that tollyth trewlye hathe a gylden thombe. The myllner answeryd and sayde it was true. Than quod the marchant: I pray the let me se thy thombe; and when the mylner shewyd hys thombe the marchant sayd: I can not perceyue that thy thombe is gylt; but it is as all other mens thombes be. To whome the mylner answered and sayde: syr, treuthe it is that my thombe is gylt; but ye haue no power to se it: for there is a properte euer incydent *vnto it*, that he that is a cockolde shall neuer haue power to se it.[2]

¶ *Of the horseman of Irelande that prayde Oconer for to hange up the frere.*   xi.

¶ ONE whiche was called Oconer, an Yrysshe lorde, toke an horsman prisoner that was one of

(1) See Brand's *Popular Antiquities*, edit. 1849, iii. 387.
(2) The reverse of the Somersetshire saying. The proverb is well known: "An honest miller hath a golden thumb;" but to this the Somersetshire folks add, "none but a cuckold can see it."

hys great enmys whiche for any request or entrety that the horsman made gaue iugement that he sholde incontynent be hanged, and made a frere to shryue hym and bad hym make hem redy to dye. Thys frere that shroue hym examyned hym of dyuers synnes, and asked him amonge other whiche were the gretteste synnes that euer he dyd. This horsman answered and sayd : one of the greatest actys that euer I dyd whiche I now most repent is that, whan I toke Oconer the last weke in a chyrche, and there I myght haue brennyd[1] hym chyrche and all, and because I had conscience and pyte of brennyng of the chyrche, I taryed the tyme so long, that Oconer escaped ; and that same deferrynge of brennynge of the chyrche and so longe taryeng of that tyme is one of the worst actes that euer I dyd wherof I moste[2] repent. This frere perceuynge hym in that mynde sayde : peace in the name of God, and change thy mynde and dye in charite, or els thou shalt neuer come in heuen. Nay, quod the horsman, I wyll neuer chaunge that mynde what so euer shall come to my soule. Thys frere perceyuynge hym thus styl contynew his minde, cam to Oconer and sayde : syr, in the name of God, haue some pyte vppon this mannys sowle, and let hym not dye now, tyl

---

(1) Burned.   (2) orig. reads *muste*.

he be in a beter mynde. For yf he dye now, he is so ferre out of cheryte, that vtterly his soule shall be dampned, and [he] shewyd hym ' what minde he was in and all the hole mater as is before shewyd. Thys horsman, herynge the frere thus intrete for hym, sayd to Oconer thus : Oconer, thou seest well by thys mannys reporte that, yf I dye now, I am out of charyte and not redy to go to heuen ; and so it is that I am now out of charyte in dede ; but thou seest well that this frere is a good man and he is now well dysposed and in charyte and he is redy to go to heuen, and so am not I. Therfore I pray the hang vp this frere, whyle that he is redy to go to heuen and let me tary tyl another tyme, that I may be in charyte and redy and mete to go to heuen Thys Oconer, herying thys mad answere of hym, sparyd the man and forgaue hym hys lyfe at that season.

By thys ye may se, that he that is in danger of hys enmye that hath no pite, he can do no beter but shew to hym the vttermost of his malycyous mynde whych that he beryth to ward hym.

¶ *Of the preest that sayd nother corpus meus nor corpus meum.* xii.

¶ THE archdekyn of Essex[1] that had ben longe in auctorite, in a tyme of vysytacyon, whan all the prestys apperyd before hym, called asyde iii. of the yonge prestys which were acusyd that thy could not wel say theyr dyvyne seruyce, and askyd of them when they sayd mas, whether they sayd corpus meus or corpum meum. The fyrst prest sayde that he sayd corpus meus. The second sayd that he sayd corpum meum. And than he asked of the thyrd how he sayde; whyche answered and sayd thus: syr, because it is so great a dout and dyuers men be in dyuers opynyons: therfore because I wolde be sure I wolde not offende, whan I come to the place I leue it clene out and say nothynge therfore. Wherfore the bysshoppe than openly rebuked them all thre. But dyuers that were present thought more defaut in hym, because he hym selfe beforetyme had admytted them to be prestys.

By this tale ye may se that one ought to take hede how he rebukyth an other lest it torne moste to his owne rebuke.

(1) Richard Rawson was Archdeacon of Essex from 1503 to 1543, and was perhaps the person here intended. See Le Neve's *Fasti*, ed. Hardy, ii. 336.

¶ Of two freres whereof the one loued nat the ele heed nor the other the tayle. xiii.

¶ Two freres satte at a gentylmans tabyll, whiche had before hym on a fastyng day an ele and cut the hed of the ele and layd it vpon one of the frerys trenchars; but the frere, bycause he wold haue had of the middle parte of the ele, sayd to the gentylman he louyd no ele hedes. Thys gentylman also cut the tayle of the ele, and layde it on the other frerys trenchar. He lyke wyse, because he wolde haue had of the myddle parte of the ele, sayde he loued no ele tayles. This gentylman, perceuynge that, gaue the tayle to hym that sayd he louyd not the hed, and gaue the hed to hym that sayd he loued not the tayle. And as fore the myddell part of the ele, he ete parte hym selfe and parte he gaue to other folke at the table; wherfore these freres for anger wolde ete neuer a morsell, and so they for al theyr craft and subtylte were not only deceyued of the best morsell of the ele, but thereof had no parte at all.

By this ye se that they that couet the best parte somtyme therfore lese the meane parte and all.

¶ *Of the welche man that shroue hym for brekynge of hys faste on the fryday.* xiv.

¶ A WELCHEMAN, dwellynge in a wylde place of Walys, cam to hys curate in the tyme of Lente and was confessyd; and when hys confessyon was in maner at the end, the curate askyd hym, and[1] he had any other thyng to say that greuyd his conscience. Which sore abasshid answered no worde a great whyle; at last by exhortacyon of his goostly fader he sayde that there was one thyng in his mynde that greatly greued his conscyence, which he was asshamed to vtter: for it was so greuous that he trowed God wold neuer forgyue hym. To whom the curate answerd and sayd, that Goddes mercy was aboue all, and bad hym not dyspayre in the mercy of God. For what so euer it was, yf he were repentant, that God wolde forgyue hym. ¶ And so by longe exortacyon at the last he shewyd it and seyde thus. Syr, it happenyd ones that, as my wyfe was makynge a chese vpon a Fryday, I wolde fayne haue sayed whether it had ben salt or fresshe, and toke a lytyll of the whey in my hande, and put it in my mouthe; and or[2] I was ware, parte of it went

(1) if.   (2) before.

A C. Mery Talys. 29

downe my throte agaynst my wyll and so I brake my faste. To whom the curate sayde: and if there be non other thynge, I warant God shall forgyue the. So whan he had well comforted hym with the mercy of God, the curate prayed hym to answere a questyon and to tell hym trueth; and when the welchman had promysed to tell the truth, the curate sayd that there were robberyes and murders done nye the place where he dwelte and diuers men found slayn; and asked hym whether *he knew ought* poyntynge[1] to any of them To whom he answeryd and sayd yes and sayd *he had ben priu*ye to many of them, and dyd helpe to robe and to slee dyuers of them. *Then the* curate asked hym, why he dyd not conffesse hym therof. The welshman *answeryd* and sayde he toke that for no synne: for it was a custome amongest *them that*, whan any boty cam of any ryche merchant rydyng, that it was but a *trewe* neyboure dede one to help another when one callyd another; and so they *held it* but for good felowshyp and neyghbourhood.

Here maye ye se that some haue remorse of conscyence of small venyall *sinnis and* fere not to do gret offencys without shame of the worled[2]

(1) appertaining or relevant.   (2) World.

or drede of *God*; and, as the comon prouerbe is, they stumble at a strawe and lepe ouer a blocke.

¶ *Of the merchaunte of London that dyd put nobles in his mouthe in hys dethe bedde.* xv.

¶ A RYCHE couetous marchant there was that dwellid in London, which euer gaderyd mony and could neuer fynd in hys hert to spend ought *vpon* hym selfe nor vpon no man els. Whiche fell sore syke, and as he laye on hys deth bed had his purs lyenge at his beddys hede, and [he] had suche a loue to his money that he put his hande in his purs, and toke out therof x or xii li. in nobles and put them in his mouth. And because his wyfe and other perceyued hym very syke and lyke to dye, they exortyd hym to be confessyd, and brought the curate vnto hym. Which when they had caused him to say Benedicite, the curate bad hym crye God mercy and shewe to hym his synnes. Than this seyck man began to sey: I crey God mercy I haue offendyd in the vii dedly synnes and broken the x commaundementes; but[1] because of the gold in his mouth he muffled so in his speche, that the curate could not well vnder-

(1) Orig. reads *and*; *but* seems to be required.

stande hym : wherfore the curat askyd hym, what he had in his mouthe that letted his spech. I wys, mayster parsone, quod the syke man, muffelynge, I haue nothyng in my mouthe but a lyttle money; bycause I wot not whither[1] I shal go, I thought I wold take some spendynge money with me : for I wot not what nede I shall haue therof; and incontynent after that sayeng dyed, before he was confessyd or repentant that any man coulde perceyue, and so by lyklyhod went to the deuyll.

By this tale ye may se, that they that all theyr lyues wyll neuer do charyte to theyr neghbours, that God in tyme of theyr dethe wyll not suffre them to haue grace of repentaunce.

¶ *Of the mylner that stale the nuttes of the tayler that stale a shepe.* xvi.

¶ THERE was a certayne ryche husbandman in a vyllage, whiche louyd nuttes meruelously well and sette trees of fylberdes and other nutte trees in his orcharde, and norysshed them well all his lyfe; and when he dyed he made his executours to make promyse to bery with him in his graue a bagge of nuttes, or els they sholde not be his

(1) Orig. reads *whether*.

executours; which executours, for fere of lesynge of theyre romes[1] fulfylled his mynde and dyd so. It happenyd that, the same nyghte after that he was beryed, there was a mylner in a whyte cote cam to this mannes garden to the entent to stele a bagge of nuttes; and in the way he met wyth a tayler in a black cote, an vnthrift of hys acquayntance, and shewyd hym hys intent. This tayler lykewyse shewyd hym, that he intendyd the same tyme to stele a shepe; and so they bothe there agred to go forwarde euery man seuerally wyth hys purpose; and after that they apoynted to make god chere eche wyth other and to mete agayn in the chyrch porch, and he that cam fyrste to tarye for the other. This mylner, when he had spede of hys nuttys, came furst to the chyrch porch, and there taryed for his felow, and the mene whyle satte styll there and knakked nuttes. It fortuned than the sexten of the church, because yt was was about ix of the cloke, cam to ryng curfue; and whan he lokyd in the porche and sawe one all in whyte knakkynge nuttes he had wente[2] it had bene the dede man rysyn owt of hys graue,

---

(1) Places or appointments. This is one of the best stories of the kind in the present or any other collection, in our own or other languages. The construction is excellent.
(2) Weened (guessed).

A C. Mery Talys. 33

knakkynge the nuttes that were beryed wyth hym, and ran home agayne in all hast and tolde to a krepyll that was in his house what he had sene. Thys crepyll, thus herynge hym, rebuked the sexten and sayd that yf he were able to go he wolde go thyder and coniure the spyryte. By my trouthe, quod the sexten, and yf thou darest do that, I wyll bere the on my neck; and so they both agreed. The sexten toke the creple on his nek, and cam in to the chyrchyarde again, and the mylner in the porch seeing[1] one comynge beryng a thynge on his necke had went[2] it had ben the tayler comynge with the shepe, and rose vp to mete them. And as he cam towarde them, he askyd and sayd: is he fat, is he fat? The sexten, heryng hym sey so, for fere cast the crepull down and sayd: fatte or lene, take hym as he is; and ranne awaye; and the creple by myracle was made hole, and ran away as fast as he or faster. Thys mylner perceyuyng that they were two, and that one ran after an other, thoughte that one had spyed the tayler stelyng the shepe, and that he had ron after hym to haue taken hym; and fearyng that one had spyed hym also stelynge the nuttes, he for feare lefte hys nuttes behynd him; and as secretly as he cowde ran home to hys myll. And anon

(1) Orig. reads *saw*. (2) Weened.

after that he was gone, the tayler cam wyth the stolen shepe vppon hys necke to the chyrche to seke the mylner; and whan he fownde there the nutte shalys,[1] he supposyd that his felow had ben ther and gone home, as he was in dede; wherfore he toke vp the shepe agayne on his necke, [and] went towarde the myll. But yet durynge this while, the sexten which ranne away went not to hys owne house, but went to the parysh prestys chamber, and shewyd hym how the spyryt of the man was rysen out of hys graue knacking nuttes, as ye haue hard before: wherfore the prest sayd that he wolde go coniure hym, yf the sexten wolde go wyth hym; and so they bothe agreed. The prest dyd on hys surples and a stole about hys necke, and toke holy water wyth hym, and cam wyth the sexten toward the church; and as sone as he entred in the chyrche yard, the talyer wyth the whyte shepe on hys neck intendyng, as I before haue shewyd yow, to go downe to the myll, met with them, and had went that the prest in his surples had ben the mylner in his whyte cote, and seyd to hym: by God! I haue hym, I haue hym! meanynge thereby[2] the shepe that he had stolen. The prest, perceyuynge the tayller all in blake and a whyte thynge on hys nek, had went it had ben

---

(1) Shells.   (2) In Orig. *by*.

the deuyll beryng away the spyryte of the dede man that was beryed, and ran away as fast as he coude, takyng the way down towarde the myl, and the sexten ronnyng after hym. Thys tayler, seying one folowyng hym, had went that one had folowed the mylner to haue done hym som hurt, and thought he wold folow, if nede were to help the milner; and went forth, tyl he cam to the mill and knocked at the myll dore. The mylner beynge wythin asked who was there. The tayler answeryd and sayd: by God! I haue caught one of them, and made hym sure and tyed hym fast by the legges. But the mylner, heryng him sey that he had hym tyed fast by the legges, had went it had ben the constable, that had taken the tayler for stelyng of the shepe, and had tyed hym by the legges; and ferid that he had come to haue taken hym also for stelynge of the nuttes: wherfore the mylner opened a bak dore, and ran away as fast as he could. The tayler, herynge the backe dore openynge, wente on the other syde of the myll, and there saw the mylner ronnyng away, and stode ther a lytyll whyle musyng wyth the shepe on his necke. Then was the parysshe preest and the sexten standynge there vnder the mylhouse hydyng them for fere, and seeing[1] the

(1) Orig. reads *saw*.

tayler agayn with the shepe on hys nek, had wende styll it had ben the deuyll wyth the spyryt of the dede man on[1] hys nek, and for fere ran awaye; but because they knew not the grounde well, the preste lepte into a dyche almoste ouer the hed lyke to be drownyde, that he cryed wyth a loude voyce : help, helpe ! Than the tayler lokyd about, and seeing[2] the mylner ronne away and the sexten a nother way, and hearing[3] the preste creye helpe, had went it had ben the constable wyth a great company cryeng for helpe to take him and to bring hym to pryson for stelyng of the shepe : wherfore he threwe down the shepe and ran away another way as fast as he coud; and so euery man was afferd of other wythout cause.

By thys ye may se well, it is foly for any man to fere a thyng to moche, tyll that he se some profe or cause.

¶ *Of the foure elementes where they shoulde sone be founde.* xvii.

¶ IN the old world when all thyng could speke, the iiii elementys[4] mette to geder for many thynges whych they had to do, because they must meddell alway one wyth a nother, and had communicacion

---

(1) Orig. reads *of.*   (2) The Orig. *saw.*   (3) Orig. *hard, i. e.* heard.
(4) There is perhaps an allusion here to the *Interlude of the Four Elements*, supposed to have been printed about 1510 by John Rastell.

to gyder of dyuers maters; and by cause they coulde not conclude all theyr maters at that season, they appoyntyd to breke communicacion for that tyme and to mete agayne another tyme. Therfore eche one of them shewed to other where theyr most abydyng was and where theyr felows shoulde fynde them, yf nede shuld requyre; and fyrste the erthe sayde: bretherne, ye knowe well as for me I am permanent alway and not remouable: therfore ye may be sure to haue me alway whan ye lyste. The wather sayde: yf ye lyst to seke me, ye shall be sure to haue me under a toft of grene rushes or elles in a womans eye. The wynde sayde: yf ye lyst to speke wyth me, ye shall be sure to haue me among aspyn leuys or els in a womans tong. Then quod the fyre: yf any of you lyst to seke me, ye shall euer be sure to fynd me in a flynt stone or elles in a womans harte.

By thys tale ye may lerne as well the properte of the iiii elementys as the properteis[1] of a woman.

¶ *Of the woman that poured the potage in the iudges male.* xviii.

¶ THERE was a iustyce but late in the reame of England callyd master Vavesour,[2] a uery homely man and rude of condycyons, and louyd neuer to spend mych money. Thys master Vauysour rode

(1) orig. reads *proprete is.* (2) *Vide infra.*

on a tyme in hys cyrcuyte in the northe contrey, where he had agreed wyth the sheryf for a certain some of money for hys charges thorowe the shyre, so that at euery inne and lodgynge this master Vauysour payd for hys owne costys. It fortunyd so, that when he cam to a certayn lodgyng he comaunded one Turpyn hys seruant to se that he used good husbondry[1] and to saue suche thynges as were left and to cary it wyth hym to serue hym at the nexte baytynge. Thys Turpyn, doyng hys maystres commandement, toke the broken bred, broken mete and all such thyng that was left, and put it in hys maysters cloth sak. The wyfe of the hous, perceyuing that he toke all suche fragmentys and vytayle wyth hym that was left, and put it in the cloth sake, she brought vp the podage that was left in the pot; and when Turpyn had torned hys bake a lytyl asyde, she pouryd the podage in to the cloth sake, whych ran vpon hys robe of skarlet and other of hys garmentys and rayed[2] them very euyll, that they were mych hurt therwyth. Thys Turpyn, sodeynly turnyng[3] hym and seeing[4] it, reuyled the wyfe therfore, and ran to hys mayster

(1) Economy.
(2) Defiled, from Fr. *rayer*, to shine and give light, as the rays of the sun, and thence to streak with lines of dirt, and so to soil. The word is not common. See Nares art *ray* (edit. 1859), and Cotgrave art *rayer* (edit. 1650.)
(3) orig. reads *turnyd*. (4) orig. reads *saw*.

and told hym what she had don : wherfore master
Vauesour incontinent callyd the wyf and seyd to
her thus: thou drab, quod he, what hast thow
don? why hast thou pourd the podage in my
cloth sake and marrd my rayment and gere? O,
syr, quod the wyfe, I know wel ye ar a iudge of
the realme, and I perceyue by you your mind is
to do ryght and to haue that is your owen ; and
your mynd is to haue all thyng wyth you that ye
haue payd for, both broken mete and other thynges
that is left, and so it is reson that ye haue ; and
therfore be cause your seruant hath taken the
broken mete and put it in your cloth sak, I haue
therin put the potage that be left, because ye haue
wel and truly payed for them. Yf I shoulde kepe
ony thynge from you that ye haue payed for, par-
aduenture ye wold troble me in the law a nother
tyme.

Here ye may se, that he that playth the nygarde
to mych, som tyme it torneth hym to hys owne
losse.

¶ *Of the wedded men that came to heuen to clayme
theyr herytage.* xix.

¶ A CERTAYN weddyd man there was whyche, whan
he was dede, cam to heuen gates to seynt Peter,
and sayd he cam to clayme hys bad heretage
whyche he had deseruyd. Saynt Peter askyd hym

what he was, and he sayd a weddyd man. Anon Saynt Peter openyd the gatys, and bad hym to com in, and sayde he was worthye to haue hys herytage, bycause he had had much troble and was worthye to haue a crowne of glory. Anon after there cam a nother man that claymyd heuen, and sayd to Seynt Peter he had hade ii wyues, to whom Saynt Peter answered and said : come in, for thou art worthy to haue a doble crown of glory : for thou hast had doble trouble. At the last there cam the thyrd, claymynge hys herytage and sayde to Saynt Peter that he had had iii wyues, and desyryd to come in. What! quod Saynt Peter, thou hast ben ones in troble and thereof delyueryd, and than wyllingly woldyst be troblyd again, and yet agayne therof delyueryd ; and for all that coulde not beware the thyrde tyme, but enterest wyllyngly in troble agayn : therfore go thy waye to Hell : for thou shalt neuer come in heuen : for thou art not worthy.

Thys tale is a warnyng to them that haue bene twyse in paryll to beware how they come therin the thyrd tyme

¶ *Of the merchaunte that charged his sonne to fynde one to synge for hys soule.* xx.

¶ A RYCHE marchant of London here was, that had one sonne that was somewhat vnthryfty. Therfore hys fader vppon hys deth bed called hym to hym, and sayde he knew well that he had ben vnthryfty; how be it, yf he knew he wold amend hys condycyons he wolde make hym hys executour and leue hym hys goods, so that he wolde promyse hym to pray for hys soule and so fynde one dayly to syng for hym: which thyng to performe hys sonne there made a faythfull promyse. After that this man made hym hys executour, and dyed. But after that hys sonne kept such ryot, that in short tyme he had wasted and spente all, and had nothynge left but a henne and a cocke that was his fader's. It fortunyd than that one of hys frendys came to hym, and sayd he was sory that he had wasted so moch, and askyd hym how he wolde performe hys promyse made to hys fader that he wolde kepe one to syng for hym. Thys yong man answered and sayde: by God! yet I wyll performe my promyse: for I wyll kepe this same cocke alyue styl, and he wyl krow euery day, and so he shall synge euery day for my faders soule; and so I wyl performe my promyse wel ynough.

By thys ye maye se, that it is wysdome for a man to do good dedys hym selfe, whyle he is here, and not to trust to the prayer and promyse of hys executours.

¶ *Of the mayde wasshynge clothes that answered the frere.* xxi.

¶ THERE was a mayde stode by a reuers syde in her smoke,[1] wasshynge clothes, and as she stouped ofttymes, her smocke cleued betune her buttockkes. By whome there cam a frere, seynge[2] her and sayde in sporte : mayde, mayde, take hede : for Bayarde bytes on the brydell.[3] Nay, wys [I], master frere, quod the mayden, he doth but wype hys mouthe, and wenyth ye wyll come and kysse hym.

By thys ye may se that womans answer is neuer to seke.

¶ *Of the thre wyse men of Gotam.* xxii.

¶ A CERTAYN man there was dwellynge in a towne called Gotam that went to a fayre iii myle for to bye shepe; and as he cam ouer a bryge he met with one of hys neyghbours and told hym whether[4] he went, and askyd hym whych way he wold bryng them. Whyche sayd he wolde brynge them ouer the same bryge. Nay, quod the other man, but thou shalt not, by God ! quod

4 lines of the original are wanting.

(1) Smock.   (2) *i.e.* who saw her.
(3) An unregistered proverb, perhaps. The meaning is tolerably clear. See *Tarlton's Newes Out of Purgatorie* (1590), edit. Halliwell, p. 93.
(4) Whither.

Presently there came a milter, who bore a sack of[1] mele vpon a horse, a neybour of theyrs, and paciently askyd them what was the cause of theyr varyaunce; which than she*wyd to hym* the mater and cause, as ye haue harde. Thys thyrde man, the mylner, *beganne* for to rebuke them by a famylyer example, and toke his sacke of mele *from* his horse backe and openyd it, and pouryd all the mele in the sacke ouer the brydge into the ronnynge ryuer; wherby all the mele was lost, and sayde thus: by my trouthe, neybours, because ye stryue for dryuynge ouer the brydge those shepe which be not yet boughte, nor wotte not where they be, me thynketh therfore there is euen as moche wytte in your hedes as there is mele now in my *sacke.*

Thys tale shewyth you, that som man takyth *upon him for to teche* other men wysdome, when he is but a fole hymselfe.

¶ *Of the graye frere that answered his penytente.*
xxiii.

¶ A MAN there was that cam to confesse hym to a *prest and tolde* hym, that he had layne with a

---

(1) I am myself responsible for these few words in italic, which I have supplied from conjecture.

yonge gentyll woman. *The prest then* asked hym in what place; and he sayde it was in * * * all nyght longe in a soft warme bed. The frere herynge that * * * thys and sayd: Now, by swete seynt Francys, then, wast thou very[1]
* * *

¶ *Of the gentylman that bare the sege borde on hys necke.* xxiv.

¶ A CHANDELER beynge a wydower, dwellynge at Holborne, *neere* London, had a fayr doughter whom a yonge gentelman of Dauys Ynne[2] woyd[3] sore to haue hys pleasure of her, whyche by longe sute to her made, at the last graunted hym, and poynted hym to com vpon a nyghte to her faders hous in the euenynge, and she wold conuey hym into her chamber secretly, which was an inner chamber within her faders chamber. So accordynge to the poyntment all thynge was performed, so that he lay wyth her all nyght, and made good chere tell about foure a clocke in the mornynge, at whyche tyme it fortunyd this yonge gentylman fell a coughynge, whych cam vpon hym so sore that he could

(1) Perhaps this story, of which we have here a fragment only, was similar to the one narrated a little farther on. See Tale 57.
(2) Thavies Inn, near St. Andrew's Church, in Holborn.
(3) Wooed.

A C. Mery Talys. 45

not refrayn. Thys wench, than fering her fader that lay in the next chamber, bad hym go put hys hede in the draught, lest that her fader shold here hym : whych after her councel rose in his shyrte, and so dyd. But than because of the sauour of the draught it causyd hym to coughe moche more and louder, that the wenchys fader herde it, and askyd of hys daughter what man it was that coughed in her chamber. She answered and said: no body. But euer this yong man coughed styll more and more, whom the fader herynge sayd : by Goddes body! hore, thou lyest ; I wyll se who is there ;— and rose out of his bedde. Thys wenche perceyued her fader rysinge, [and] cam to the gentylman and sayde : take hede syr to your selfe : for my fader comyth. This gentylman, sodeynly therwyth abasshyd, wolde haue pullyd his hede oute of the draughte hole, which was [so] very streyghte for hys hede that he pullyd the sege borde vp therwyth, and, [it] hangyng about his neck, ran vpon the fader beynge an olde man, and gaue hym a great fall and bare *him to the ground.*

8 *lines wanting.*

there was two or thre skyttysh horses whych, when they se this gentylman ronnyng, start[ed] asyde and threwe downe the cart wyth colys, and drew *backe* and brake the carte rope, wherby the colys fell out, some in one place and *some in* another; and after the horses brake theyr tracys and rannc, some towarde Smythfelde and som toward Newgate. The colyar[1] ran after them, and was an houre and more, or[2] euer he coulde gette his horses to gyder agayne; by which tyme the people of the strete were rysen and cam to the *place*, and saw yt strawyn with colys. Euery one for hys parte gaderyd vp *the colys, tyll the* most parte of the colys were gone, or the colyar had got his horses *agayne.* Duryng *thys* whyle the gentylman went thrugh Seynt Andrews *Chyrch Yarde towarde* Dauys Inne, and there met with the sexten commynge to attend to *ring the bell for* morow mas: whych, whan he saw the gentylman in the *Chyrche Yarde in hys* shyrt wyth the draught borde[3] about his neck, had wend[4] *it had ben a spryt, and c*ried: alas, alas, a spryt! and ran back again to his house almost atte b * * for fere was almoste out of his wytte that he was the worse *a long tyme af*ter. This gentilman, than, because dauys inne gatys were not open, *ranne to the b*acksyde and lept ouer the garden wal; but, in lepyng, the draught-bord so troubled hym, that he fell downe into the gardyn and had almoste

(1) orig. reads *that the colyar.*   (2) before.
(3) the seat of the commode.   (4) weened.

broken his necke; and ther he lay styll, tyll that the pryncypall cam into the garden; which, wan he saw hym lye there, had wente some man had ben slayne and there caste ouer the wall, and durst not come nye him, tyll he had callyd vp hys companye which, when many of the gentylmen[1] wer com to gether loked well vppon hym, and knewe hym, and after releuyd hym; but the borde that was about hys necke caused his hed so to swell, that they coulde not gette it of, tyll they were mynded to cutte it of with hatchettys. Thus was the wenche well iaped,[2] and for fere she ranne from her fader; her faders arme was hurte; the colyar lost his coles; the sexton was almost out of hys wyt; and the gentylman had almost broke his necke.

¶ *Of the merchantes wyfe that sayd she wolde take a nap at sermon.* xxv.

¶ A MARCHANTYS wyfe there was in Bowe parysh in London, somewhat slepte in age, to whom her mayde cam on a Sonday in Lente after dyner and sayde: maystres, quod she, they rynge at Saynte Thomas of Acres, for there shall be a sermon

(1) orig. reads *gentylman*.
(2) mocked, made a jest of. See Nares (edit 1859) *in voce*.

prechyd anon; to whome the mastres answered and sayde: mary! Goddys blessynge haue thy harte for warnynge me thereof; and because I slepte not well all this nyght, I pray the brynge my stole with me: for I wyll go thyder to loke, whether I can take a nappe there, whyle the preest is prechynge.

By this ye may se, that many one goth to chyrch as moch for other thynges as for deuocyon.

¶ *Of the woman that said and she lyued another yere she wolde haue a cockoldes hatte of her owne.* xxvi.

Of the above tale but a few words remain in the fragment.

¶ *Of the gentylman that wysshed his tothe in the gentylwomans tayle.* xxvii.

¶ A GENTYLMAN and gentylwoman satte to gyder talkyng, *which gentylman* had great pain in one of his tethe, and hapnyd to say *to the gentylwo*man thus: I wys, maystres, I haue a tothe in my hede which *greuyth me u*ery sore: wherfore I wold it were in your tayl. She, heryng him *say this*, *answe*ryd thus: in good fayth, syr, yf your tothe were in my tayle it coulde *do it but lytle* good;

but yf there be any thynge in my tayle that can do your tothe good, I wolde it were in your tothe.

By this ye may se that a womans answere is seldome to seke.[1]

¶ *Of the Welcheman that confessyd hym howe he had slayne a frere.* xxviii.

¶ In the tyme of Lente, a Welcheman cam to be confessyd of his curate; whych in his confessyon sayde that he had kylled a frere; to whome the curate sayd he coulde nat assoyle hym. Yes, quod the Welchman, yf thou knewest all, thou woldest assoyle me well ynoughe; and when the curate had commandyd hym to shew hym all the case, he sayd thus: mary, there were ii freres; and I myght haue slayn them bothe, yf I had lyst; but I let the one scape: therfore mayster curate set the tone agaynst the tother, and than the offence is not so great but ye may assoyle me well ynoughe.

By this ye may se, that dyuers men haue so euyll and larg conscyence that they thynke, yf they do one good dede or refrayn from doynge of one euyll synne, that yt ys satysfaccyon for other *synnes* and ofencys.

(1) This moral is also attached to Tales 21, 44, and 56, in all which cases the lady's rejoinder is not less opposed to modern notions of female delicacy.

¶ Of the Welcheman that coude nat gette but a lytell male. xxix.

¶ THERE was a company of gentylmen[1] in Northamptonshyre which wente to hunte for dere in the porlews[2] in the gollet besyde Stony Stratford, amonge which gentylmen there was one which had a Welchman to his seruante, a good archer; whiche, whan they cam to a place where they thought they *should find dere*, apoynted thys Welchman to stand *still, and forbade him in* any wyse to shote at no rascal[3] *dere but to make sure of the greate male and* spare not. Well, quod this Welchman, *I will do so. Anon cam by many greate dere and* Rascall; but euer he lette them go, and toke no hede to them; and within an houre after he saw com rydynge on the hye-waye a man of the contrey, whych had a boget hangynge at hys sadyll bowe.[4] And whan this Welcheman had espyed hym, he bad hym stande, and began to drawe his bow and bad hym delyuer that lytell male that hunge at his sadyll bowe. Thys man, for fere of hys lyfe, was glad to delyuer hym hys boget, and so dyd, and than rode hys waye, and was glad he was so

(1) orig. reads *gentylman*. (2) purlieus.
(3) a lean beast not worth hunting—*Nares*.
(4) The jest here, such as it is, lies in the play on the words male (of the deer) and the mail, or post.

escapyd. And when this man of the contrey was gone, thys Welcheman was *very glad* and wente incontynente to seke hys mayster, and at the laste founde hym wyth hys companye; and whan he saw hym he came to hym, and sayd thus: mayster, by cottes plut and her nayle! I haue stande yonder this two hourys, and I colde se neuer a male but a lytell male that a man had hangynge at his sadell bow, and thet I haue goten, and lo here it is; and toke his master the boget whiche he had taken away from the forsayd man, for the whiche dede bothe the mayster and the seruante were afterwarde in greate trouble.

By this ye may lerne, yt is greate folye for a mayster to putte a seruaunte to that besynes whereof he can nothynge skyll and wherin he hath not ben usyd.

¶ *Of the gentyll woman that sayde to a gentyll man : ye haue a berde aboue and none benethe.* xxx.

¶ A YONGE gentylman of the age of xx yere, somwhat dysposed to myrth and gaye, on a tyme talked wyth a gentylwoman whyche was ryght wyse and also mery. Thys gentylwoman, as she talked with hym, happenyd to loke vpon hys berde which was but yonge and somewhat growen vpon the ouer lyppe, and but lyttell growen benethe as all other yonge mennys berdes comynly vse to grow, and sayd to hym thus: syr, ye haue a berde aboue and none beneth; and he, herynge her say so sayde in sporte: maystres, ye haue a berde beneth and none aboue. Mary, quod she, than set the tone agaynst the tother. Which answere made the gentylman so abasshed, that he had not one worde to answere.

¶ *Of the frere that sayde our Lorde fed fyue M. people with iii. fysshys.* xxxi.

¶ THERE was a certayn White Frere whiche was a very glotton and a great nyggyn,[1] whiche had an vngracyouse boy that euer folowed hym and bare his cloke, and what for the freres glotony and for his chorlysshnes the boy, where he wente, cowlde scante gette meate ynoughe: for the frere wolde eate almoste all hym selfe. But on a tyme the frere made a sermone in the contry, wherin he touched very many myracles whyche Cryste dyd afore hys passyon, amonge which he specyally rehersyd the myracle whyche Cryste did in fedynge fyue thousande people with fyue louys of brede and with iii lytell fysshes; and this frerys boy

(1) niggard.

A C. Mery Talys. 53

which caryd not gretely for hys mayster * *, *by reason that* hys mayster was so great a churle, *cryed out aloude* that all the church harde, and sayd : by *my faith, then, there were no* fryers there ! whyche answere made all *the people laughe, so* that for shame the frere wente out of the * * * * * he than departyd out of the churche * * * *.

By thys ye may se that it is honeste * * depart with suche as he hath to them * *

¶ *Of the frankelyn that wold haue had the frere gone.* xxxii.

¶ A RYCHE fraynklyn dwellyn in the countie *of* * * * *had a frere in his* house, of whom he could neuer be ryd any *meanes, but he wold tarrye by the* space of a senyght[1] and wold neuer depart ; wherfore *the franklyn was sore greuud and sadly* wery of hym. On a tyme as he and hys wyfe and this frere *were togydder, he* faynyd hymselfe very angry wyth hys wyfe, in somoche that *he smote* her. Thys frere perseyuyng well what they ment sayd * * * I haue bene here this seuenyght whan ye were frendys, and *I will tarrye a* forte- nyght lenger but I wyll se you frendys agayne, or

(1) a week.

I depart. *The franklyn*, perceyuynge that he coude no good nor wold not depart by none other meanes, answeryd hym shortely and sayd: by God! frere, but thou shalt abyde here no longer; and toke hym by the shulders, and thrust hym out of the dorys of the house.

By this ye may se, that he that wyl lerne no good by examples in a maner to hym shewyd, is worthy to be taught wyth open rebuke.

¶ *Of the prest that sayd Our Lady was not so curyous a woman.* xxxiii.

¶ In the towne of Bottelley dwellyd a mylner, whiche had a good homely wenche to his doughter, whome the curate of the nexte towne louyd, and, as the fame went, had her at hys pleasure. But on a tyme thys curat prechyd of those curyouse wyues now a dayes, and whether it were for the nonys,[1] or whether it cam oute at all adventurys, he had peuyd to say thus in hys sermon: ye wyues, ye be so curyous in all your warkes, that ye wot not what ye meane, but ye shold folow Oure Lady. For Our Lady was nothynge so curyous as ye be; but she was a good homely wenche lyke the mylners doughter of Botteley. At whych sayng all the parishons made gret laughyng, and specyally they that knew that he louyd that same wenche.

By this ye may se, it is gret foly for a man that is suspectyd with any person to praise or to name the same parson openly, lest it bryng hym in forther sclaunder.

¶ *Of the good man that sayde to his wyfe he had euyll fare.* xxxiv.

¶ A FRERE Lymytour[1] come into a pore mannys howse in the countrey, and because thys pore man thought thys frere myght do hym some good, he therefore thought to make hym good chere. But bycause hys wyfe wold dresse hym no good mete for coste, he therfore at dyner tyme sayd thus: by God! wyfe, bycause thou dyddest dresse me no good mete to my dyner, were it not for mayster frere, thou shouldest haue halfe a dosyn strypes. Nay, syr, quod the frere, I pray you spare not for me; wherwyth the wyfe was angry, and therfore at souper she caused them to fare wors.

¶ *Of the frere that had hys chylde make a laten.* xxxv.

But very few words remain of this Tale.

[1] Mendicant friar.

¶ *Of the gentylman that asked the frere for his beuer.* xxxvi.

¶ *In the terme* tyme a good old gentylman, beyng a lawyer, cam to Lon*don to the* terme; and as he cam he hapenyd to ouertake a frere, which *was an v*nthrift and went alone wythout hys beuer : wherfore this *gentylman asked* thys frere, where was hys beuer that shold kepe hym compa*ny, and sayd it was* contrary to his relygyon to go alone, and it wolde cause people to suppose hym to be som apostata or som vnthryft. By God, syr, quod the *frere! my beuer* commaundeth hym unto your master-shyp. Why, quod the gentylman, I knowe hym not. Than (quod the frere to the gentylman), ye are the more fole to aske for hym.

By thys tale ye may se, that he that geueth counsell to any vnthryft, *and tech*eth hym hys dutye, shall haue oftymes but a mock for his labour.

¶ *Of the thre men that chose the woman.* xxxvii.

¶ THRE gentylmen cam into an Inne, where a fayre woman was tapster : wherfore, as these thre satte there makynge mery, eche of them kyssed her, and made good pastyme and plesure. Howbeit one spake merley[1] and sayde : I can not se how this gentylwoman is able to make pastyme and pleasure to vs all thre excepte that she were departed in thre partes. By my trouthe, quod one of them, yf that she myght be departed, than I wolde chuse for my parte her hed and her fayre face, that I myghte alway kysse her Than quod the seconde : I wolde haue the breste and harte : for there lyeth her loue. Than quod the thyrd : then ther is nothyng left for me but the loynys, buttockes and legges ; I am contente to haue it for my parte. And whan these gentylmen had passed the tyme there by the space of one hour or ii, they toke theyr leue and were goynge awaye ; but, or they went, the thyrd man whych had chosen the bely and the buttockys did kys the tapyster and bad her farewell. What! quod the fyrste man that had chosen the face and the mouth, why dost thou so ? thou dost me wronge to kysse my parte that I haue chosen of her. O ! quod the other, I pray the be nat angry : for I am contente that thou shal kys my parte for it.

(1) Merrily

¶ *Of the gentylman that taught his cooke the medycyne for the tothake.* xxxviii.

¶ In Essex there dwellyd a mery gentylman, whyche had a coke callyd Thomas that was greatly dysseasyd with the tothake, and complaynyd to hys mayster thereof; whych sayd he had a boke of medecins and sayd he wold loke vp hys boke to se whether he could fynd any medecyn therin for it, and so sent[1] one of hys doughters to hys study for hys boke, and incontynent lokyd uppon yt a long season; and than sayd thus to hys coke: Thomas, quod he, here is a medesyn for your tothake; and yt ys a charm; but yt wyl do you no good except ye knele on your knees, and aske yt for Sent Charyte. Thys man, glad to be relesyd of hys payn, kneled and sayd: mayster, for Seint Charyte, let me haue that medecyne. Than, quod thys gentylman, knele on your knees and say after me; whyche knelyd down and sayd after hym as he bad hym. Thys gentylman began and sayd thus :—

"The son on the Sonday."
"The son on the Sonday," quod Thomas.
"The mone on the Monday."

(1) orig. reads *send*.

A C. Mery Talys. 59

"The mone on the Monday."
"The Trynyté on the Tewsday."
"The Trynyté on the Tewsday."
"The wyt on the Wednysday."
"The wyt on the Wednysday."
"The holy holy Thursday."
"The holy holy Thursday."
"And all that fast on Fryday."
"And all that fast on Friday."
"—— in thy mouthe on Saterday."

Thys coke Thomas,[1] heryng hys mayster thus mokkyng hym, in anger stert vp and sayd: by Goddys body! mokkyng churle, I wyll neuer do the seruyce more; and went forth to hys chamber to gete hys gere to geder to thentent to haue gon thens by and by; but what for the anger that he toke wyth his mayster for the mok that he gaue hym, and what for labor that he toke to geder hys gere so shortly togeder, the payne of the tothake went from hym incontynent, that hys mayster cam to hym and made hym to tarry styll, and tolde hym that hys charme was the cause of the ease of the payne of the tothake.

By thys tale ye may se, that anger oftymes puttyth away the bodely payne.

(1) orig. reads Thomas coke. In the orig. the text runs on in the above passage, which is generally done in old books to save room.

¶ *Of the gentylman that promysed the scoler of Oxforde a sarcanet typet.* xxxix.

¶ A SKOLER of Oxford latley made Mayster of Art cam in to the cyte of London, and in Poulys mette with the sayd mery gentleman of Essex, which was euer disposyd to play many mery pageants,[1] wyth whom before he had bene of famylyer accoyntaunce and prayd hym to give hym a sercenet typet. This gentylman, more lyberall of promyse than of gyfte, grauntyd hym he should haue one, yf he wold com to hys lodgyng to the sygne[2] of the Bull wythout Byshops gate in the next mornynge at vi of the cloke. Thys scoler thankyd hym, and for that nyght departyd to hys lodgyng in Flete Strete, and in the mornyng erely as he poyntyd cam to hym to the sygne of the Bull. And as [soon as] thys gentylman saw hym, he bad hym go wyth hym in to the Cyte, and he sholde be sped anon; whyche incontynent went togyder, tyll they[3] cam in to seynt Laurence Church in the Jury, where the gentylman espyed a preste raueshyd to masse[4] and [he] told

(1) tricks and pranks. (2) orig. reads *synne*. (3) orig. reads *he*.
(4) Intently engaged in the celebration of mass. "St. Lawrence Jewry," says Mr. Cunningham (*Handbook of Lond.* 471,) "stood in King Street, Cheapside. It was destroyed in the Fire of 1666, and was rebuilt by Sir C. Wren."

the skoller that "yonder is the preste that hath the typet for you," and bad hym knele downe in the pew, and he shold speke to hym for it. And incontynent thys gentylman went to the preest and sayd : syr, here is a skoller, a kynnysman of myne, gretly dyseasyed wyth the chyncough.[1] I pray you, whan masse is donne, gyue hym iii draughtys of your chales. The preest grantyd hym, and tornyd hym to the skoler, and sayd : syr, I shall serue you as sone as I haue sayd masse. The skoler than taryed styll and herd the mas, trusting that whan the masse was done, that the preste wold giue hym hys typet of sarcenet. Thys gentylman in the meane whyle departyd out of the chyrche. Thys preste, whan mas was done, putte wyne in the chales, and cam to the skoler knelyng in the pew, profferyng hym to drynk of the chales. Thys skoler lokyd upon hym, and musyd and sayd: why, master parson, wherfore profer ye me the chales ? Mary, quod the prest, for the gentylman told me ye were dysseasyd with the chyncough, and prayd me therfor that for a medecyne ye might drynk of the chales. Nay, by seynt mary, quod the scoler, he promysyd me ye shulde delyuer me a tipet of sarcenet. Nay, quod the preest, he spake to me of no typet, but he desyred me to

(1) Hooping-cough.

gyue yow drynk of the chales for the chyncough. By Goddis body, quod the scoler, he is, as he was euer wont to be, but a mokkyng wretch, and if[1] I lyue I shall quyte hym; and so departid out of the church in great anger.

By thys tale ye may percyue, it is no wysdom for a man to truste to a man to do a thing, that is contrary to hys old accustumyd condycyons.

¶ *Of mayster Skelton that brought the bysshop of Norwiche ii fesauntes.* xl.

¶ It fortuned ther was a great varyance bitwen the bysshop of Norwych and one master Skelton[1] a poyet lauryat, in so much that the bysshop commaundyd hym that he shuld not come in his gatys. Thys mayster Skelton dyd absent hym selfe for a long seson; but at the laste he thought to do hys dewty to hym, and studyed weys how he myght obtayne the bysshopys fauour, and determynyd hem self that he wold come to hym wyth some present and humble hym self to the byshop; and [he] gat a cople of fesantes and cam to the bysshuppys place, and requyryd the porter he might come in to speke wyth my lord. This porter, knowyng his

(1) orig. reads *ever*.
(2) The celebrated poet. The bishop was of course Bishop Nykke, Nikke, or Nyx, as the name is variously spelled. He held the see from 1501 to 1536.

A C. Mery Talys. 63

lordys pleasure, wold not suffer him to come in at the gatys : wherfor thys mayster Skelton went on the baksyde to seke some other way to come in to the place. But the place was motyd, [so] that he cowlde se no way to come ouer except in one place, where there lay a long tree ouer the motte in maner of a brydge that was fallyn down wyth wynd : wherfore thys mayster Skelton went a long vpon the tree to come ouer; and whan he was almost ouer hys fote slypyd for lak of sure fotyng, and [he] fel in to the mote vp to the myddyll. But at the last he recoueryd hym self, and as wel as he coud dryed hymself ageyne, and sodenly cam to the byshop, beyng in hys hall than lately rysen from dyner, whyche, whan he saw Skelton commyng sodenly, sayd to hym : why, thow catyfe, I warnyd the thow shuldys neuer come in at my gatys and chargyd my porter to kepe the out. Forsoth, my lorde, quod Skelton, though ye gaue suche charge and though your gatys by neuer so suerly kept : yet yt ys no more possible to kepe me out of your dorys than to kepe out crowes or pyes : for I cam not in at your gatys, but I cam ouer the mote, [so] that I haue ben almost drownyd for my labour; and shewyd his clothys how euyll he was arayed, whych causyd many that stode therby to laughe apace. Than quod Skelton : yf it lyke

your lordeshyp, I haue brought you a dyshe to
your super, a cople of Fesantes. Nay, quod the
byshop, I defy the and thy Fesantys also, and,
wrech as thou art, pyke the out of my howse, for I
wyll none of thy gyft how   *   *   *   *
Skelton, than consyderynge that the bysshoppe
called hym fole so ofte, sayd to one of hys famy-
lyers therby that, thoughe it were euyll to be
christened a fole, yet it was moche worse to be
confyrmed a fole of suche a bysshoppe : for the
name of confyrmacyon must nedes abyde Therfore he ymagened howe he myghte auoyde that
confyrmacyon, and mused a whyle; and at the
laste sayde to the bysshope thus : if your lordeshype knewe the names of these fesantes ye wold
be contente to take them. Why, caytefe, quod the
bisshoppe hastly and angrey, *what* be theyr names?
Y wys, my lorde, quod Skelton, this fesante is
called Alpha, which is in primys—the fyrst; and
this is called O, that is novissimus, the last; and
for the more playne vnderstandynge of my mynde,
if it plese your lordeshype to take them, I promyse
you this alpha is the fyrste that euer I gaue you,
and this O is the laste that euer I wyll gyue you
whyle I lyue. At which answere all that were
by made great laughter, and they all d*esired the
Bishoppe* to be good lorde vnto him for his merye

conceytes, at which *earnest entrety, as it* wente, the bysshope was contente to take hym vnto his fauer agayne.

By thys tale ye may se, that mery conceytes dothe *a man more* good than to frete hymselfe with a*nger* and melancholy.

¶ *Of the yeman of garde that sayd he wolde bete the carter.* xli.

¶ A YOMAN of the kynges garde, dwellynge in a vyllage besyde London, had a very fayre yonge wife. To whome a carter of the towne, *a mery* fellowe, resorted and laye with her dyuers tymes, whan her husbande was on garde; and thys was so openly knowen that all the towne spake therof. *A certaine yonge* man of the towne well acquoyntyd with thys yeman *told him* that suche a carter hadde layne by his wyfe. To whome *this yeman of the garde* sware by Goddes body, if he mette with hym it *should go harde but he wolde bete him well.* *Hey*, quod the yonge man, if ye go streyght euen nowe the *right way*, ye *shall* ouertake him dryuyng a carte laden with haye towarde London; wherfore the yeman of the garde incontynent rode after this carter, and within shorte space overtoke him and knewe him well ynoughe, and incontynent called the carter to him and sayd thus: Syrra, I vnderstande that thou doste lye euery nyght with my wyfe, whan I am from home. Thys carter beynge no thynge afrayde of hym answered, ye, marry, what than? What than, quod the yeman of garde! By Goddys harte! hadst thou nat tolde me truth, I wolde haue broke thy hede. And so the yeman of garde retourned, and no hurte done, no stroke stryken nor proferyed.

By this ye may se, that the greatyst crakers somtyme, whan it commeth to the profe, be moste cowardes.

¶ *Of the fole that saide he had leuer go to hell than to heuen.* xlii.

¶ A FOLE there was, that dwelled with a gentylman in the countrey, whiche was called a great tyraunte and an extorcyoner. But this fole loued his mayster meruaylously, because he cherysshed hym so well. It happened   *   *

3 lines wanting.

to heuen: for I had leuer go to hell. Than the other asked hym why he had leuer go to hell. By my trouthe, quod the fole: for I wyll go with my master; and I am sure my master shall go to hell. For euery man seyth he shall go to the deuyll in hell; and therfore I wyll go thyder with hym.

¶ *Of the plowmannys sonne that sayde he sawe one make a gose to creke sweetly.* xliii.

¶ THERE was a certayn plowmans son of the contrey of the age of xvi yeres, that neuer coming moche amonge company but alway went to plough and husbandry. On a tyme this yonge lad went to a weddyng with his fader, where he se one lute[1] vpon a lute; and whan he came home at nyght his moder asked hym, what sporte he had at weddynge. This lad answeryd and sayd: by my trouth, moder, quod he, there was one that brought a gose in his armes and tykled her so vpon the neck, that she crekyd the sweetlyest that I hard gose creke in my lyfe.

¶ *Of the maydes answere that was with chylde.* xliv.

¶ AT a merchauntes house in London there was a mayde whiche was great with chylde, to whom the maystres of the house cam, and comaunded[2] her to tell her who was the fader of the chylde. To whom the mayde answered: forsooth, nobody.

(1) *Lute*, as a verb, appears to be obsolete. We still say *to fiddle* and no doubt *to lute* was formerly just as much in use.
(2) Orig. reads *and that commanded*.

Why, quod the maystres, it is not possyble but som man is the fader thereof? To whom the mayd answered: why, maystres, why may I not haue a chyld without a man as well as hennys lay eggys withhout a cocke?

By this ye may se it is harde to fynde a woman wythout an excuse.

¶ *Of the seruaunt that rymyd with hys mayster.* xlv.

¶ A GENTLEMAN there was dwellynge nygh Kyngston upon Tamys, and rydynge in the contrey with his seruaunt which was *not the* quyckest felowe, but rode alway sadly[1] by *his maysters side and uttered uery fewe wordys.* Hys mayster sayd to him: *wherefore rydyst* thou so saddly? I wolde have the tell me some tale to beguyle the tyme with. By my trouthe, mayster, quod he, I can tell no tale. Then sayd his mayster: canst thou not synge? No by my trouthe, quod he, I coulde neuer synge in all my lyfe. Quod the mayster: canst thou ryme? No, by my trouthe, quod he, I can not; but yf ye wyll begyn to ryme, I wyll folow as well as I can. By my trouth, quod the mayster, that is well; therfore I wyll begyn to make a ryme. Let me se

(1) Quietly.

how well thou canst folowe thy mayster meanwhyle; and then [he] began to ryme thus :—

"Many mennys swannys swymme in Temmys,
And so do myne."

Then quod the seruant :—

"And many a man lyeth by other mennys wyues,
And so do I by thyne."[1]

What dost thou, horeson, quod the mayster? By my trouthe, mayster, no thynge, quod he, but make vp the ryme. But quod the mayster: I charge the tell me why thou sayest so? Forsothe Mayster, quod he, for nothynge in the worlde but to make vp your ryme. Than quod the mayster: yf thou doist for nothynge ellys, I am content. So the mayster forgaue hym hys saynge, all thoughe he sayd trouthe peraduenture.

¶ *Of the Welcheman that delyuered the letter to the ape.* xlvi.

5 *first lines wanting.*

fauoure to his seruant and commaunded his seruant shortely to br*ynge hym an* answere. This

(1) This, to save space, is printed like prose in the orig.; but it was evidently meant to be verse.

Welcheman came to the chefe Iustyce' place, and at *the gate saw* an ape syttynge there in a cote made for hym, as they use to *apparell apes* for disporte. This Welchman dyd of hys cappe, and made curtsye *to the ape and* sayd: my mayster recommendeth hym to my lorde youre father, and sendeth hym here a letter. This ape toke this letter and opened it, and *lokyd theron*, and after lokyd vpon the man, makynge many mockes and moyes, *as the proper*tyes of apes is to do. This Welcheman, because he vnde*rstood hym* nat, came agayne to his mayster accordynge to his commaundes, *and tolde hym he* delyuered the letter vnto my lorde chefe Iustyce' sonne, *who was at the gate* in a furred cote. Anone his mayster asked hym what *answere he broughte. The man* sayd he gaue hym an answere; but it was other Frenche or *Laten: for he understode* him nat. But, syr, quod he, ye nede nat to fere: for I saw *in his counte*naunce so moche, that I warrante you he wyll do your errande to my lorde his father. This gentylman in truste therof made not a*nye further suite*, for lacke wherof his seruaunte, that had done the felonye, within a monthe after was rayned at the kynges benche and caste, and afterwarde hanged.

By this ye may se that euery wyse man ought

to take hede, that *he sende nat a fo*lysshe seruaunte vpon a hasty message that is a matter of *nede*.

¶ *Of hym that solde ryght nought.* xlvii.

¶ A *certaine* felowe there was whiche profered a dagger to sell to a fellowe, *the* which answered hym and sayd, that he had ryght nought *to giue* therfore ; wherefore the other sayde that he shulde haue hys dagger *upon c*ondycyon that he shulde gyue and delyuer vnto hym therefore *within iii* dayes after ryghte nought, or els forty shyllynges in money : wher*on the* other was contente. Thys bergayne thus agreed, he that shulde del*yuer* his ryght noughte toke no thoughte, vntyll suche tyme that the day apoynted drewe nye. At the whiche tyme he began to ymagen, howe he myght *delyuer* this man ryght nought. And fyrst of all he thought on a feder, a straw, a pynnes poynte, and suche other ; but nothynge could he deuyse but that it was somwhat ; wherfore he came home all sadde and pencyfe for sorowe of losynge of his xl. shyllynges, and coulde nother slepe nor take reste, wherof hys wyfe, beynge agreued, demaunded the cause of his heuynes ; which at the last after many denayes tolde her all. Well, syr, quod she, lette me here with alone and gette ye forthe a—towne ; and I shall handell this matter well ynoughe. This man folowynge his wyfes counsell wente forthe of the

5 lines wanting.

Therfore, syr, quod she, put your hande in yonder potte, and take your money. This man beynge glad thrust his hande in it, supposyng to haue taken xl shyllynges of money, and thrust his hande thoroughe it vp to the elbowe. Quod the wyfe than : syr, what haue ye there? Mary, quod he, ryghte nought. Syr, quod she, than haue ye youre bergayne, and than my husbande hathe contented you for his dagger accordynge to his promyse.

By this ye may se, that oftentymes a womans wytte at an extremyte *is moche* better than a mans.

¶ *Of the frere that tolde the thre chyldres fortunes.* xlviii.

¶ THERE was *a frere* lymyttour whyche wente a lymyttynge to a cer*tayne* towne, wherin dwellyd a certayne ryche man of whome he ne*uer coulde* gette the value of an hal[f]peny : yet he thought he wolde go thyder and assaye hem.[1] And as he

(1) *i. e.* him. The Orig. reads *them.*

wente thyderwarde, the wyfe stand*yng at the* dore, perceyuynge hym commynge a farre of, thoughte that he *was commynge* thyther, and by and by ranne in and badde her chyldren standyng *thereby*, that if the frere asked for her, say she was nat within. The frere *sawe her* runne in and suspected the cause, and came to the dore and asked for the wyfe. The chyldren, as they were bydden, sayde that she was nat within. Than stode he styll lokynge on the chyldren; and at the laste he called to hym the eldeste and badde hym let hym se his hande; and whan he *saw his* hande : O Jesu! quod he, what fortune for the is ordayned! *Then he asked the* seconde sonne to se his hande and, his hande sene, the frere sayd : *O Jesu! what* destenye for the is prepared. Than loked he in the thyrde sonnes *hand. O God!* quod he, thy desteny is hardest of all; and therwith wente he his way. The *wyfe*, heryng these thinges, sodenly ranne out and called the frere againe, *and pray*de hym to come in, and after to sytte downe, and sette before hym *all the vita*ile that she had. And whan he had well eaten and dronken, she bes*ought* hym to tell her the destenyes of her chyldren; which at the last after many *difficulties* tolde her that the fyrste shulde be a beggar, the seconde a thefe, the thyrde a homicyde; whiche she hearynge fell downe in a soone[1] and toke it greuouslye. The frere comforted her and said that, thoughe these were theyr fortunes, there myght be remedy had. Than she besought of him[2] his counsell. Than said the frere: you must make the eldest that shalbe a beggar a frere, and the seconde that shalbe a thefe a man of lawe, and the thyrde that shalbe an homicyde a phisicyon.

By this tale ye may lerne, that they that will come to the speche or presence of any persone for theyr owne cause, they muste fyrste endeuer them selfe to shewe suche matters as those persones most delyte in.

¶ *Of the boy that bare the frere his masters money.* xlix.

4 lines wanting.

Ye, quod the frere. Than wente the man to the boye and sayd: syr, thy mayster byddeth the gyue me xl pens. I wyll nat, quod the boye. Than called the man with an hye voyce to the frere and sayd: syr, he sayeth he wyll not. Than quod the frere: bete him; and whan the boye

(1) Swoon.   (2) Orig. reads *besought him of*.

harde his mayster say so, he gaue the man xl pens.

By this ye may se, it is foly for a man to say ye or nay to a matter, excepte he knewe surely what the matter is.

¶ *Of Phylyp Spencer the bochers man.* 1.

¶ A CERTAYNE bocher dwellynge in Saynt Nicolas[1] Flesshambles in London, called Poule, had a seruaunte called Peter. Thys Peter on a Sonday was at the churche herynge masse; and one of his felowes, whose name was Phylyppe Spencer, was sente to call him at the commaundement of his maister. So it happened at the tyme that the curat *preched*, and in his sermonde touched many auctoryties of the holy scriptures, amonge all, the wordes of the pystles of saynt Poule ad[2] phylypenses : howe [we] be nat onely bounde to beleue in Chryste but also to suffre for Chrystes sake; and [he] sayd these wordes in the pulpet : what sayeth Poule ad Phylyppenses to

---

(1) Orig. reads *Nocolas*. The Church of St. Nicholas Shambles, which formerly stood in the neighbourhood of Newgate Market, was pulled down at the Reformation. See Cunningham, *Handbook of London*, in voce.

(2) Orig. reads *and*.

this ? Thys yonge man, that was called Philyppe Spenser, hadde went he had spoken of him [and] answered shortely and sayd : mary, syr, he bad Peter come home and take his parte of a podynge, for he shulde go for a Calfe anone. The curate herynge this, was abasshed, and all the audyence made great laughter.

By thys ye may se, that it is no token of a wyse man to gyue a soden answere to a questyon, before he knowe surely what the matter is.

¶ *Of the courtear and the carter.* li.

¶ THERE came a courtyer by a carter, the whiche in derysyon preysed the carters backe, legges, and other membres of his body meruaylously, whose gestynge the carter perceyued and sayde, he had another properte than the courtyer espyed in hym ; and whan the courtyer had demanded what it shulde be, he lokyd asyde ouer hys shulder vpon the courtyer and sayde thus : lo ! syr, this is my propertie. I haue a walle eye in my hede : for I neuer loke ouer my shulder thys wyse but lyghtlye [1] I spye [2] a knaue.

By this tale a man may se, that he that useth to deryde and mocke other folkes, is somtyme him selfe more deryded and mocked.

(1) Quickly.   (2) Orig. reads *lyghtlye espye.*

A C. Mery Talys. 77

¶ *Of the yong man that prayd his felow to teche hym hys paternoster.* lii.

¶ A YONGE man of the age of xx yere, rude and unlerned, in the tyme of Lente came to his curate to be confessed; whiche, whan he was of his lyfe serched and examyned could not saye his Pater noster: wherfore his confessoure exorted him to lerne his Pater noster and shewed him what an holy and goodly prayer it was and the effecte therof and the vii peticyons therin contayned. *The i. sanctificetur &c. halowed be thy name. The ii. adueniat regnum &c. thy kingdome come The iii. Fiat voluntas &c. thy will be done in earth as it is in heuen. The iv. Panem nostrum &c. geue*[1] *us* our dayly sustenaunce alway and helpe vs as we helpe[2] them that haue nede of us. The v. Dimitte &c. Forgyue vs our synnes done to the as we forgyue them that trespas agaynste vs. The vi. Et ne nos. Let vs nat be ouercome with euyll temptacyon. The vii. Sed libera &c. But delyuer us from all euyll. amen. And than his confessour, after this exposicyon to hym made, injoyned hym in penaunce to faste euery Fryday on brede and water, tyll he had his Pater noster well and sufficiently

(1) Singer's ed. reads *yeve*.
(2) Orig. ed. and Singer read *we haue and helpe them*.

lerned. This yonge man, mekely acceptyng his penaunce, so departed and came home to one of his companyons, and sayde to his felowe : so it is that my gostely father hathe gyuen me in penaunce to faste euery Fryday [on] brede and water, tyll I can say my Pater noster. Therfore I pray thee teche me my Pater noster, and by my truthe I shall therfore teche the a songe of Robyn Hode that shall be worth xx of it.

By thys tale ye may lerne to knowe the effecte of the holy prayer of the Pater noster.

¶ *Of the frere that prechyd in ryme expownynge the ave maria.* liii.

¶ A CERTAYNE frere there was whiche, vpon Our Lady day the Annuncyacion, made a sermon in the Whyte Freres in London, and began his antetexte thys wyse. Aue Maria gracia plena dominus tecum &c. These wordes, quod the frere, were spoken by the aungell Gabryell to Oure Ladye, whan she conceyued Christe; which is as moche to saye in our mother tonge as : all hayle, Mary, well thou be; the sonne of God is with the. And furthermore the aungell sayde: thou shall conceyue and bere a sonne, and thou shalt call his name Jesum ; and Elyzabeth thy swete cosyn, she shall

A C. Mery Talys. 79

conceyue the swete Saynt John. And so [he] proceded styll in his sermon in suche fonde ryme, that dyuers and many gentylmen of the court that were there began to smyle and laughe. The frere that perceyuyng said thus: Maysters, I pray you, harke; I shall tell you a narracyon. There was ones a yonge preest, that was nat all the best clerke, sayd masse and redde a colect thus: Deus qui vigenti filii tui &c. wherfore he shulde haue said vnigeniti filii tui &c; and after, whan masse was done, there was suche a gentylman, as one of you are, nowe that had herde this masse, came to the preest and sayde thus: syr, I pray you tell me how many sonnes had God Almyghty? Quod the preest: why aske you that? Mary, syr, quod the gentylman, I suppose he had xx sonnes: for ye sayd right nowe: Deus qui viginti filii tui.[2] The preest, perceyuynge how that he deryded hym, answered hym shortely and said thus: howe many sonnes so euer God Almyghty had, I am sure that thou arte none of them: for thou scornyst the worde of God. And so sayde the frere in the pulpet: no more are ye none of the chyldren of God: for ye scorne and laughe at me nowe, that preche to you the worde of God whiche

3 lines wanting.

(1) This portion of the tale is repeated in *Scoggin's or Scogin's Jests.*

By this ye may[1] perceyue wel that the best, the wysyst and the most holyest matter that is, by fond pronuncyacion and otterauns, may be marryd nor shall not[2] edyfye to the audyence. Therfore euery proces shold[3] be vtteryd wyth wordys and countenaunce conuenyent to the matter.

Also yet by thys tale they that be vnlearnyd in the laten tonge may know the sestence[4] of the Aue Maria.

¶ *Of the curat that prechyd the artycles of the Crede.* liv.

¶ IN a wyllage in Warwykshyre there was a parysh prest, all though he wer no great clarke nor graduat of the vnyuersyte, yet he prechid to hys paryshons vppon a Sonday, declaryng to them xii artycles of the Crede; shewyng them that the furst artycle was to beleue in God the fader almyghty maker of heuen and erth; the second, to beleue in Jesu Cryste hys onely son our Lorde coequal wyth the fader in all thynges perteynyng to the deyte; the thyrd, that he was conceyuyd of the holy goost, borne of the

---

(1) I have supplied these four words from conjecture. They are not in the original nor in Singer's reprint.
(2) The double negative is very common in old English books.
(3) Orig. reads *wold.*
(4) Essence?

vyrgyn Mary; the fourthe, that he suffred deth under Pons pylate and that he was crucyfyed, dede and beryed; the fyft, that he descended to hell, and fet[1] out the good sowlys that were in feyth and hope, and than the thyrd day rose from deth to lyfe; the syxt, [that] he assendyd into heuen to the ryght syde of God the fader, where he syttyth; the seuynth, that he shall come at the day of dome to judge both us that be quyk and them that be dede; the eyght, to beleue in the Holy Gost equall God wyth the fader and the sone; the nynth, [to beleue] in the holy churche Catholyk and in the holy communyon of sayntes; the tenth, [to beleue] in the remyssion of synnys; the levynth, [to beleue] in the resurreccyon generall of the body and soule; the twelfth [to beleue] in euerlastynge lyfe that God shall rewarde them that be good. And [he] sayd to his paryshons further, that these artycles ye be bounde to beleue: for they be trewe of auctoryte. And yf you beleue not me, than for a more surete and suffycyent auctoryte go your way to Couentre, and there ye shall se them all playe in Corpus Cristi playe.

By redynge of this tale, they that understand no Laten may lerne to knowe the xii articles of the fayth.

(1) Fetched.

¶ Of the frere that prechyd the x commaunde-
mentis. lv.

¶ A LYMYTOUR of the Gray Freres in London prechyd[1] in a certaine vyllage in the contrey in the tyme of his lymytacyon, and had prechyd a sermon which he had lernyd by hart, that of the declaring of the x. commaundementis. The fyrst, to beleue in one God and to honoure him aboue all thynges. The seconde, to swere not in vayn by hym nor none of his creatures. The thyrde, to absteyne from wordely operacyon on the holy day, thou and all thy seruauntys of whome thou hast cherg. The fourthe, to honour thy parentys and to help them in theyr necessyte. The fyft, to sle no man in dede nor wyll, nor for no hatred hurte his bodye nor good name. The syxte, to do no fornycacyon actuall nor by no vnlefull[2] thought to desyre no fleshly delectacyon. The seuenthe (eighth), to stele nor depryue no mannes goodes by thefte. *The ninth, not to bear false witness against thy neighbour. The tenth, not*[3] to couete nor desyre no mannes goodes vnlefullye. Thou shalt not desyre thy

---

(1) Orig. reads *whych prechyd*, which the context will scarcely allow.
(2) Unlawful.
(3) The words in italics are supplied by me from conjecture. They are not in orig. or in Singer's reprint; but it is evident what the context requires.

neyghbours wyfe for thyne owne apetyte vnlaufully. And because this frere had preched this sermonde so often, one that had herde it before tolde the freres seruaunte, that his maister was called frere John x. Commaundementes; wherfore this seruaunte shewed the frere his mayster therof, and aduysed him to preche some sermonde of some other matter: for it greued him to here his maister so deryded and to be called frere John x. Commaundementes. For euery man knoweth [quod he] what ye wyll say, as sone as euer ye begyn, because ye haue prechyd it so ofte. Why than, quod the frere, I am sure thou knowest well whiche be the x commaundementes that hast herde them so ofte declared. Ye, syr, quod the seruaunte, that I do. Than, quod the frere, I pray the reherse them vnto me nowe. Mary, quod the seruaunte, they be these. Pride, couetise,[1] slouthe, enuy, wrathe, glotony and lechery.

By redyng thys tale ye may lerne to knowe the x commaundementes and the vii dedely synnes.[2]

(1) Covetousness. Orig. reads *covetous*.
(2) Whitford, in his *Werke for Householders*, 1533, says:—" yet must you have a lesson to teche your folkes to beware of the vii pryncipall synnes, whiche ben communely called the seven dedely synnes, but in dede they doue call them wronge: for they be not alway dedely synnes. Therfore they sholde be called capytall or pryncipall synnes, and not dedely synnes. These ben theyr names by ordre after our dyvysion Pryde, Envy, Wrath, Covetyse, Glotony, Slouth, and Lechery."

¶ *Of the wyfe that bad her husbande ete the candell fyrste.* lvi.

¶ THE husbande sayde to his wyfe thus wyse : by this candell, I dremed thys nyght that I was cockecolde. To whom she answered and sayd : husbande, by this brede, ye are none. Than sayd he : wyfe, eate the brede. She answered and sayd to her husbande : than eate you the candell : for you sware fyrste.

By this a man may se, that a womans answer is *neuer to seke.*

¶ *Of the man of lawes sonnes answer.* lvii.

¶ A WOMAN demaunded a questyon of a little chylde, sonne unto a man of lawe, of what crafte his father was; whiche chylde sayde, his father was a craftye man of lawe.

By this tale a man may perceyue, that somtyme peraduenture yonge Innocentes speke truely vnaduysed.

¶ *Of the frere in the pulpet that bad the woman leue her babelynge.* lviii.

¶ IN a certayne parrysshe churche in London, after the olde laudable and accustomed maner, there was a frere Mynor, all thoughe he were nat the best clerke nor coulde nat make the best sermondes, yet by the lycence of the curate he there prechyd to the Parysshons. Among the whyche audyence there was a wyfe at that tyme lytell disposed to contemplacyon, [who] talked wyth a gossype of hers of other femenyne tales so loude that the frere harde and somwhat was perturbed therwith. To whome therfore openly the frere spake and sayd: thou woman there in the tawny gowne, holde thy peace and leaue thy babelynge; thou troublest the worde of God. This woman therwith sodenly abasshed, because the frere spake to her so openly, that all the people her behelde, answered shortly and said: I beshrowe his harte that babeleth more of us two. At the which seyng the people dyd laughe, because they felte but lytell frute in hys sermonde.

By this tale a man may lerne to beware howe he openly rebuketh any other, and in what audyence, lest it come to his owne reprofe.

¶ *Of the Welchman that cast the Scotte into the see.*
lix.

5 first lines wanting.

they toke many great interpryses and many shyppes and many prisoners of other realmes that were theyr enemyes. Amonge the whiche they happened on a season to take a Scottes shype; and dyuers Scottes they slewe and toke prisoners, amonge whome there was a Welcheman that had one of the Scottes prysoners, and bad him that he shulde do of his harneys, whiche to do the Scotte was very lothe; howe be it for feare at the laste he pulled it of with an euyll wyll, and sayd to the Welcheman: and if thou wylte nedes haue my harneys, take it there, and cast it ouer the borde into the see. The Welcheman, seynge that, sayd: by Cottes blud and her nayle,[1] I shall make her fette[2] it agayne; and toke him by the legges, and caste hym after ouer the borde into the see.

By this tale a man may lerne, that he that is subiecte to another, ought to forsake his owne wyll and folowe his wyll and comaundement that so hathe subieccyon ouer him, leste it turne to his great hurte and damage.

(1) i. e. By God's blood and His nail. (2) Fetch.

¶ *Of the man that had the dome wyfe.* lx.

¶ THERE was a man that maryed a woman whiche had great ryches and beautie; howe be it she had suche an impedyment of nature, that she was domme and coulde nat speke. Whiche thinge made him to be ryght pensyfe and sadde; wherfore, vpon a day as he walked alone ryght heuy in harte, thynkynge vpon his wyfe, there came one to him and asked hym, what was the cause of his heuynesse; whiche answered that it was onely because his wife was borne domme. To whome this other sayde: I shall shewe the sone a remedye and a medecyne therfore, that is thus: go take an aspen lefe and laye it vnder her tonge this nyght, she beynge a slepe; and I warante the that she shall speke on the morowe. Whiche man, beynge glad of this medycyne, prepared therfore and gathered aspyn leaues; wherfore he layde thre of them vnder her tonge, whan she was a slepe. And on the morowe whan he hymselfe awaked, he, desyrous to knowe howe his medecyne wrought, beynge in bedde with her, he demaunded of her howe she dyd; and sodenly she answered and sayd: I beshrowe your harte for wakenynge me so erly; and so by the virtue of that medycyne she was restored to her speche. But in conclusyon her speche so encreased day by day, and she was so curste of condycyon, that euery daye she brauled and chydde with her husbande so moche, that at the laste he was more vexed, and hadde moche more trouble and disease with her shrewde wordes, than he hadde before whan she was dome. Wherfore, as he walked another tyme abrode, he happened to meate agayne with the same persone that taughte *hym howe to make his wyfe speke*[1]

2 *or* 3 *lines wanting.*

and more wery of her nowe than I was before, whan she was domme; wherfore I praye you teche me a medycyne to modefye her, that she speke nat so moche. This other answered and sayd thus: syr, I am a deuyll of hell; but I am one of them that haue leste power there. All be it yet I haue power to make a woman to speke, but and if a woman begyn ones to speke, I, nor all the deuyls in hell that haue the more power, be nat able to make a woman to be styll, nor to cause her to leaue her spekynge.

By thys tale ye may note, that a man ofte tymes desyreth and coueteth moche that thynge, that ofte turneth to his displeasure.

(1) These words in Italics I have supplied from conjecture. They are not in orig. or in Singer.

¶ *Of the Proctour of Arches that had the lytel wyfe.*
lxi.

¶ ONE askyd a Proctour of the Arches, lately before maryed, why he chose so lytel a wyfe; whiche answered: because he had a texte sayenge thus: ex duobus malis minus[1] est eliendum, that is to saye in englyshe, amonge euyll thinges the leste is to be chosen.

¶ *Of ii nonnes that were shryuen of one preste.* lxii.

¶ IN the tyme of Lente there came two nonnes to saynte Johnns in London bycause of the great pardon, there to be confessed. Of the whyche nonnes, the one was a young lady and the other was olde. This yonge lady chose fyrst her confessour, and confessed her that she hadde synned in lechery. The confessour asked, with whome it was; she sayd it was with a lustye gallante. He demaunded where it was; she sayd: in a plesaunte grene herber. He asked further: whan it was. She sayd: in the mery moneth of Maye. Than sayd the confessour this wyse: a fayre yonge lady, with a lusty galante, in a plesaunte herber, and in

(1) orig. reads: *ex duobus malis minus malis.*

the mery moneth of Maye! Ye dyd but your kynde! Nowe, by my truthe, God forgyue you, and I do; and so she departed. And incontynent the olde nonne mette with her, askynge her howe she lyked her confessour; whiche sayd he was the best gostly father that euer she hadde and the most easyest in penaunce-geuyng. For comfort wherof this other nonne went to the same confessour and shroue her lykewyse, that she had synned in lechery. And he demaunded with whome. Whiche sayde: with an old frere. He asked where. She said: in her olde cloyster. He asked: what season. She sayde; in Lente. Than the confessour sayd: an old ——, to lye with an old frere, in her olde cloyster, and in the holy tyme of Lente! by cockes body,[1] if God forgyue the, yet wyll I neuer forgyue the. Which wordes caused her to departe all sadde and sore abasshed.

By this tale men may lerne, that a vicyous acte is more abhomynable in one person than in another, in one season than in another, and in one place than in an other.[2]

(1) By God's body.
(2) If meant as quiet irony, this moral is admirable.

A C. Mery Talys. 91

¶ *Of the esquyer that sholde haue ben made knyght.*
lxiii.

4 lines of the original are wanting.

and the trumpettes began to blowe, a yonge squyer of Englande rydynge on a lusty courser of whych horse the noyse of the trumpettes so prycked the corage, that the squyer could nat him retayne; so that agaynste his wyll he ranne vpon hys enemyes. Whyche squyer, seynge none other remedy, sette his spere in the rest and rode throughe the thyckest of hys enemyes, and in conclusyon had good fortune, and saued hym selfe alyue without hurte; and the Englysshe hooste folowed and had the victorye. And after, whan the felde was wonne, this kynge Edwarde called the squyre and badde hym knele down, *and he* wolde make hym knyght, because he valyauntely was the man that day, which with the moost couragyous stomake aduentured fyrste vpon theyr enemyes. To whome the squyer thus answered: if it lyke your grace to make any one knyghte therfore, I beseche you to make my horse knyght, and nat *me: for certes* it was his dede, and nat myne, and full sore agaynst my wyll. Whiche answere the kynge herynge refrayned to promote hym to the order of knyghthode, reputynge hym in maner but for a cowarde; and euer after fauored hym the lesse therfore.

By this tale a man may lerne, howe it is wysedome *when he is* in good credence to kepe hym[self] therein, and in no wyse to dysable[1] hym selfe to moche.

¶ *Of him that wolde gette the maystrye of his wyfe.*
lxiv.

¶ A YONGE man, late maryed to a wyfe, thought it was good polecye to gette the maystrye of her in the begynnynge, came to her, the potte sethynge ouer the fyre, all thoughe the meate therein were nat ynoughe soden [and] commaunded[2] her to take the potte fro the fyre; whiche answered and said that the meate was nat redy to eate. And he said agayne: I wyll haue it taken of for my pleasure. This good woman, lothe yet to offende hym, sette the potte besyde the fyre, as he badde. And anone after he commaunded her to sette the potte behynde the dore, and she said agayne: ye be nat wyse therin. But he precysely said, it shuld be so, as he bad. And she gentylly againe dyd

(1) disparage.
(2) orig. is here apparently very corrupt; it reads: "all thoughe the meat therein were nat ynoughe, soden*lye* commaunded," &c.

A C. Mery Talys. 93

his commaundement. This man, yet nat satisfyed, comaunded her to set the pot a-hygh vpon the henne roste. What! quod the wyfe, I trowe ye be madde. And he fyerslye than comaunded her to sette it there, or els he sayd she shulde repente it. She, somwhat afrayde to moue his pacyence, toke a ladder, and sette it to the rost[1] and wente her selfe vp the ladder, and toke the potte in her hande, prayeng her husbande than to holde the ladder faste for [fear of] slydynge; whiche so dyd. And whan the husbande loked up, and sawe the potte stande there on hyght, he sayd thus: Lo! nowe standeth the potte there, as I wolde haue it. This wyfe hearynge

4 lines wanting

¶ *Of the penytent that sayd the shepe of God haue mercy upon me.* lxv.

¶ A CERTAYNE confessour, in the holy tyme of Lente, enioyned his penytente to saye dayly for his penaunce this prayer: Agnus Dei miserere mei, whiche was as moche to saye in englysshe as the Lambe of God haue mercye vpon me. This penytente acceptynge his penaunce departed, and that tyme twelfe monthe after came agayne to be confessed of the same confessoure, whiche demaunded

(1) planted it against the roost.

of him whether he had fulfylled his penaunce that he hym enioyned the laste yeare. *Than* he sayde thus: ye, syr, I thanke God I haue fulfylled it. For I haue sayd thus to daye in the mornynge and so dayly: the shepe of God haue mercy vpon me. To whome the confessour said: nay, I bad the say: Agnus Dei miserere mei, that is, the Lamb of God haue mercy vpon me. Ye, syr, quod the *penytente*, ye say truthe; that was the laste yeare. But now it is a twelfemonthe *since*, and it is a shepe by this tyme. Therfore I muste nedes say nowe: the shepe of God haue mercy vpon me.

By this tale ye may perceyue, that if holy scripture be expowned to the lay people onely in the lytterall sence, peraduenture it shall do lytell good.

¶ *Of the husbande that sayd he was John Daw.*
lxvi.

¶ It *happened* dyuers to be in communicacyon, amonge whome there was a curate or a parysshe preest and one John Dawe, a parisshon of his; whiche ii had communicacyon more busy than other in thys maner. This preest thought that one myght nat by felynge knowe one from· a nother in the darke. John Dawe his parysshone,

A C. Mery Talys. 95

[being] of the contrary opinyon, layde with his curate for a wager xl pence; whervpon the parysshe preest, wyllynge to proue his wager, wente to this John Dawes house in the euenynge, and sodenly gate hym to bedde with his wyfe; where, whan he began to be somwhat busye, she felynge his crowne sayde shortely with a loude voyce: by God! thou art nat John Dawe. That hearynge, her husbande answered: thou sayest trouthe, wyfe, I John Dawe am here.[1] Therfore, mayster persone, gyue me the money: for ye haue loste your xl. pence.

By this tale ye may lerne to perceyue, that it is no wysedome for a man to be couetous of wynnynge of any wager to put in ieopardye a thynge, that maye turne him to greatter displeasure.

¶ *Of the scoler of Oxforde that proued by souestry ii chykens iii.* lxvii.

¶ A RYCHE Frankelyn in the contrey hauynge by his wyfe but one chylde and no mo, for the great affeccyon that he had to his sayd chylde founde hym at Oxforde to schole by the space of ii or iii yere. Thys yonge scoler, in a vacacyon[2] tyme, for his disporte came home to his father. It for-

(1) orig. reads *I am here John Dawe.*   (2) orig. reads *vocacyon.*

tuned afterwarde on a nyght, the father, the mother and the sayd yonge scoler

<small>5 *lines wanting.*</small>

I haue studyed souestry, and by that scyence I can proue, that these ii chekyns in the dysshe be thre chekyns.[1] Mary, sayde the father, that wolde I fayne se. The scoller toke one of the chekyns in his hande and said : lo ! here is one chekyn, and incontynente he toke bothe the chekyns in his hande iointely and sayd : here is ii chekyns ; and one and ii maketh iii : ergo here is iii chekyns. Than the father toke one of the chekyns to him selfe, and gaue another to his wyfe, and sayd thus : lo ! I wyll haue one of the chekyns to my parte, and thy mother shal haue a nother, and because of thy good argumente thou shalte haue the thyrde to thy supper : for thou gettyst no more meate here at this tyme; whyche promyse the father kepte, and so the scoller wente without his supper.

By this tale men may se, that it is great foly to put one to scole to lerne any subtyll scyence, whiche hathe no naturall wytte.

<small>(1) The same story is to be found in *Scogin's Jests*, with a trifling variation. *Scogin's Jests* were published before 1565. Several of the anecdotes, here narrated, were re-produced in that and other collections. See also *Joake upon Joake*, 1721, where the present story is told of King Charles the Second, Nell Gwynne, and the Duchess of Portsmouth. In this version the Duchess is the sufferer.</small>

A C. Mery Talys. 97

¶ *Of the frere that stale the podynge.*[1] lxviii.

¶ A FRERE of London there was that on a Sonday in the mornynge yerly[2] in the somer season came fro London to Barnette to make a colacyon,[3] and was there an houre before hye masse began; and bycause he wolde come to the churche honestly, he wente fyrst to an ale house there to wype his shoes and to make him selfe clenly. In the whyche house there were podynges to sell, and dyuers folkes there brekynge theyr faste, and eatynge podynges. But the frere brake his faste in a secrete place in the same house. This frere sone after came to the church, and by lycence of the curate entered into the pulpet to make a colacyon or sermon. And in his sermon there he rebuked sore the maner of them that met to breke theyr faste on the Sonday before hye masse, and said it was called the deuyls blacke brekefast. And with that worde spekynge, as he dyd caste his armes out to make his countenaunce, there fell a podyng out of his sleue, whiche he hym selfe had stolen a lytell before in the same alehouse; and whan the people saw that, and specially they that brake

---

(1) This story, as already mentioned in the Introduction, is taken from the tale of the "Vickar of Bergamo" in *Tarlton's Newes out of Purgatorie* (1590). See Halliwell's ed. of *Tarlton's Jests, &c.* p. 82 (Shakesp. Soc.).   (2) Early.   (3) Homily.

H

theyr faste there the same mornynge, and knewe well that the wyfe had complayned howe she had one of her podynges stolen, they laughed so moche at the frere, that he incontynente wente downe out of the pulpet for shame.

By this tale a man may se that, whan a precher dothe rebuke any synne or vyce wherin he is knowen openly to be gyltie him selfe, suche prechynge shall lytell edefye to the people.

¶ *Of the frankelyns sonne that cam to take ordres.* lxix.

¶ A CERTAYNE scoler there was, intendynge to be made a preest, whyche hadde nother great wytte nor lernynge, came to the bysshoppe to take orders, whose folysshenes the bysshoppe perceyuynge, because he was a ryche mannes sonne wolde nat very strongly oppose him, but asked him thys *questyon: Noye had thre sonnes, Sem, Came, and Japhete; nowe tell me, who was Japhetes father? But the scoler was all abashed, and knew nat what to answere: wherefore the bysshoppe sayde: get the home and consider awhile,* and come agayne and soyle[1] me this questyon, and thou shalte haue orders. This scoler so departed and came home to his father, and shewed hym the cause of the

(1) Satisfy, a very rare word.

hynderaunce of his orders. Hys father, beyng angry at his folisshenes, thought to teche hym the solucyon of this questyon by a familier example, and called his spanyels before hym, and sayd thus: Thou knowest well, Colle my dogge hathe these iii. whelpes, Ryg, Trygge and Tryboll. Muste nat all my dogges nedes be syre to Tryboll? Than quod the scoler: by God! father, ye [have] sayd trouthe. Let me alone nowe; ye shall se me do well ynoughe the nexte tyme. Wherfore on the morowe he wente to the bysshoppe agayne, and sayd he coulde soyle his questyon. Than sayd the bysshoppe: Noye had thre sonnes, Sem, Came,[1] and Japhete. Now, tell me who was Japhetes father. Mary, syr, quod the scoler, if it plese youre lordeshyppe, Colle my fathers dogge.

By this tale a man may lerne, that it is but loste tyme to teche a fole any thynge, whiche hathe no wytte to perceyue it.

¶ *Of the husbandman that lodgyd the frere in his own bedde.* lxx.

¶ It fortuned so that a frere, late in the euenynge, desyred lodgynge of a poore man of the countrey,

(1) Ham.

the whiche for lacke of other lodgyng, glad to harborowe the frere, lodged him in his owne bedde. And after, he and his wyfe, the frere beynge a slepe, came and laye in the same bedde; and in the mornynge after the poore man rose and went to the market, leauyng the frere in the bedde with his wyfe. And as he wente he smiled and laughte to hym selfe; wherfore hys neyghbours demaunded of hym, why he so smyled. He answered and sayd : I laughe to thynke, howe shamefaste the frere shal be whanne he waketh, whome I left in bedde with my wyfe.

By this tale a man may lerne, that he that ouershoteth hym selfe doth folysshely : yet he is more fole to shewe it openly.

¶ *Of the preste that wolde say two gospels for a grote.* lxxi.

¶ SOMTYME there dwelled a preest in Stretforde vpon Auyne of small lernyng, which vndeuoutly sange masse and oftentymes twyse on one day. So it happened on a tyme, after his seconde masse was done in shorte space, nat a myle from Stretforde there mette with hym dyuers marchaunte men whiche wolde haue harde masse, and desyred hym to synge masse and he shuld haue a grote;

whiche answered them and sayd : syrs, I wyll say masse no more this day; but I wyll say you two gospels for one grote, and that is dogge chepe [for] a masse in any place in Englande.

By this tale a man may se, that they that be rude and unlerned regarde but lytell the meryte and goodness of holy prayer.

¶ *Of the coutear that dyd cast the frere ouer the bote.* lxxii.

Too much damaged to decypher.

¶ *Of the frere that prechyd what mennys sowles were.* lxxiii.

A PRECHER in pulpet whiche prechyd the worde *of God, amonge other* matters spake of mennes soules and sayd *that the soule was so* subtyll that a thousande soules myght daunce *on the space of the nayle of a* mannes fynger. Amonge which audyence there was a mery conceyted *fellow* of small deuocyon that answered and sayde thus : mayster doctour, if a thousande soules may daunce on a mannes nayle, I praye you than, where shall the pyper stande?

By this tale a man may se, that it is but foly to shewe or to teche vertue to them, that haue no pleasure nor mynde therto.

¶ *Of the husbande that cryed ble under the
bed.* lxxiv.

IN London there was a certayne artifycer hauyng a fayre wife, to whom a lusty galante made pursute to accomplisshe his pleasure. This woman, denyeng, shewed the matter vnto her husband whiche, moued therewith, bad his wyfe to appoynte him a tyme to come secretly to lye with her all nyght, and with great crakes and othes sware that, agaynst his comyng, he wolde be redy harneysed and wolde put him in ieopardye of his lyfe, except he wolde make hym a great amendes. Thys nyght was then appoynted; at whiche tyme thys courtyer came at his houre, and entred in at the chamber, and set his two-hande sworde downe, and sayde these wordes: stande thou there, thou sworde, the dethe of thre men! This husbande lyenge vnder the bedde in harneys, herynge these wordes, lay still for fere. The courtyer anone gat him to bed with the wyfe about his prepensed busynesse; and within an houre or two the husbande, beynge wery of lyenge, beganne to remoue hym. The courtyer, that hearynge, asked the wyfe what thinge that was that remoued vnder the bedde; whiche, excusyng the matter, sayd it was a lytell shepe, that was wonte dayly to go about the house; and

A C. Mery Talys. 103

the husbande, that herynge, anone cryed *ble*, as it had ben a shepe. And so in conclusyon, whan the courtyer sawe his tyme, he rose and kissed the wyfe, and took his leaue and departed. And as sone as he was gone the husbande arose; and, whan the wyfe loked on him, somwhat abasshed began to make a sad countenance; and [she] sayde; alas! syr, why did you * *

The remainder of this tale is wanting.

By this tale ye may se, that he is not wyse that will put his confydence *in bosters and* great crakers, whiche ofte tymes wyll do but ly*tell, when it comes to* the poynte.

¶ *Of the shomaker that asked the colyer what tydynges in hell.*[1] lxxv.

¶ A SOUTER[2] syttynge in his shope, that sawe a colyer come by, *deryded hym*, because he was so blacke, and asked hym, what newes from hell and

(1) The blackness of colliers was employed of course from a very early period as a ground for satirical insinuations as to their connexion with the Evil One. In 1568, Ulpian Fulwell, a distinguished writer of the Elizabethan era, published *A Pleasant Interlude intituled Like will to Like quoth the Devil to the Collier;* and in the old play of *Grim the Collier of Croydon*, the epithet grim was intended to convey a similar idea. In *Robin Goodfellow His Mad Pranks and Merry Jests*, 1628 however, *Grim* is the name of a Fairy.

(2) Shoemaker or Cobbler. Lat. *Sutor.*

howe the deuyll fared. To whome the colyer answeryd hym: he was well, whan I sawe hym laste; for he was rydynge *and waited* but for a souter to plucke on his botes.

By this ye may se that he, that vseth to deryde other folkes is somtyme him selfe more deryded and mocked.

¶ *Of Seynt Peter that cryed cause bobe.* lxxvi.

¶ I FYNDE wrytten amonge olde gestes,[1] howe God mayde Saynt Peter porter of heuen, and that God of hys goodnes, sone after his passyon, suffered many men to come to the kyngdome of Heuen with small deseruynge; at whiche tyme there was in heuen a great company of Welchemen, whyche with their crakynge and babelynge troubled all the other. Wherfore God sayde to saynte Peter, that he was wery of them, and that he wolde fayne haue them out of heuen. To whome saynte Peter sayd: Good Lorde, I warrente you, that shal be

(1) It is not very usual to find this word in its jocular sense spelled in this manner. It continued to be used in its original signification (*action* or *exploit*) even to the Restoration, perhaps later. The most recent example of its employment with which the Editor has happened to meet is at p. 29 of Mauley's *Iter Carolinum*, 1660, where the writer speaks of "His Majesties Gests from Newcastle to Holdenby in Feb. 1646.'' These *gests* were certainly no *jests*. Since the former part of this note was written, a more recent instance of the use of *gest* in the sense in question has occurred to the Editor in the *Life and Gests of S. Thomas Cantilupe, Gant*, 1674. 8vo.

done. Wherfore saynt Peter wente out of heuen gates and cryed wyth a loud voyce *Cause bobe*, that is as moche to saye as rosted chese, whiche thynge the Welchemen herynge, ranne out of Heuen a great pace. And when Saynt Peter sawe them all out, he sodenly wente into Heuen, and locked the dore, and so sparred all the Welchemen out

By this ye may se, that it is no wysdome for a man to loue or to set his mynde to moche vpon any delycate or worldely pleasure, wherby he shall lose the celestyall and eternall ioye.

¶ *Of hym that aduenturyd body and soule for hys prynce.* lxxvii.

¶ Two knyghtes there were which wente to a standynge fylde with theyr prynce; but one of them was confessed before he wente, but the other wente into the felde without shryfte or repentaunce. Afterwarde thys prynce wanne the fylde, and had the victory that day; wherfore he that was confessed came to the prynce, and asked an offyce and sayd that he had deserved it, for he had done good seruice and aduentured that day as farre as any man in the felde. To whome the other that was unconfessed answered and sayd : nay, by the masse, I am more worthy to haue a rewarde than he : for he aduentured but his body for your sake, for he durst nat go to the felde tyll he was confessed ; *but I that was unconfessed adventured my soule.*¹ * * * *

The remainder of this tale is wanting.

¶ *Of the parson that stale the mylners elys.* lxxviii.

Too imperfect to decypher.

¶ *Of the Welchman that saw one* xls. *better than God.* lxxix.

¶ A WELCHMAN on a tyme went to churche to *be shryued, and chanced* to come in euyn at the sacryngtime.² When he had *confessed him* he went home, wher one of his felowes askyd hym wh*ether he had seen God* Almighty to day ; which answerd and sayd : nay, but I saw *one forty shillings better.*

¶ *Of the frere that said dyryge for the hoggys soule.* lxxx.

¶ UPON a tyme certayn women in the countrye were ap*poynted*³ *to de*ryde and mokke a frere limi-

---

(1) The words in Italics are supplied from conjecture. They are not in orig. or in Singer.
(2) Sacrament.
(3) Prepared, *i. e.* had made themselves ready.

tour, that vsed moche to *trouble them;* whereupon one of them, a lytyll before the frere came, *tooke a hogge,* and for dysport leyd it under the borde after the manner of a corse ; a*nd told the* frere it was her good man and dysyrd hime to say dirige for his soule. *Where*fore the frere and his felaw began Placebo and Dirige and so fo*rth, thorough* the seruyse full devowtly, which the wyues so heryng could not re*fraine* them selfe from lawghynge and went in to a lytyll parler to lawgh *more* at theyr pleasure. These freris somwhat suspected the cause, and quikly, *or* that the women were ware, lokyd under the borde, and spying[1] that it was an hog, sodenly toke it bytwene them and bare it homeward as fast as they might. The women, seyng that, ran after the frere and cryed : com agayn, maester frere, come agayne, and let it allone. Nay by my faith, quod the frere, he is a broder of ours, and therefore he must nedys be buryed in oure cloyster. And so the frerys gate the hog.

By this ye may se, that they that use to deride and mok other, somtyme it tornyth to theyre owne losse and damage.

(1) Orig. reads *spyed.*

¶ *Of the parson that sayde masse of requiem for Crystes soule.* lxxxi.

¶ A CERTAYN prest there was that dwellyd in the cuntry which was not very well lernyd. Therfore on Ester-Euyn he sent his boy to the prest of the next town, that was ii. myle from thens, to know what masse he sholde synge on the morowe. This boy came to the sayd prest, and dyd his maysters errande to hym. Then quod the prest: tel thy mayster that he must   *   *

Several lines wanting.

masse he shuld synge on the morowe. By my trothe, *quod the boy*, I have forgotten it; but he bad me tell you it began * * * * *Then quod the prest:* I trowe thou sayest trewth: for now I remem*ber me it is the masse of requiem :* for God Almyghty dyed upon Good Fry*day*, and it *is meet we shulde say masse* for hys soule.

By thys tale ye may se, that when one fole sendyth another fole on hys er*rand, hys* besynes folyshly sped.

¶ *Of the herdeman that sayde: ryde apace, ye shall haue rayn.* lxxxii.

¶ *A certayne skoler of Oxenford* which had studied the iudicials of astronomy, *upon a tyme as he* was rydyng by the way, came[1] by a herdman; and *he asked thys herdm*an how far it was to the next town. Syr, quod the herd*man, it is rather* past a mile and an half; but, sir, quod he, ye nede to ryde *apace: for ye shal h*aue a shower of rayn, or ye com thider. What, quod the skoler, *maketh ye say so?* There ys no token of rayn: for the cloudes be both fayr and clere. *By my troth*, quod the herdman, but ye shall fynd it so. The skoler then rode forth, *and it chanced* or he had ryden half a myle forther, there fell a good showre of rayn *and*[2] *thys* skoler was well washyd and wett to the skyn. The skoler then tornyd *hym backe, and* rode to the herdman, and desyryd hym to tech him that connyng. *Nay*, quod the herdman, I wyll not tech you my connynge for nought. Than *the skoler* profferyde hym xl shyllyngs to teche hym that connynge. The herd*man, after* he had reseyuyd hys money, sayd thus: syr, se you not

---

(1) Orig. reads *which came*.
(2) Singer's conjectural reading is *that*; but *and* seems to me to be the word required.

yonder *blacke* ewe with the whyte face? Yes, quod the skoler. Suerly, quod the herdman, when she daunsith and holdeth up her tayle, ye shall haue a showre of rayn within half an howre after.[1]

By this ye may se, that the connyng of herdmen and shepardes, as touchinge alteracyons of weders, is more sure than the iudicials of astronomy.

¶ *Of hym that sayde: I shall haue neuer a peny.* lxxxiii.

¶ In a certayne towne, there was a rych man that lay on his deth bed at poynte of deth, whyche chargyd hys executours to dele[2] for hys soule a certayne some of money in pence, and on thys condicion chargyd them as they would answere afore God, that euery pore man that cam to them and told a trew tale shulde haue a peny, and they that said a fals thing shuld haue none; and in the dole-tyme there cam one whych sayd that God was a good man. Quod the executours: thou shalt haue a peny, for thou saist trouth. Anone came a nother and said, the deuil was a good man. Quod the executours: there thou lyest; therefore thou shalt haue nere a peny. At laste came on[e] to the executors and said thus: ye shall gyue me

(1) See *Scoggin's Jests* (reprint 1796), p. 47. (2) Count out.

nere a peny: which wordes made the executors
amasyd, and toke aduysment whyther they shuld
* * * *

The end of this tale is wanting.

¶ *Of the husbande that sayde hys wyfe and he
agreed well.* lxxxiv.

Too imperfect to decypher.

¶ *Of the prest that sayde Comede episcope.* lxxxv.

¶ IN the tyme of visitacyon a bysshoppe, whi*che
was maryed*[1] and had gote many chyldren, prepared
to questyon a preest what rule he kepte, whiche
preest had a le*man* * * * * * and by her had
two or thre small chyldren. In shorte *tyme before
the By*sshoppes commynge, he prepared a rowme
to hyde his *leman and children* ouer in the rofe of
his hall; and whan the bysshoppe was *come and dis-
coursing* with him in the same hall, hauynge x of
his owne chyldren about him, *the preest*, who coude
speke lytell lytyn or none, bad the bysshoppe in

(1) These two words are not in orig. or in Singer; but they seem to be what the context requires.

latyn * * * * Comede,[1] episcope. This woman in rofe of the house, hearing *the preest say* so, had went[2] he had called her, byddynge her: come, Ede; and *answered him* and sayde: shall I brynge my chyldren with me also? The bysshoppe, *hearing* this, sayde in sporte: vxor tua sicut vitis abundans in lateribus domus tuæ. The preest than, halfe amasyd, answerd and sayd: filii tui sicut nouellæ oliuarum in circuitu mensæ tuæ.

By this ye may se, that they, that haue but small lernyng, som tyme speke truely unaduysed.

¶ *Of the woman that stale the pot.* lxxxvi.

¶ ON Ashe Wednesday in the mornynge, was a curate of a churche whyche had made good chere the nyght afore and sytten up late, and came to the churche to here confessyon, to whome there came a woman; and among other thynges she confessed her that she had stolen a potte. But than, because of greate watche that this preest had, he there sodenly felle aslepe; and whan this woman sawe him nat wyllynge to here her, she rose and went her waye. And anone an other woman kneled down to the same preest and began to say: Benedicite; wherwith this preest sodenly

(1) Orig. reads *Comode*.   (2) Weened.

A C. Mery Talys.

awaked, and wenynge she had ben the other woman,[1] sayd all angerly, what! arte thou nowe at Benedicite agayne? tell me, what dyddest thou whan thou haddest stolyn the potte?

¶ *Of mayster Whyttynton dreme.*[2] lxxxvii.

¶ Sone after one maister Whyttington had bylded a colege, on a nyght as he slepte, he dremed that he satte in his church and many folkes there also; and further he dremed that he sawe Our Lady in the same church with a glas of goodly oyntemente in her hande goynge to one askynge him what he had done for her sake; which sayd that he had sayd Our Ladyes sauter[3] euery daye: wherfore she

(1) Orig. reads *and* after *woman*.
(2) The celebrated Sir Richard Whittington. In his *If you know Not me you know No Body*, Part ii, 1606, Heywood introduces the following dialogue respecting Whittington between Dean Nowell and Old Hobson, the haberdasher of the Poultry :—
  "*Dr. Now.* This Sir Richard Whittington, three times Mayor,
  Son to a knight, and 'prentice to a mercer,
  Began the library of Gray-friars in London,
  And his executors after him did build
  Whittington College, thirteen almshouses for poor men,
  Repair'd Saint Bartholomew's, in Smithfield,
  Glazed the Guildhall, and built Newgate.
    Hob. Bones a me, then, I have heard lies;
  For I have heard he was a scullion,
  And rais'd himself by venture of a cat.
    Dr. Now. They did the more wrong to the gentleman."
(3) Psalter.

I

gaue him a lytel of the oyle. And anone she wente to another * * *

Several lines wanting.

he had buylded a great college, and was very gladde in hys mynde. *Whan that Oure Ladye cam to hym*, she asked him what he hadde suffred for her *sake*, *this* questyon made him greatly abashed, because he had nothing to *answer*: *wherefore Our Lady* him informed that for all the great dede of buyldynge *of a colege he must haue no parte of* that goodly oyntemente.

By this ye may perceue, that to suffre for Goddes sake is more *acceptable to God than to buyld or* gyue great goodes.

¶ *Of the prest that killed his horse called modicus.*
lxxxviii.

¶ *A certayne Bysshoppe* appoynted to go on visytacion to a preeste's; *and, bycause he* would haue the preest do but lyttel coste vpon him, he told him to prepare but lytell meate saying thus: Preparas * * * * * *modicus*. This preest whyche understode hym nat halfe well, had *some desire*,[1] wherfore he thoughte to obtayne the bysshoppes fauour; *and therfore againste* the bys-

(1) Wanting in orig. and left blank by Singer. I have supplied them from conjecture.

shoppes comynge kylled his horse that was *called Modicus*, whereof the bysshoppe and his seruauntes ete parte; whiche, *whan the bys*shoppe knewe afterwarde, was greatly displeased.

By this ye may se, that many a fole dothe moche coste in makyng *good chere* at dyners, whiche hathe but lytell thanke for his laboure.

¶ *Of the Welcheman that stale the Englysshmans cocke.* lxxxix.

¶ A WELCHEMAN dwellynge in Englande fortuned to stele an Englysshemans cocke, and set it on the fyre to sethe; wherefore thys Englysheman, suspecting the Welcheman, came to his house, and sawe the cocke sethyng on the fyre and said to the Welcheman thus: syr, this is my cocke. Mary, quod the Welcheman; and if it be thyne, thou shalte haue thy parte of it. Nay, quod the Englyssheman, that is nat ynoughe. By cottes blut and her nayle! quod the Welcheman, if her be nat ynoughe nowe, her will be ynoughe anone: for her hath a good fyre under her.

¶ *Of hym that brought a botell to a preste.* xc.

¶ CERTAYNE vycars[1] of Poules, disposed to be mery on a Sonday at hye masse tyme, sente

(1) Priests.

another madde felowe of theyr acquointance unto a folysshe dronken preest to gyue hym a bottell, whiche man met with the preest upon the toppe of the stayres by the chauncell dore, and spake to him and sayd thus : syr, my mayster hath sente you a bottell to put your drynke in, because he can kepe none in your braynes. This preest, therwith beynge very angry, all sodenly toke the bottell, and with his fote flange it downe into the body of the churche upon the gentylmans hede.[1]

¶ *Of the endytement of Jesu of Nazareth.* xci.

¶ A CERTAYNE Jury in the countye of Myddelsex was enpaneled for the kynge to enquere of all endytements, murders, and felonyes. The persones of this panell were folyshe, couetous and unlerned : for who so euer wolde gyue them a grote, they wolde affyne and verifye his byll, whether it were true or fals, withoute any profe or euydence; wherefore one that was * * * *

Some lines wanting.

the Jury loking on the grote and nothing on the byll as was their *custome*, which byll whan it was

(1) Orig. reads *gentylmens*.

presented into the courte, *the judge* said openly before all the people : lo ! syrs, here is the *straungest byll euer* presented by an enquest : for here they haue indyted *Jesu of Nazareth* for stelyng of an asse. Which whan the people harde it, it *made them all to laughe*, and to wonder at the folysshenes and shamefull periury *of the Jury.*

By this ye may se, it is great parell [1] to enpanell *men upon an* enquest, whiche be folysshe and haue but small *witte or honesty.*

¶ Of the frere that preched agaynst them that rode on the Sonday. xcii.

¶ IN a certayne parryshe, a frere preched and *said moche* againt them, that rode on the Sonday euer lokyng upon *one that was there*, spurred redy to ryde. This man, perceuyng that *the frere loked at* hym, sodenly halfe in angre answered the frere thus : *I meruayle that ye say so* moche agaynste them that ryde on the Sonday : for Christe *rode into Jerusalem* on Palme Sonday, as thou knowest well it is wrytten * * * *To* whome the frere sodenly answered and sayd thus : *but knowe ye not also what came* thereof ? Was he nat hanged on

(1) Peril.

the Fryday after. Whiche hear*ing all them that were* in the churche fell on laughynge.

¶ *Of the one broder that founde a purs.* xciii.

¶ THERE was a certayne man that had two sonnes unl*yke eche other.* For the eldyst was lustye and quycke, and vsed moch*e betimes to* walke into the fyldes. Than was the yonger slowe, and vsed *moche* to lye in his bed as long as he myght. So on a day the elder, as *he was vsed*, rose erly and walked into the fyldes ; and there by fortune he founde a purse of money, and brought it home to his father. His father, whan he had it, wente strayght to hys other sonne yet lyenge than in his bed and sayd to him : o thou slogarde, quod he, seyst thou nat thyne eldest brother, howe he by hys erly rysyng had founde a purse with money whereby we shall be greatly holpen all our lyfe, whyle thou sluggynge in thy bedde dost no[1] good but slepe ? He than wyst nat what to say, but answered shortly and said : father, quod he, if he that hathe loste the purse and money had lyne in hys bedde that same tyme that he loste it, as I do nowe, my brother had founde no purse nor money to day.

(1) Orig. reads *thou sluggynge in thy bedde dost thou no good* which repetition of *thou* seems unnecessary.

By this ye may se, that they that be accustomed in vyce and synne will alwaye fynde one excuse or other to cloke therewyth theyr vyce and vnthryftynes.

¶ *Of the answere of the mastres to the mayde.* xciv.

¶ A CERTAYNE wyfe there was, whiche was somwhat fayre, and, as all women be that be fayre, was somwhat proude of her beautye; and as she and her mayde satte together, she, as one that was desyrous to be praysed, sayd to her thus : I, faythe, Jone, howe thynkest thou ? am I nat a fayre wyfe ? Yes, by my trouth, maistres, quod she, ye be the fayrest that euer was excepte * * *

The end is wanting.

¶ *Of the northern man that was all harte.* xcv.

Of this tale but a small fragment remains.

¶ *Of the burnynge of olde John.* xcvi.

¶ *In a certayne* towne there was a wife somewhat aged, that had beryed *her husbande*, whose name was John, whome she so tend*erlye loued in his* lyfe, that after hys dethe she caused an ymage of tymber *to be made in forme* and persone as lyke to hym as coulde be; whiche ymage *she kept carefully* under her bedde; and euery nyghte she caused her mayde to *wrap the ymage in a shete* and lay it in her bedde; and called it olde John. Thys *widowe had* a prentyse whose name was John; whiche John wolde fayne *haue married hys* maystres, nat for no great pleasure, but onely for her good *substance: for she* was ryche. Wherefore he ymagened howe he myght obtayne hys *desire and so dyd* speke to the mayde of the house, and desyred her to lay hym in his maystres bedde for one nyghte in stede of the pycture,[1] and promysed her a good rewarde for her laboure; whyche mayde ouer nyghte wrapped the sayde younge man in a shete, and layde hym in his maysters bedde, as she was wonte to laye the pycture. Thys wydowe was wonte euery nyght, before she slepte and dyuers tymes whan she waked, to kysse the sayde pycture of olde John: wherefore the sayde nyghte she kyssed the sayde yonge man, beleuynge that she hadde kyste the picture. And he sodenly sterte,[2] and toke her in his armes, and so well pleased her than, that olde John from

---

(1) Not here put as a painting, but in a general sense, as a representation.

(2) The old perfect of *start*. The orig. reads *starte*.

thens forth was clene out of her mynde, and [she] was contente that this yonge John shulde lye with her styll all that nyghte, and that the pycture of olde John shulde lye styll under the bedde for a thynge of noughte. After thys in the mornynge, thys wydowe, intendynge to please this yonge John whyche had made her so good pastyme all the nyght, bad her mayde go dresse some good mete for their brekefast to feaste therwith her yonge John. This mayde, whan she had longe sought for wode to dresse the sayde mete, told her maystres that she coude fynde no wode that was drye, except onelye the pycture of olde John that lyeth under the bed. * * * * * * * *

Some lines wanting.

and dressyd the brekfast; and so olde John *was brenyd; and* from thens forth yong John occupyed *his place.*

¶ *Of the courtear that ete the hot custarde.* xcvii.

¶ A CERTAYNE merchaunt and a courtear, *being upon a time together* at dyner hauing a hote custerd, *the courtear being* somwhat homely of maner toke *parte of it and put it* in hys mouth, whych was so hote that made him *shed teares. The* merchaunt, lokyng on him, thought that he had *ben weeping, and asked hym why* he wept. This curtear, not wyllynge [it] to be kno*wn that he had brent his* mouth with the hote custerd, answered and said, sir : q*uod he, I had* a brother whych dyd a certayn offence wherfore he was hanged ; *and, chauncing* to think now vppon his deth, it maketh me to wepe. This merchaunt thought the courtear had said trew, and anon after the merchaunt was disposid to ete *of the custerd,* and put a sponefull of it in his mouth, and brent his mouth also, that his *eyes watered.* This courtear, that perceuyng, spake to the merchaunt and seyd : sir, quod *he, pray* why do ye wepe now ? The merchaunt perseyued how he had *bene deceiued* and said[1] : mary, quod he, I wepe, because thou wast not hangid, *when that* thy brother was hangyd.

¶ *Of the thre pointes belonging to a shrewd wyfe.* xcix.

¶ A YONG man, that was desirous to haue a wyf, cam to a company *of Phi*losofers which were gadred to gider, requiring them to gif *him their opinion* howe he might chose him sich a wyf that

---

(1) Singer inserts *answered* before *and said*: but the word does not appear to be required.

wer no shrew. Th*ese Philos*ofers with gret study and delyberacion determinid and shewd this man that there *were iii esp*ecial pointes, wherebi he shuld sure know if a woman were a shrew. The *i point is* that if a woman have a shril voyce, it is a gret token that she is a shrew. The ii point is that, if a woman have a sharp nose, then most commenly she is a shrew. *The* iii point that neuer doth mis is[1] that if she were [a] kerchefer,[2] ye may be sure she is a shrew.

¶ *Of the man that paynted the lamb upon his wyfes bely.* c.

¶ A CONNING painter ther was dwelling in London, which had a fayre yong wife, and for thingis that he had to do went ouer se ; but because he was somwhat jelous, he praed his wyfe to be content, that he might paint a lamb upon her bely, and praed her it might remain ther, til he cam home

(1) Orig. reads *the iii point is that never mis that &c*
(2) A very costly article of female dress during the reigns of the Tudor and Stuart sovereigns. It constituted part of the head-gear, and from the way in which it was worn by some women, was calculated to convey a notion of skittishness. In the *New Courtly Sonet of the Lady Greensleeves*, printed in Robinson's "Handful of Pleasant Delites," 1584, the lover is made to say to his mistress :—
 " I bought three kerchers to thy head,
 That were wrought fine and gallantly :
 I kept thee both at board and bed,
 Which cost my purse well-favourdly."

again; wherewith she was content. After which lamb so painted he departid; and sone after that, a lusti yong merchaunt, a bacheler, came and woed his wyf, and obteined her fauor, so that she was content he shuld lye with her; which resortid to her and had his plesure oftymes; and on a time he toke a pensell, and to the lamb he painted ii hornys, wening to the wif that he had but refreshed the old painting. Than at the last, about a yere after, her husband cam home again, and the first night he lay with his wyfe, he loked uppon his wifes bely, and saw the ii hornes painted there. He said to his wif, that some other body had ben besy there, and made a new painting:
for the picture that he painted had no
hornes and this hath hornes; to
to whome this wif shortly
* * * *

cetera desunt.

Here endeth the booke of a C. mery Talys. Imprinted at London at the sygne of the meremayde at powlys gate nexte to chepesyde.

¶ *Cum priuclegio Regali.*

ADDITIONAL NOTES AND ILLUSTRATIONS.

A C, MERY TALYS.

Introduction, vi.—I might have mentioned that Taylor the Water-Poet cites *The Hundred Merry Tales* as one of the authorities employed by him in the composition of his *Sir Gregory Nonsense His Newes from No Place*, 1622 (Taylor's Works, 1630), and see also Epistle Dedicatory to Meredith's *Eusebius*, 1577.

P. 19.—This story is found in the *Ducento Novelle* of Celio Malespini, printed at Venice, 1609, 4°.

P. 22. *Of the Woman that sayd her Woer cam too late.*
"If thou be slow to speake, as one I knew,
Thou wouldst assure thy selfe my counsels true;
Hee (too late) finding her upon her knees
In Church, where yet her husbands coorse she sees,
Hearing the Sermon at his funerall,
Longing to behold his buriall,
This sutor being toucht with inward love,
Approached neare his lovely sute to move,
Then stooping downe he whispered in her eare
Saying he bore her love, as might appeare,
In that so soone he shewed his love unto her,
Before any else did app[r]och to woo her,
Alass (said she) your labour is in vaine,
Last night a husband I did entertaine."
—*Uncasing of Machivils Instructions to his Sonne*, 1613, Sign. C 3.
Stories of this kind are of very common occurrence in the modern collections of facetiæ.

P. 23. "When Davie Diker diggs, and dallies not,
When smithes shoo horses, as they would be shod,
When millers toll not with a golden thumbe."
—*The Steel Glas, a Satyre*, by George Gascoigne, Esquire (1576),
Sign. H 3 verso.
A writer in the *Retrospective Review*, New Series, ii. 326, states that thi story of the "Miller with the golden thumb" "is still (1854) a favourite in Yorkshire."

I *

P. 30. *Stumble at a Straw, &c.*—This proverb is quoted in *Machivils Instructions to his Sonne*, 1613, p. 16.

P. 35. *Of the good man that sayd to his wyfe, &c.*
" Dr. *South*, visiting a Gentleman one morning, was ask'd to stay Dinner, which he accepted of; the Gentleman stept into the next Room and told his Wife, and desired she'd provide something extraordinary. Hereupon she began to murmer and scold, and make a thousand Words ; till at length, Her husband, provok'd at her Behaviour, protested, that if it was not for the Stranger in the next Room, he would kick her out of Doors. Upon which the Doctor, who heard all that passed, immediately stept out, crying, *I beg, Sir, you'll make no Stranger of me.*"
—*Complete London Jester*, ed. 1771, p. 73.

P. 44. *Draught hole.*—See Dekker's *Guls' Horn Book*, 1609, ed. Nott, p. 121-2-3.

P. 47. *Saynte Thomas of Acres.*
"A the Austen fryers
They count us for lyers :
And at Saynt Thomas of Akers
They carpe us lyke crakers."
—Skelton's *Colin Clout* (Works, ed. Dyce, i. 357).
This tale is imitated in *Hobson's Conceits*.

P. 60. *Of the gentylman that promysed the scoler of Oxforde a sarcenet typet.*—Sarcenet, at the period to which this story refers, was a material which only certain persons were allowed to wear. See Nicolas' note to a passage in the *Privy Purse Expenses of Elizabeth of York*, p. 220. This jest is transplanted by Johnson, with very little alteration, into the *Pleasant Conceits of Old Hobson*, 1607.

P. 78. *Therefore I pray thee, teche me my Pater noster, and by my truthe, I shall therfore teche thee a songe of Robyn Hode that shall be worth xx of it !*
The following passage from a poem, which has been sometimes ascribed to Skelton, is a curious illustration of this paragraph :—
'Thus these sysmatickes,
And lowsy lunatickes,
With spurres and prickes
Call true men heretickes.
They finger their fidles,
And cry in quinibles,
Away these bibles,
For they be but ridles !

> And give them Robyn Whode,
> To red howe he stode
> In mery grene wode,
> When he gathered good,
> Before Noyes ffloodd!
> *The Image of Ipocrysy*, Part iii.

P. 84. *Of the wyfe that bad, &c.*
Of swearing between a wyfe and her husband.
" Cis, by this candle in my sleep I thought
One told me of thy body thou werf nought.
Good husband, he that told you ly'd, she said,
And swearing, laid her hand upon the bread.
Then eat the bread, quoth he, that I may deem
That fancie false, that true to me did seem.
Nay, sir, said she, the matter well to handle,
Since you swore first, you first shall eat the candle."
Wits Interpreter, the English Parnassus. By John Cotgrave,
1662, p. 286.

P. 87. *Of the man that had the dome wyfe.*
" A certain man, as fortune fel,
A woman tungles wedded to wive,
Whose frowning countenānce perceivīg by live
Til he might know what she ment he thought long,
And wished ful oft she had a tung.
The devil was redy, and appeered anon,
An aspin lefe he bid the man take,
And in her mouth should put but one,
A tung, said the devil, it shall her make ;
Til he had doon his hed did ake ;
Leaves he gathered, and took plentie,
And in her mouth put two or three.
Within a while the medicine wrought :
The man could tarry no longer time,
But wakened her, to the end he mought
The vertue knowe of the medicine ;
The first woord she spake to him
She said : 'thou whoresonne knave and theef,
How durst thou waken me, with a mischeef!
From that day forward she never ceased,
Her boistrous bable greeved him sore :

>   The devil he met, and him intreated
>   To make her tungles, as she was before;
>   'Not so,' said the devil, 'I will meddle no more.
>   A devil a woman to speak may constrain,
>   But all that in hel be, cannot let it again.'"
>   *Schole-house of Women*, 1542 (Utterson's *Select Pieces of Early
>   Popular Poetry*, ii. 74).

P. 89. *Of the Proctour of arches that had the lytel wyfe.*
"One ask'd his Friend, why he, so proper a Man himself, marry'd so small a Wyfe? *Why*, said he, *I thought you had known, that of all evils we should chuse the least."—Complete London Jester*, ed. 1771, p. 65.

P. 92. *Of him that wolde set, &c.*
In the *Scholehouse of Women*, 1542, the same story is differently related:—

> "A husband man, having good trust
> His wife to him bad be agreeable,
> Thought to attempt if she had be reformable,
> Bad her take the pot, that sod over the fire,
> And set it aboove upon the astire.
>   She answered him: 'I hold thee mad,
> And I more fool, by Saint Martine:
> Thy dinner is redy, as thou me bad,
> And time it were that thou shouldst dine,
> And thou wilt not, I will go to mine.
> 'I bid thee (said he) vere up the pot.'
> 'A ha! (she said) I trow thou dote.'
>   Up she goeth for fear, at last,
> No question mooved where it should stand
> Upon his hed the pottage she cast,
> And heeld the pot stil in her hand,
> Said and swore, he might her trust,
> She would with the pottage do what her lust."

As this story in the *C. Mery Talys* is defective in consequence of the mutilation of the only known copy, the foregoing extract becomes valuable, as it exhibits what was probably the sequel in the prose version, from which the author of the *Scholehouse of Women* was no doubt a borrower.

P. 101. *If a thousande soules may dance on a mannes nayle.*—This is a different form of the common saying that a thousand angels can stand on the point of the needle. "One querying another, whether a thousand angels might stand on the point of a needle, another replied, 'That was a *needles* point.'"—Ward's *Diary*, ed. 1839, p. 94.

P. 106. Scot, in his *Discovery of Witchcraft*, 1584, ed. 1651, p. 191, has a story, which bears the mark of being the same as the one here entitled: "Of the parson that stale the mylner's elys." The passage in Scot, which may help to supply the unfortunate *lacuna* in the *C. Mery Talys*, is as follows:—

"So it was, that a certain Sir John, with some of his company, once went abroad jetting, and in a moon-light evening, robbed a miller's weire and stole all his eeles. The poor miller made his mone to Sir John himself, who willed him to be quiet; for he would so curse the theef, and all his confederates, with bell, book, and candel, that they should have small joy of their fish. And therefore the next Sunday, Sir John got him to the pulpit, with his surplisse on his back, and his stole about his neck, and pronounced these words following in the audience of the people:—

'All you that have stolne the millers eeles,
Laudate Dominum de coelis,
And all they that have consented thereto,
Benedicamus Domino.'

Lo, (saith he) there is savoe for your eeles, my masters."

P. 108. *Of the parson that sayde masse of requiem, &c.*—This story is also in *Scoggin's Jests*, 1626, and perhaps the lacunæ may be supplied from that source. Thus (the words supplied from *Scoggin's Jests* are in italics):—

"Then quod the prest: tel thy mayster that he must *say the Masse which doth begin with a great R*. [when the boy returned, the Prest asked him whether the Parson had told him what] masse, &c."

And again, a line or two lower down, there can be no doubt, on a comparison of Scoggin's Jests, p. 74, what the missing words are. We ought to read:—"but he bad me tell you it began *with a great R*."

Tales, and quicke

answeres, very mery,

and pleasant to

rede.

MERY
Tales, Wittie
Questions
and Quicke Answeres,
Very pleasant to
be Readde.

IMPRINTED
at London
in Fleete strete, by
H. Wykes.
1567.

The Table.

	PAGE
Of hym that rode out of London, and had his seruaunt folowynge hym on foote. i.	15
¶ *Of hym that preached on saynte Christofers day.* ii.	16
¶ *Of the frenche man that stroue with the Janwaye for his armes.* iii.	*ib.*
¶ *Of the curate that sayde our lorde fedde fyue hundred persones.* iiii.	17
¶ *Of hym that profered his doughter to one in maryage.* v.	18
¶ *Of the men of the countrey, that came to London to bye a crucifixe of wodde.* vi.	*ib.*
¶ *Of hym that folowed his wyfe to buryeng.* vii.	19
¶ *Of hym that felle in to the fyre.* viii.	*ib.*
¶ *Of hym that vsed to calle his seruaunte the kynge of fooles.* ix.	20
¶ *Of the yonge woman, that sorowed so greatly the deathe of her husbande.* x.	21
¶ *Of hym that kyssed the fayre mayde with the longe nose.* xi.	*ib.*

	PAGE
¶ *Of the vplandysshe mans answere concernyng the steple and pulpytte.* xii.	23
¶ *Of the beggers aunswere to mayster Skelton the poete.* xiii.	ib.
¶ *Of the chaplen that sayde our ladye mattens lyenge in his bedde.* xiiii.	24
¶ *Of hym that loste his purse in London.* xv.	25
¶ *Of the marchaunt that loste his boudget betwene ware and London.* xvi.	26
¶ *Of him that was called kockold.* xvii.	27
¶ *Of the iolus man.* xviii.	28
¶ *Of the fat woman that sat and solde frute.* xix.	ib.
¶ *Of a poller that begyled a preste.* xx.	29
¶ *Of Papirius pretextatus.* xxi.	31
¶ *Of the corrupte man of lawe.* xxii.	33
¶ *Of kynge Lowes of Fraunce and the husbandman Conon.* xxiii.	34
¶ *Of a picke thanke, that thought to begyle the same moste prudent kynge.* xxiiii.	37
¶ *Of Thales the great astronomer, the whiche felle in to a diche.* xxv.	38
¶ *Of the astronomer that theues robbed.* xxvi.	39
¶ *Of the plough man that wolde saye his pater noster with a stedfast mynde.* xxvii.	ib.
¶ *Of him that dreamed he founde golde.* xxviii.	40
¶ *Of the crakynge yonge gentyll man that wolde ouerthrowe his enemys a myle of.* xxix.	42
¶ *Of him that fell of a tre and brake a rybbe in his syde.* xxx.	44
¶ *Of the fryer that brayed in his sermon.* xxxi.	45

	PAGE
¶ The oration of th ambassadour that was sent to Pope Urban. xxxii.	46
¶ Of the ambassadour that was sent to the prince Agis. xxxiii.	47
¶ The answere of Cleomenes to the Samiens ambassadour. xxxiiii.	ib.
¶ Of the wyse man Piso, and his seruant. xxxv.	48
¶ Of the marchant that made a wager with his lorde. xxxvi.	49
¶ Of the scrowes that the frier gaue out against the pestilence. xxxvii.	51
¶ Of the physition that vsed to wryte bylles ouer nyght called resceytes. xxxviii. . . .	52
¶ Of him that wolde confesse him by a lybell in wrytynge. xxxix.	53
¶ Of the hermite of Padowe. xl.	54
¶ Of the vplandissh man that saw the kyng. xli.	56
¶ Of the courtier that bade the boye to holde his horse. xlii.	57
¶ Of the deceytfull scriuener. xliii.	ib.
¶ Of him that sayde he beleued his wyfe better than other, that she was chaste. xliiii. . .	59
¶ Of him that paid his det with cryeng bea. xlv.	60
¶ Of the woman that appeled from kynge Philip to kynge Philip. xlvi.	62
¶ Of the olde woman that prayd for the welfare of the tyran Denyse. xlvii.	63
¶ Of the phisitian Eumonus. xlviii.	64
¶ Of Socrates and his scoldynge wyfe. xlix. .	65
¶ Of the phisitian that bare his pacient on hand he had eaten an asse. l.	ib.

	PAGE
¶ *Of the inholders wyfe, and her ii louers.* li. .	67
¶ *Of hym that healed franticke men.* lii. . . .	68
¶ *Of hym that sayd he was nat worthy to open the gate to the kynge.* liii.	70
¶ *Of Mayster Uauasour, and Turpyn his manne.* liiii.	ib.
¶ *Of hym that sought his wyfe, that was drowned, agaynst the streme.* lv.	72
¶ *Of hym that at a skyrmyssh defended hym valiauntly with his feete.* lvi.	73
¶ *Of hym that wolde gyue a songe to the tauerner for his dyner.* lvii.	74
¶ *Of the foole that thought him selfe deed, whan he was a lyue.* lviii.	75
¶ *Of the olde man and his sonne that brought his asse to the towne to sylle.* lix.	78
¶ *Of him that sought his asse, and rode upon his backe.* lx.	80
¶ *The answere of Fabius to Liuius.* lxi. . . .	81
¶ *The answere of Poltis the kynge of Trace to the Troyan ambassadours.* lxii.	82
¶ *The wyse answere of Haniball to kynge Antiochus concerninge his ryche army.* lxiii. .	83
¶ *The wordes of Popilius the Romayn ambassadour to Antiochus the kynge.* lxiiii. . . .	ib.
¶ *Of hym that loued the marchantes wyfe.* lxv. .	84
¶ *Of the woman that couered her heed, and shewed vp her tayle.* lxvi.	86
¶ *How Alexander was monisshed to slee the firste that he mette.* lxvii.	86
¶ *How the aunciente cyte of Lamsac was saued from destruction.* lxviii.	87

Table. xi

                                            PAGE

¶ *Howe Demosthenes defended a mayde.* lxix. . 88
¶ *Of him that desyred to be a gentylman.* lxx. . 89
¶ *Of the gentyllman and his shrewd wife.* lxxi. 90
¶ *Of the two yonge men that rode to Walsyngham to gether.* lxxii. 91
¶ *Of the yong man of Brugis and his spouse.* lxxiii. 92
¶ *Of him that made as he hadde ben a chaste lyuer.* lxxiiii. 93
¶ *Of him that the olde roode fell on.* lxxv. . . 94
¶ *Of the wydowe that wolde not wedde for bodely pleasure.* lxxvi. 95
¶ *Of the couetous ambassadour, that wolde here no musike for sparinge of his purse.* lxxvii. ib.
¶ *Howe Denyse the tyran of Syracuse serued a couetouse man.* lxxix. 97
¶ *Of the old man that quyngered the boy oute of the aple tre with stones.* lxxx. 98
¶ *Of the ryche man that was sycke and wolde not receyue a glyster.* lxxxi. 99
¶ *Of him that feyned him selfe deed, to proue what his wyfe wolde do.* lxxxii. . . . . ib.
¶ *Of the poure man, in to the whose house theues brake by nyght.* lxxxiii. 101
¶ *Of him that shulde haue ben hanged for his scoffinge and his iestynge.* lxxxiiii. . . . ib.
¶ *Of him that had his goose stole.* lxxxv. . . 102
¶ *Of the begger that sayde he was of kynne to kynge Phylip of Macedone.* lxxxvi. . . . 103
¶ *Of Dantes answere to the iester.* lxxxvii. . . ib.
¶ *Of hym that had sore eies.* lxxxviii. 104

	PAGE
¶ Of the olde woman that had sore eies. lxxxix.	105
¶ Of hym that had the custody of a warde. xc.	106
¶ Of the excellente peynter, that hadde foule chyldren. xci.	ib.
¶ Of the scoffer that made one a southsayer. xcii.	107
¶ Of the marchant of Florence, Charles. xciii.	ib.
¶ Of the chesshire man called Eulyn. xciiii.	108
¶ Of hym that desyred to be sette vpon the pyllorye. xcv.	109
¶ Of the wydowes daughter, that was sente to the abbot with a couple of capons. xcvi.	111
¶ Of the two men that dranke a pynte of whyte wyne to gether. xcvii.	112
¶ Of the doctour that desyred to go with a fouler to catche byrdes. xcviii.	114
¶ Of hym that undertoke to teache an asse to spelle and rede. xcix.	115
¶ Of the fryer that confessed the fayre woman. c.	116
¶ Of the chapplen of Louen called syr Antonye that deceyued an vserer. ci.	118
¶ Of the same chaplen and his spiter. cii.	119
¶ Of the olde manne that putte hym selfe in his sonnes handes. ciii.	121
¶ Of hym that had a flye peynted in his shilde. ciiii.	122
¶ Of th emperour Augustus and the olde men. cv.	123
¶ Of Phocions oration to the Atheniens. cvi.	ib.
¶ Of Demosthenes and Phocion. cvii.	124
¶ Of the aunswere of Phocion to them that brought hym a great gyfte from Alexander. cviii.	ib.

		PAGE
¶ *Of Denyse the tyran and his sonne.* cix.	. . .	125
¶ *Of Pomponius the Romayne that was taken and brought before Mithridates.* cx.	. . .	ib.
¶ *Of Titus and the scoffer.* cxi.	. . . . . .	126
¶ *Of Scipio Nasica, and Ennius the poete.* cxii.		ib.
¶ *Of Fabius Minutius and his sonne.* cxiii.	.	127
¶ *Of Aurelian the emperour, that was displeased, by cause the citie Tyana was closed agaynste him.* cxiiii.	. . . .	128
¶ *Of the Nunne forced that durst not crie.* cxv.		129
¶ *Of him that sayde he was the Diuelles man.* cxvi.	. . . .	ib.
¶ *Of the vplandishe priest, that preached of Charitie.* cxvii.	. . . .	130
¶ *An other sayinge of the same preest.* cxviii.	. .	131
¶ *Of the fryer that praysed sainct Frauncis.* cxix.	. . . .	133
¶ *Of hym that warned his wife of wasshynge her face in foule puddell water.* cxx.	. . . .	ib.
¶ *Of the husband man that caused the iudge to geue sentence agaynst him selfe.* cxxi.	. .	134
¶ *Of the Italian frier that shoulde preach before the B. of Rome and his cardinals.* cxxii.	.	ib.
¶ *Of the doctour that sayd, in Erasmus workes were heresies.* cxxiii.	. . . .	136
¶ *Of the frier that preached at Paules crosse agaynst Erasmus.* cxxiv.	. . . . . .	137
¶ *Of an other frier that taxed Erasmus for writyng Germana theologia.* cxxv.	. . .	138
¶ *Of an other that inueighed agaynst the same Erasmus.* cxxvi.	. . . .	ib.

	PAGE
¶ *Of kyng Richarde the iii. and the Northern man.* cxxvii.	139
¶ *Of the Canon and his man.* cxxviii.	140
¶ *Of the same Canon and his sayd man.* cxxix.	ib.
¶ *Of the gentilman that checked hys seruant for talke of ryngyng.* cxxx.	141
¶ *Of the blynde man and his boye.* cxxxi.	142
¶ *Of him that sold two lodes of hey.* cxxxii.	ib.
¶ *How a mery man deuised to cal people to a playe.* cxxxiii.	145
¶ *How the image of the dyuell was lost and sought.* cxxxiiii.	148
¶ *Of Tachas, kyng of Aegypt, and Agesilaus.* cxxxv.	149
¶ *Of Corar the Rhetorician, and Tisias hys scoler.* cxxxvi.	150
¶ *Of Augustus and Athenodorus the Phylosopher.* cxxxvii.	151
¶ *Of the frenche kyng and the brome seller.* cxxxviii.	152
¶ *An other tale of the same frenche kyng.* cxxxix.	153
¶ *What an Italyan fryer dyd in his preaching.* cxl.	155

TALES

AND

QUICKE ANSWERES.

¶ *Of hym that rode out of London and had his seruaunt folowynge on foote.* i.

¶ THERE was a manne on a tyme that rode v myle out of London, and had his seruaunt folowyng after hym on fote, the whiche came so nere, that the horse strake hym a great stroke vpon the thye. The seruaunte, thynkynge to be reuenged, toke and threwe a great stone at the horse, and hytte his mayster on the raynes of the backe, who thought it had bene his horse. He within a whyle loked backe and chydde his seruaunte, bycause he came haltynge so farre behynde. The seruaunt aunswered: Sir, your horse hath gyuen me suche a stroke vpon my thygh, that I can go no faster. Trewely, sayde his mayster, the horse is a great kyckar, for lyke-wyse with his hele right nowe[1] he gaue me a great stroke vpon the raynes of my backe.

¶ Of hym that preched on saynt Chrystophers day. ii.

¶ A FRYERE that preached vpon a saynt Christofers daye, greatly laudynge saynte Christopher, sayde : what a prerogatyue hadde he here in erthe in his armes to beare our Sauioure! was there euer any lyke hym in grace? A homely blount felowe, heryn ghym aske twyse or thryse that question so ernestly, answered : yes, mary: the asse that bare both hym and his mother.

¶ Of the frenche man, that stroue with the Janway for his armes. iii.

¶ THERE was one amonge the Janwayes[2] that the Frenche kyng had hyred to make warre agaynst the Englysshe men, which bare an oxe heed paynted in his shelde : the whiche shelde a noble man of France challenged : and so longe they stroue, that they must needs fyght for it. So, at a day and place appoynted, the frenche gallaunt came into

(1) Just now.   (2) The Genoese.

Quicke Answeres. 17

the felde, rychely armed at all peces.[1] The Janway all vnarmed came also in to the felde, and said to the frenche man : wherfore shall we this day fyght ? Mary, sayd the frenche man, I wyll make good with my body, that these armes were myne auncetours' before thyne. What were your auncetours' armes, quod the Janwaye? An oxe heed, sayd the frenche man. Than, sayde the Janwaye, here needeth no batayle : for this that I beare is a cowes heed.

By thys tale ye perceyue howe nycely the vayne braggynge of the frenche man was deryded.

¶ *Of the curate that sayde our Lorde fedde U. C. persons.* iiii.

¶ A CERTAYNE curate, preachynge on a tyme to his parysshens sayde, that our Lorde with fyue loues fedde v hundred persones. The clerke, herynge hym fayle,[2] sayde softely in his eare : Sir, ye erre ; the gospell is v. thousande. Holde thy peace, foole, said the curate ; they wyll scantly beleue, that they were fyue hundred.

---

(1) At all points.   2) Make a mistake.

¶ *Of hym that profered his doughter in mariage.* v.

¶ THERE was a man vpon a tyme, whiche profered his doughter to a yonge man in mariage, the which yonge manne refused her, sayenge, that she was to yonge to be maryed. I wys, quod her foolysshe father, she is more able than ye wene. For she hath borne iii. children by our parysshe cleeke.

Lo, by this tale ye se, that foles can nat telle what and whan to speake: therfore it were best for them to kepe alway silence.

¶ *Of them that came to London to bye a Crucifixe.* vi.

¶ THERE were certayne men vpon a tyme sent out of a village to London to bye a Crucifixe of wodde. The Caruer that they came to, seynge and herynge by theyr wordes, that they were but folysshe blount felowes, asked them, whether they wolde haue the ymage a lyue or elles deade; whiche question so abasshed them, that they went a syde to deuyse whether[1] was beste. So whan they had spoken priuely to gether, they came to the caruer

(1) Which of the two.

agayne and said they wold haue the image a lyue: for, if theyr neighbours at home were nat so contente, they myghte lyghtly[1] kylle hym.

¶ *Of hym that folowed his wyfe to buryenge.* vii.

¶ A MAN, that wepynge folowed his wyfe to buryenge, rebuked his lyttel sonne, that wente with hym, because he sange, sayenge that he was peuysshe and madde to synge at his mothers buryenge, but he shulde rather be sory and wepe. The chylde answered: father, seynge ye gyue to these prestes money to synge at my mothers buryenge, why be ye angry with me, that aske you nothynge for my syngynge? His father aunswered: the preestes offyce and thyne is nat all one.

By thys tale ye may perceyue that all thynges beseme nat euery body.

¶ *Of hym that felle into the fyre.* viii.

¶ A FELOWE, that was frowarde to his wyfe, vsed to be oute drynkynge many tymes verye late. So on a nyghte he taryed so longe oute, that his wyfe wente to bedde, and badde her mayde make a

(1) A too literal translation of the French word *legierement*, which ought here to have been rendered *readily*, rather than *lightly*.

good fyre, and tarye vp for hym. About xij. of the clocke home he came, and as he stode warmynge him by the fyre his hede was so tottye,[1] that he felle into the fyre. The mayde, seing him fall, ranne vp cryenge to her maistres, and sayd : Alas ! my maister is fallen and lyeth longe straughte in the fyre. No force,[2] mayde, said her maistres, let him lye and take his pleasure in his owne house, where so euer him listeth.

¶ *Of him that vsed to cal his servant the kinge of foles.* ix.

¶ THERE was a man that had a dulle lumpisshe felow to his seruant, wherfore he vsed commonly to call him the kinge of fooles. The felow at laste waxed angry in his minde to be alway so called and sayde to his mayster: I wolde that I were the kinge of foles : for than no man coulde compare with me in largenes of kingedome, and also you shulde be my subiect. By this one may perceiue, that to moch of one thing is not good : many one calleth an other fole, and is more fole him selfe.

(1) Giddy.   (2) No matter.

¶ *Of the yonge woman that sorowed so greatly her husbondes deth.* x.

¶ THERE was a yonge woman, the whiche for her husbande, that laye a dyenge, sorowed oute of all measure, wherfore her father came often to her and sayde : daughter, leaue your mourninge : for I haue prouyded for you a nother husbande, a farre more goodly man. But she did nat onely continue in her sorowe, but also was greatly displeased, that her father made any motion to her of an other husbande. As sone as she had buryed her husbande, and the soule masse was songe, and that they were at dyner, betwene sobbynge and wepynge she rowned[1] her father in the eare, and sayde : father, where is the same yonge man, that ye said shuld be min husbande ? Lo, thus may ye se, that women sorowe ryght longe, after theyr husbondes be departed to God.

¶ *Of him that kissed the mayd with the longe nose.*
xi.

¶ A BABLYNGE gentylman, the whiche on a tyme wolde haue bassed[2] a fayre mayde, that had nat the leest nose, sayde : how shulde I kysse you : youre nose wyll not suffre our lyppes to mete? The mayden, waxinge shamfast and angrye in her

(1) Whispered—*Singer.*   (2) Kissed, from the French word,

mynde (for with his scoffe he a lyttell touched her) answered on this wyse : syr, if ye can not kysse my mouth for my nose, ye may kysse me there as I haue nere a nose.

Ye may by this tale lerne, that it is folye so to scoffe, that youre selfe therby shulde be laughed to scorne agayne. One that is ouer-couetous ought nat to attwite[1] an other of prodigalite. Thou arte her brother (sayd Alcmeon to Adrastus) that slewe her husbande. But he blamed nat Alcmeon for an others faute, but obiected against him his owne. Thou hast with thy hande (sayd he) slayne thin owne mother. It is nat ynough to haue rebukes redie, and to speke vyle wordes agaynst other : for he, that so shuld do, ought to be without any vyce. For of all men, sayth Plutarchus, he ought to be innocent and haue the lyfe vnculpable, that wolde reprehende the fautes of other. The lyttell morall boke[2] saythe :

It is a foule thynge worthye rebuke and blame
A vyce to reprehende and do the same.

(1) *i.e.* twit or taunt.

(2) *Parvus et Magnus Catho*, printed by Caxton, n. d. 4to. Chaucer. in his *Miller's Tale* (*Chaucer's Works*, ed. Bell, i. 194), describes the old carpenter of Oxford, who had married a young girl, as having neglected to study [*Magnus*] *Catho*, which prescribed that marriages ought to take place between persons of about the same age.

"' He knew not Catoun, for his wyt was rude,
That bad man schulde wedde his similitude."

No doubt both *Cato and Parvus Cato* circulated in MS. before the invention of printing. The former was printed by Caxton in 1483-4. See Blades (*Life and Typography of William Caxton*, ii. 53-4).

Quicke Answeres. 23

¶ *The Uplandisshe mans answere, concerninge the steple and pulpit* xii.

¶ IN a certayne place, on a tyme the perysshyns[1] had pulled downe theyr steple, and had buylded it vp newe agayne, and had put out theyr belles to be newe-founded : and bycause they range nat at the bysshops entrynge into the village, as they were wont and acustomed to do, he asked a good homely man, whether they had no belles in theyr steple : he answered : no! Than, sayde the bysshop, ye may sylle aweye[2] your steple. Why so, and please your lordship sayd the man? Bycause hit stondeth vacant, said the bysshop. Than sayde the man, we may well sylle away an other thinge, that we haue in our churche. What is that, sayd the bysshop? That is a pulpit, quod he. For this vii yere ther was no sermon made therin.

¶ *Of the beggers answere to M. Skelton the poete.* xiii.

¶ A POURE begger, that was foule, blacke and lothlye to beholde, cam vpon a tyme vnto mayster Skelton the poete, and asked him his almes. To

(1) Parishioners. This jest is included by Johnson in his *Pleasant Conceits of Old Hobson, the Merry Londoner*, 1607 (reprinted 1843, p. 17). (2) Sell away.

whom mayster Skelton sayde : I praye the, gette the awaye fro me : for thou lokeste as though thou camest out of helle. The poure man, perceyuing he wolde gyue him no thynge, answerd : For soth, syr, ye say trouth, I came oute of helle. Why dyddest thou nat tary styl there, quod mayster Skelton? Mary, syr, quod the begger, there is no roume for suche poure beggers as I am; all is kepte for suche gentyl men as ye be.

¶ *Of the chaplen, that sayde our lady matens a bed.*
xiiii.

¶ A GERTAYNE lorde's chaplen bosted on a tyme, syttynge at his lorde's table, that he sayde our lady matyns euery morninge besyde all his other seruice and orisons. The lorde, to proue whether his chaplen did as he sayde, arose yerly on a morninge, and went to his chaplen's chamber, and called him, saying : where be ye, syr wylliam? Here, and please your lordshyp (quod he), in my bedde. Why, sayd the lorde, I thought ye had ben vp and sayenge of our lady matyns. I am nowe sayinge it, quod the chappleyn. What! lienge in your bedde, quod the lord? why, syr, sayd the chapplain, where shudde women be serued but a bedde?

Quicke Answeres. 25

¶ *Of him that lost his purse in London.* xv.

¶ A CERTAYN man of the countre, the whiche for busines came vp to London, lost his purse as he wente late in the euenynge; and by cause the somme therin was great, he sette vp bylles in dyuers places that, if any man of the cyte had founde the purse, and wolde brynge it agayne to him, he shulde haue welle for his laboure. A gentyll man of the Temple wrote vnder one of the byls, howe the man shulde come to his chamber, and tolde [him] where. So, whan he was come, the gentyll man asked him fyrst what was in the purse; secondli, what countrey man he was, and thirdly, what was his name? Syr, quod he, xx nobles was inne the pourse; I am halfe a walshe man; and my name is John vp Janken.[1] John vp Jankyn (sayde the gentyll man), I am gladde I knowe thy name: for so longe as I lyue, thou nor none of thyn name shal haue my purse to kepe; and nowe fare well, gentyll John vp Jankyn. Thus he was mocked to scorne and went his way.

Hereby ye may perceyue, that a man can not haue a shrewde tourne, but otherwhyle a mocke withall.

(1) John ap Jenkin.

26   *Tales and*

¶ *Of the marchaunt that lost his bodgette betwene Ware and Lon[don]*. xvi.

¶ A CERTAYNE marchant betwene Ware and London lost his bodget and a c li. therin, wherfore he caused to proclayme in dyuers market townes, that who so euer[1] founde the sayde bodget, and wolde bryng it agayne, shulde haue xx li. for his labour. An honeste husbandeman, that chaunsed to fynde the sayde bodget, brought it to the baily[2] of Ware, accordynge to the crye, and required his xx li. for his labour, as it was proclaymed. The couetous marchant, whan he vnderstode this, and that he muste nedes pay xx li. for the fyndynge, he sayd, that there was an c and xx li. in his bodgette, and so wolde haue hadde his owne money and xx li. ouer. So longe they stroue, that the matter was brought before mayster Vauasour the good Judge. Whan he vnderstode by the bayllye, that the crye was made for a budget with an c li. therin, he demanded where hit[3] was ? Here, quod

---

(1) The original has *who so ever that*.
(2) Baillie or magistrate, from the old French word *bailli*.
(3) This form of *it*, though it does not occur in the *C Mery Tales*, is very common in old English works; see the *Seven Sages*, edited by Wright, 1845, for the Percy Society, and the *Anglo-Saxon Passion of St. George*, 1850 (Percy Soc.).

the bailly, and toke it vnto him. Is it iust an
c li. sayde the Judge? Ye, trulye, quod the baillye.
Holde, sayde the Judge (to him that founde the
bodget), take thou this money vnto thyne owne
vse: and if thou hap to fynde a bodgette with a
c and xx li. therin, brynge it to this honest mar-
chante man. It is myn; I lost no more but an
c li. quod the marchant. Ye speke nowe to late,
quod the Judge.

By this tale ye may vnderstande, that they that
go about to disceyue other, be often tymes disceyued them selfe. And some tyme one fallethe
in the dytche, that he him selfe made.

¶ *Of him that was called cuckolde.* xvii.

¶ A CERTEYNE man, whiche vpon a tyme in company betwene ernest and game was called cuckolde,
went angerly home to his wife and sayde: wyfe,
I was this day in company called kockolde;
whether am I one or nat? Syr, truly, sayde she,
ye be none. By my fayth (sayde he), thou shall
swere so vpon this boke; and helde to her a boke.
She denyed it longe; but whan she sawe there was
no remedy, she sayde: well, sythe I must nedes
swere, I promyse you by my faythe, I will swere
truly. Yea, do so, quod he. So she toke the boke

in her hande and sayd : By this boke, syr, ye be a cokolde. By the masse, hore, sayd he, thou lyest! thou sayste it for none other cause but to anger me.

By this tale ye may parceyue, that it is nat best at all tymes for a man to beleue his wife, though she swere vpon a boke.

¶ *Of the iolous man.* xviii.

¶ A MAN that was ryght iolous on his wyfe, dreamed on a nyght as he laye a bed with her and slepte, that the dyuell aperd vnto him and sayde : woldest thou nat be gladde, that I shulde put the in suretie of thy wife? Yes, sayde he. Holde, sayde the dyuell, as longe as thou hast this rynge vpon thy fynger, no man shall make the kockolde. The man was gladde therof, and whan he awaked, he founde his fynger in * * * * * * * *.

¶ *Of the fatte woman that solde frute.* xix.

¶ As a greate fatte woman sate and solde frute in a Lente, there came a yonge man bye, and behelde her frute ernestly, and specially he caste his eyes on her fygges. She asked him, as was her gyse : syr, wyll ye haue any fygges; they be fayre and good? And whan she sawe he was content, she sayde, howe manye? wyll ye haue fyue li? He was content. So she wayed him oute fyue li. into his lappe: and whyle she layde aside her balaunce, he wente his waye faire and softely. Whan she tourned to haue taken her[1] money, and sawe her chapman go his waye, she made after apace, but faster with her voice than with hir fote. He, dissemblinge the mater, wente styll forth on. She made suche a cryenge and folkes gathered so faste, that he stode styll. So in the preace he shewed to the people all the matter, and said: I bought nothing of hir; but that that she vnbyd gaue me, I toke; and if she wyll, I am contente to go before the Justice.

¶ *Of a poller that begyled a prest.* xx.

¶ VPON a tyme in Andwarpe a false pollynge[2] felowe came vnto a certeyne preste, that hadde his purse hangynge at his gyrdell strouttinge[3] oute full of money that he a lytell before had resceyued, and gentilly gretynge hym sayde: good Mayster, our parysshe preste bad me bye him a palle[4] (which

---

(1) The original has *whan she turned her to have taken money.*
(2) Cheating.
(3) The word seems to be here used in a rare sense. The meaning is *bulging.*
(4) This word (Latinè *pallium*) was originally used in a special and exclusive signification.

is the vppermoste vestement, that a preste syngeth masse in); if it wolde please you to go with me, I were moche bounde to you: for our curat and you be of one stature. The preste was contente. Whan they came there where he wolde bye it, the palle was broughte forth, and the preste dyd it on: the poller loketh and toteth[1] thereon, and preyseth it, but he layde a wyte,[2] that it was to shorte before. Nay, quod the syller, the faute is nat in the vestement, hit is the strouttinge purse vnderneth that beareth hit up. Shortely to speake, the prest dyd of his purse, and layde hit by, and than the vestiment they behelde agayne. Whan the poller sawe the preste was tourned, he snatched vp the purs, and toke his legges and to go.[3] The preste rounne after with the vestement on his backe: and the vestement-maker after the prest. The prest bad stop the thefe, the siller bad stop the prest, the poller bade holde the mad preste, and euery man wende[4] he had ben mad in dede, bicause he had the vestement on his backe; and so whyle one letted an other, the false poller went his waye.

(1) Singer explains this to mean *gazeth*.
(2) Found fault with it.
(3) There is probably some corruption here. We ought perhaps read: "and toke *to* his legges *as if* to go."
(4) Weened.

Quicke Answeres. 31

¶ Of Papirius pretextatus. xxi.

¶ AULUS GELLIUS[1] reherseth, how the Senatours of Rome on a tyme helde a great counsaile. Before which tyme the senatours chyldren, called of their garmentes *Pueri pretextati*, vsed to come into the parlemente house with theyre fathers. So at this tyme a chylde, called Papyrius, cam in with his father and herde the great counsayl the which was straytely commaunded to be kept secrete, tyll hit was decreed. Whan this chylde came home, his mother asked him what the counsaile was. The chylde answered, hit oughte nat to be tolde. Now was his mother more desyrous to knowe hit than she was before; wherfore she enquered more straitly and more violentlye. The chylde, beinge sore constrayned of his mother, shortelye deuysed a propre merye leasynge.[2] It is reasoned in the parlemente (quod he), whether of both[3] shulde be more profytable for the comon welth, a man to haue ii wiues or els a woman ii husbandes. Whan she harde him saye so, her mynde was pacified: and forth-with she wente and tolde hit to the other matrones.

(1) *Noctes Atticæ*, translated by Belue, vol. i. p. 86. The *Historie of Papyrius Prætextatus* is related in the 18th Novel of the 1st Tome of Painter's *Palace of Pleasure*.
(2) Deceit, or what would now be called *a white lie*.
(3) *i.e.* which of the two.

On the morowe, a great company of the moste notable wyues of Rome came to the parlemente house weping, and humbly prayeng, that rather one woman shuld be maryed vnto ii men than ii wemen to one man. The Senatours entringe into the court, what with the sodayn assembling of the wyues and of their request, were right sore astonied. Than the childe Papyrius stode forth, and enformed the senatours, how his mother wold haue compelled him to vtter the secrete counsayle : and howc he, to contente her mynde, feyned that leasynge. For which dede the Senatours right hyghly commended the childes fydelite and wytte. And forth-with they made a law, that no child after that (saue only Papirius) shuld come in to the parlement house with his father. And for his great prudence in that tender age he hadde gyuen to hym, to his great honour, this surname *Pretextatus*.

Whereby ye may se, that the hygh treasure of man, and greattest grace, resteth in well-ordrynge of the tonge. The moste prudent poete Hesiodus sayth : The tonge shulde not ronne at large, but be hydde as a precious treasure : for, of all the membres of man, the tonge yll-ordered is the worste. The tonge blasphemeth God. The tonge slaundereth thy neyghbour. The tonge breaketh peace, and stereth vp cruell warre, of all thynges

Quicke Answeres. 33

to mankynde moste mischefull; the tonge is a broker of baudrye; the tonge setteth frendes at debate; The tonge with flatterynge, detraction and wanton tales enfecteth pure and clene myndes; the tonge without sworde or venome strangleth thy brother and frende; and brefely to speake, the tonge teacheth cursed heresyes, and of good Christiens maketh Antichristes.

¶ *Of the corrupte man of lawe.* xxii.

¶ THERE was a man of lawe, whiche on a tyme shulde be iudge betwene a poure man and a ryche: the poure man came, and gaue hym a glasse of oyle (whiche was as moche as his powèr wold stretche to] and desyred, that he wolde be good in his matter. Yes, quod he, the matter shall passe[1] with the. The riche man, perceyuynge that, sente to the same iudge a fatte hogge, and prayed hym to be fauorable on his syde. Wherfore he gaue iudgement agaynst the poure man. Whan the poure man sawe that he was condemned, pytously complaynyng he sayd to the Judge: syr, I gaue you a glasse of oyle, and ye promysed by your faith, the matter shulde passe with me. To whom the iuge sayde: for a trouth there came a hogge

(1) Go easily.

into my house, whiche founde the glasse of oyle, and ouerthrewe and brake it: and so through spyllynge of the oyle I cleane forgot the.

> Wherby ye may se, that euermore amonge
> The ryche hath his wyll, the pore taketh wronge.

¶ *Of kynge Lowes of France, and the husbandman.*
xxiii.

¶ WHAT tyme kynge Lowes of Fraunce, the xi of that name, bycause of the trouble that was in the realme, kepte hym selfe in Burgoyne, he chaunced by occasion of huntinge to come acqueynted with one Conon a homely husbande man, and a plaine meanynge felowe, in whiche maner of men the hygh princes greatly delyte them. To this man's house the kynge ofte resorted from huntynge. And with great pleasure he wolde eate radysshes rotes with hym. Within a whyle after, whan Lowes was restored home, and had the gouernaunce of France in his hande, this husbandeman was counsailed by his wyfe to take a goodly sorte of radysshe rotes and to go and gyue them to the kyng, and put him in mind of the good chere, that he had made hym at his house. Conon wolde nat assente therto. What folysshe woman! quod he, the greate princes remembre nat suche smalle pleasures. But for all that she wolde not reste, tyll Conon chose out a great syght[1] of the fayrest rootes, and toke his iourney towarde the courte. But as he went by the way, he yete vp all the radysshes save one of the greattest.

Conon peaked[2] into the courte, and stode where the kynge shulde passe by: By and by the kynge knewe hym, and called hym to hym. Conon stepte to the kynge and presented his rote with a gladde chere. And the kynge toke it more gladly, and bad one, that was nerest to hym, to laye it vp amonge those iewels that he best loued; and than commaunded Conon to dyne with hym. Whan dyner was done, he thanked Conon: and whan the kyng sawe that he wolde departe home, he commaunded to gyue hym a thousande crownes of golde for his radisshe rote. Whan this was knowen in the kinges house, one of the court gaue the kyng a propre mynion[3] horse. The king, perceiuing that he dyd it, bicause of the liberalite shewed vnto Conon, with very glad chere he toke the gyft, and counsailed with his lordes, howe and with what

(1) This old phrase is still in colloquial use. "A good sight better," or a "great sight more," are well understood terms among us, though vulgar.

(2) A rare word as a verb, though the adjective *peakish* is common enough in old English writers. By *peaked* we must understand "stole" or got admission by stealth.

(3) A literal rendering of the Fr. *mignon*, delicate or dainty.

gyft he myght recompence the horse, that was so goodly and faire. This meanewhile the pickethank had a meruailous great hope, and thought in his mynde thus : if he so wel recompensed the radysshe rote, that was gyuen of a rusticall man, howe moche more largely wyl he recompence suche an horse, that is gyuen of me that am of the courte? Whan euery man had sayde hys mynde, as though the kynge had counsayled aboute a great weyghty matter, and that they hadde longe fedde the pycke-thanke with vayne hope, at last the kyng sayd: I remembre nowe, what we shal gyue hym; and so he called one of his lordes, and badde hym in his eare go fetche hym that that he founde in his chambre (and told hym the place where) featly[1] folded vp in sylke. Anone he came and brought the radysshe roote, and euen as it was folded vp, the kyng with his owne hande gaue it to the courtier, sayenge : we suppose your horse is well recompensed with this iewell, for it hath cost vs a thousande crownes. The courtier went his way neuer so glad, and whan he had vnfolded it, he found none other treasure but the radysshe rote almoste wethered.[2]

(1) Neatly.
(2) The germ of this and the following story may be found in Lane's *Arabian Tales and Anecdotes*, p. 112.

¶ *Of an other picke-thanke, and the same kinge.*
xxiiii.

¶ VPON a time a seruant of the fornamed kinges, seynge a louce crepe vpon the kynges robe, kneled downe and put vp his hande, as though he wolde do somwhat, and as the kynge bowed hym self a lyttell, the man toke the louce, and conueyed her away priuely. The kynge asked hym what it was, but he was ashamed to shew. So moche the kyng instanted[1] hym, that at laste he confessed hit was a louce. Oh! quod the kynge, it is good lucke: for this declareth me to be a man For that kynde of vermyne principally greueth mankynde, specially in youth. And so the kynge commanded to gyue him fyfty crownes for his labour.

Nat longe after, an other, seynge that the kynge gaue so good a rewarde for so smalle a pleasure, came and kneled downe, and put vp his hande, and made as though he toke and conueyed some what priuelye awaye. And whan the kynge constrayned him to tell what hit was, with moche dissemblyng shamfastnes he sayd, hit was a flee. The kynge, perceyuinge his dissimulation, sayd to him : what, woldest thou make me a dogge? and

(1) Importuned.

so for his fifty crownes, that he prooled[1] for, the kinge commaunded to gyue him fiftye strypes.

Wherby ye maye note, that there is great difference betwene one that doth a thynge of good will and mynde, and hym that doth a thynge by crafte and dissymulation; whiche thinge this noble and moste prudent prince well vnderstode. And one ought to be well ware[2] howe he hath to do with highe princes and their busynes. And if *Ecclesiast*[*es*] forbid, that one shall mynde none yll to a kynge, howe shulde any dare speake yll?

¶ *Of Thales the astronomer that fell in a ditch.*
xxv.

¶ LAERTIUS wryteth,[3] that Thales Milesius wente oute of his house vpon a time to beholde the starres for a certayn cause: and so longe he went backeward, that he fell plumpe in to a ditche ouer the eares; wherfore an olde woman, that he kepte in his house laughed and sayde to him in derision: O Thales, how shuldest thou haue knowlege in heuenly thinges aboue, and knowest nat what is here benethe vnder thy feet?

(1) Prowled. (2) CarefuL
(3) Diogenes Laertius (*Lives of the Philosophers*, translated by Yonge, 1853, p. 18).

¶ *Of the astronomer that theues robbed.* xxvi.

¶ As an astronomer that satte vpon a tyme in the market place of a certayne towne, and toke vpon him to dyuine and to shewe what theyr fortunes and chaunses shuld be, that came to him: there came a felow and tolde him (as it was in deede) that theues had broken in to his house, and had borne away all that he hadde. These tidinges greued him so sore, that all hevy and sorowefullye he rose vp and wente his waye. Whan the felowe sawe him do so, he sayde: O thou folissh and madde man, goest thou aboute to dyuine other mennes matters, and arte ignorant in thine owne?

This tale (besyde the blynde errour of suche foles) toucheth them, that handell theyr owne matters lewdly, and wyll entermedle in other mens. And Cicero saythe: That wyse man, that can nat profytte him selfe, hath but lytell wysdome.

¶ *Of the plough man that sayde his pater noster.* xxvii.

¶ A RUDE vplandisshe ploughman, on a tyme[1] reprouynge a good holy father sayd, that he coude

(1) The orig. reads *whiche on a tyme*. I have therefore ventured to strike out the unnecessary word.

saye all his prayers with a hole mynde and stedfaste intention, without thinkyng on any other thynge. To whome the good holy man sayde : Go to, saye one *Pater noster* to the ende, and thynke on none other thinge, and I wyll gyue the myn horse. That shall I do, quod the plough man, and so began to saye : *Pater noster qui es in celis,* tyll he came to *Sanctificetur nomen tuum,* and than his thought moued him to aske this question : yea, but shal I haue the sadil and bridel withal ? And so he lost his bargain.

¶ *Of him that dreamed he fonde golde.* xxviii.

¶ THERE was a man, that sayde in company vpon a tyme, howe he dreamed on a nyghte, that the deuyll ledde him in to a felde to dygge for golde. Whan he had founde the golde, the deuyll sayde : Thou canste not carye hit a waye nowe, but marke the place, that thou mayste fetche hit an other tyme. What marke shall I make, quod the man ? S**** ouer hit, quod the deuyl : for that shall cause euery man to shonne the place, and for the hit shall be a speciall knowlege. The man was contente, and dyd so. So whan he awaked oute of his slepe, he parceyued, that he had foule defyled his bedde. Thus betwene stynke and dyrte vp he rose, and

Quicke Answeres. 41

made him redy to go forth: and laste of all he put on his bonette, wherin also the same nighte the catte hadde s*** ; For great stinke wherof he threwe away his couer knaue,[1] and was fayne to wasshe his busshe.[2] Thus his golden dreame tournędde all to dyrte.[3]

Tibullus sayth: Dreames in the nyght begylen, and cause fearefull myndes to drede thynges that neuer shalbe. But yet Claudian sayeth: Dreames in sondrye wyse fygured gyueth warnynge of vnluckye thynges. And Valerius Maximus wryteth that, as Hamylcar besiged the cyte of Syracuse, he dreamed, that he harde a voyce saye, that he the nexte daye shulde suppe with in the cyte. Wherfore he was ioyfull, as thoughe the victorye from heuen had ben to him promised. And so [he] apparayled his hooste to assaute the towne: in whiche assaute he chaunced to be taken in his lodgynge by them of the cyte, and so bounden lyke a prysoner, they ledde hym in to theyr cite. Thus he more disceyued by hope, than by his dreme, supped that nyghte within the citie as a prisoner, and nat as a conquerour, as he presumed

(1) A cant term for a bonnet. (2) Thick bushy hair.
(3) See Brand's *Popular Antiquities*, ed. 1849, iii. 132, where Brand cites Melton's *Astrologaster, or the Figure-Caster*, 1620, to show that to dream of the devil and of gold was deemed an equally lucky portent. To dream of gold is also pronounced a happy omen in the *Countryman's Counsellor*. 1633.

in his mynde. Alcibiades also hadde a certayne vision in the nyghte of his miserable ende.

This tale sheweth that dreames sometyme come to passe by one meane or other. And he that desyreth to knowe more of dreames wrytten in our englysshe tonge, let hym rede the tale of the nounnes preste, that G. Chauser wrote: and for the skeles howe dreames and sweuens[1] are caused, the begynnynge of the Boke of Fame, the whiche the sayde Chauser compiled with many an other matter full of wysedome.

¶ *Of the crakynge yonge gentyll man, that wold ouerthrowe his enmyes a myle of.* xxix.

¶ A YONGE gentyl man in a cite that was beseged, rebuked the other and called them cowherdes, bycause they wolde nat issue out and fight with their enmyes. So he armed at all peces lepte on horsebacke, and galopte out at the gates. Whan he,

---

(1) Dreams. Thus Chaucer, in the opening lines of the *House of Fame* (called in the old editions and in the present text the *Boke of Fame*), says:—

"God turne us every dreme to goode!
For hyt is wonder thing, be the roode,
To my wytte, what causeth swevenes
Eyther on morwes, or on evenes."

For examples of the later use of the word, see Nares by Halliwell and Wright, art. *Sweven*.

thus crakynge,[1] hadde prycked on aboute a myle, he encountred with manye, that retourned home from the skyrmysshe sore wounded; wherfore he beganne to ryde a softer pace. But whan he harde the hydous noyse, and sawe a myle frome hym howe fyerslye they of the citie and theyr enmyes assayled eche other, he stode euen stylle. Than one, that harde his crakynge before, asked hym, why he rode no nere[r] to fyghte with their enmyes. He answered and sayde: Trewly I fynde nat my selfe so able and stronge in armes, that my harte wyl serue me to ryde any nere[r] to them.

Wherby may be noted, that nat onely the force of the mynde, but also of the body, shulde be wel consydred. Nor one shulde nat bragge and bost to do more than he maye welle atcheue. There be many, whiche with their wordes slee[2] theyr enmyes a great waye of, but whan they se theyr enmye, they put on a sure breste plate and a gorget of a myle of lengthe. Plutarche wryteth that, whan Memnon made warre for Darius agaynste Alexander, he harde one of his souldyours crake and speake many yll wordes agaynst Alexander; wherfore he rapte hym on the pate with a iauelynge, sayenge: I hyred the to fyght agaynste Alexandre, and not to crake and prate.

1) Boasting.   (2) Singer reads *flee*.

Otherwhyle sayth Quintus Curtius, the couetousnes of glory and insaciable desire of fame causeth, that we thynke nothing ouermoche or ouer hard. But Salust saith : Before a man enterprise any feate, he ought fyrst to counsayle : and after to go in hande there with nat heedlynge[1] nor slowly.

¶ *Of hym that fell of a tre and brake his rybbe.*
xxx.

¶ THERE was a husbande man whiche, on a tyme, as he clymbed a tree to gette downe the frute, felle and brake a rybbe in his syde. To comforte hym there came a very merye man whiche, as they talked to gether sayde, he wolde teache hym suche a rule that, if he wold folowe it, he shuld neuer falle from tree more. Marye, sayde the hurte man, I wolde ye hadde taught me that rule before I felle : neuer the lesse, bycause it may happe to profyte me in tyme to come, lette me here what it is. Than the other sayd : Take hede, that thou go neuer downe faster than thou wentest vp, but discende as softly as thou clymmest vp ; and so thou shalt neuer fall.

By this tale ye may note, that abidyng and

(1) Headlong.

slownesse otherwhile are good and commendable, specially in those thynges, wherin spede and hastines cause great hurte and damage. Seneca saythe: A sodayne thynge is nought.

¶ *Of the frier that brayde in his sermon.* xxxi.

¶ A FRYER, that preached to the people on a tyme, wolde otherwhyle crie out a loude (as the maner of some fooles is) whiche brayenge dyd so moue a woman that stode herynge his sermone, that she wepte. He, parceyuyng that, thought in his mynde her conscience being prycked with his wordes had caused her to wepe. Wherfore, whan his sermon was done, he called the woman to hym, and asked what was the cause of her wepynge, and whether his wordes moued her to wepe or nat? Forsoth, mayster (sayde she), I am a poure wydowe : and whan myne husbande dyed, he lefte me but one asse, whiche gotte parte of my lyuynge, the whiche asse the wolues haue slayne : and nowe, whan I hard your hyghe voyce, I remembred my selye asse : for so he was wonte to braye bothe nyghte and daye. And this, good mayster, caused me to wepe. Thus the lewde brayer, rather than preacher, confuted with his folysshenes, wente his way; which, thinkynge for his brayenge lyke an asse to be reputed for the beste preacher, deserued well to here hym selfe to be compared to an asse.

> For truely one to suppose hym selfe wyse
> Is vnto folysshenes the very fyrste gryce.[1]

¶ *The oration of the ambassadour sent to Pope Urban.* xxxii.

¶ OUT of the towne of Parusyn were sente vpon a tyme thre ambassadours vnto our holye father Pope Urban, whom they founde sycke in his bed. Before whose holynes one of the sayde ambassadours had a longe and a tedious oration, that he had deuysed by the way; the whiche, er it was ended, ryght sore anoyed the popes holynesse. Whan he hadde all sayde, the pope asked: Is there anye thynge elles? An other of the thre, percevuynge howe greately the ambagious[2] tale greued the popes holynes to here it out, sayde: Moost holy father, this is all the effecte, and if your holynes spede vs nat forthewith, my felowe shall telle his tale agayne. At whiche sayenge the pope laughed, and caused the ambassadours to be spedde incontinent.

(1) Step, from the Latin *grassus* or *gressus*.
(2) Circumlocutory.—SINGER.

By this tale one maye lerne, that superfluous wordes ought dilygently to be auoyded, specially where a matter is treated before an hygh prince.

¶ *Of the ambassadour sent to the prince Agis.* xxxiii.

¶ NAT moch vnlike the forsayd tale, Plutarche reciteth that, whan the ambassadour of the Abderites had at laste ended a longe tale to the prynce Agis, he asked what answere he shulde make to them that sent him? Say vnto them (quod the prince), whan thou comest home, that all the longe tyme that thou didest dispende in tellynge thy tale, I sate styll and harde the paciently.

¶ *The answere of Cleomenes to the Samiens ambassadour.* xxxiiii.

¶ PLUTARCHE rehersethe also, that what tyme an ambassadour, that was sente frome the Samiens, had made a longe oration vnto Cleomines, to perswade him to make warre to Polycrates, he answered the ambassadour on this maner of wyse: I remembre nat, what thou sayddest in the begynnyng of thy tale, and therfore I vnderstand nat the myddis; and thy conclusion pleaseth me nat.

Wherby we may perceyue, that the noble wyse

men loue fewe wordes. And as the Rhetoriciens say: amonge the vices of an oratoure, there is none more hurtefull than the superfluous heape of wordes.

¶ *Of the wyse man Piso and his seruant.* xxxv.

¶ A CERTAYN wise man called Piso, to auoyde greuous ianglynge, commaunded that his seruauntes shulde saye nothinge, but answere to that that thei were demaunded, and no more. Vpon a daye the sayde Piso made a dyner, and sente a seruaunt to desire Clodius the Consull to come and dyne with him. Aboute the houre of diner al the guestes came saue Clodius, for whom they taryed tyll hit was almoste nyght, and euer sente to loke if he came. At laste Piso sayde to his seruaunt: diddest thou byd the Consull come to dyner? Yes, truely, sayde he. Why cometh he nat than, quod Piso? Mary, quod the seruaunt, he sayde he wolde nat. Wherfore toldest me nat so incontinent, quod Piso? Bycause, quod the seruaunt, ye dyd nat aske me.

By this tale seruauntes may lerne to kepe theyr maisters biddyng: but yet I aduise maysters therby to take hede, howe they make an iniunction.

¶ Of the marchant that made a wager with his lord. xxxvi.

¶ A CERTAYNE marchaunt, before his lorde that he was subiecte vnto, amonge other thynges praysed his wyfe, and sayde, that he neuer harde her lette a *****. Wherat the lorde meruailed, and sayd it was impossible: and so layde and ventred a souper with the marchant, that before thre monethes were ended, he shulde here her lette a ***** or twayne. On the morowe, the lorde came to the marchaunt, and borowed fyfty crownes, the whiche he promysed trewely to repay agayne within viij dayes after. The marchaunt ryght sore agaynst his wylle lent it, and thoughtfully abode, tyll the daye of payment was come: and than he wente to his lorde and requyred his moneye. The lorde, makynge as though he had hadde more nede than before, desyred the marchaunt to lende hym other fyftye crownes, and promysed to paye all within a monethe. And all though the good man denyed hit longe, yet for feare lest he shulde lose the first somme, with moche grutchynge he lente hym the other fyfty crownes. And so wente home to his house ryghte heuye and sorowfull in his mynde. Thus thynkynge and dredynge diuers thynges, he passed many nyghtes awaye without slepe. And as he laye wakyng, he harde his wyfe nowe and than rappe out *****. At the monethes' ende the lorde sente for the marchant, and asked him, if he neuer sythe harde his wyfe let a *****. The marchant aknoweleginge his folye, answered thus: Forsothe, syr, if I shulde for euery ***** paye a souper, all my goodes and landes wolde nat suffice therto. After whiche answere, the lorde payde the marchant his money, and the marchant payde the souper.

Here by ye maye se, that many thinges passe by them that slepe, and it is an old sayenge: He that slepeth, byteth no body. By this tale ye may note also that they, the whiche fortune swetelye enbraceth, take theyr reste and slepe soundely; And contrarye wyse, they that bene oppressed with aduersite, watche sorowefullye whan they shulde slepe. This man, which for a very folisshe thing preysed his wyfe, afterwarde whan a lyttell care beganne to crepe aboute his stomacke, he perceiued that faute in her ryght great. The morall boke, called Cato,[1] counsayleth vs to watche for the more parte: For moche slomber and slepe is the norisshinge of vice.

(1) Vide supra, p. 22.

Quicke Answeres.

¶ *Of the friere that gaue scrowes agaynst the pestilence.* xxxvii.

¶ AMONGE the limitours [1] in the cyte of Tiburtine (Tivoli), was a certayne friere, which vsed to preache about in the villages to men of the countrey : and for as moch as they greately suspecte[d] that a plague of pestilence shulde come amonge them, he promysed eche of them a lytell scrowe:[2] which he sayde was of suche a vertue, that who so euer bare hit hangynge aboute his necke xv dayes shulde nat dye of the pestilence. The folisshe people trustynge herevpon, euerye one after his power gaue him money for a scrowe ; and with a threde of a mayden's spynninge, they hanged hit aboute their neckes. But he charged them that they shuld nat open it tyll the xv dayes ende: for, if they did, he sayde hit had no vertue. So whan the frire hadde gathered moche moneye, he wente his waye. Soone after (as the desyre of folkes is

---

(1) A word used by Chaucer. It signifies a person licensed to preach and beg within a certain *limit*. There was an order of mendicant friars.

"Lordings, ther is in Engelond, I gesse,
A mersschly land called Holdernesse,
In which there went a lymytour aboute,
To preche and eek to begge, it is no doubte."
                CHAUCER'S *Sompnour's Tale;* Works, ed. Bell. ii. 103.

(2) Scrowl.

to knowe newes) the sayd scrowes were redde, in which was writen in Italian speche :

Donna, si fili et cadeti lo fuso,
Quando ti pieghi, tieni lo culo chiuso.(1)

Which is to saye in englysshe : woman, if thou spynne, and thy spyndell falle awaye, whan thou stoupest to reache for him, holde thyne **** close. He sayde, that this passed all the preceptes and medicines of the phisitians.

By whiche tale one may lerne, that all is nat gospell that suche wanderers about saye, nor euerye word to be beleued : For often tymes :—

Gelidus jacet anguis in herbâ.

¶ *Of the phisition, that vsed to write bylles ouer eue.* xxxviii.

¶ A CERTAYNE phisitian of Italy vsed ouer night to write for sondry diseasis diuers billes, called resceitz, and to put them in a bag al to gether. In the morning whan the vrins (as the custome is) were brought to him, and he [was] desired to showe some remedy, he wolde put his hand in to the bag, and at al auentures take oute a bille. And in takinge oute the bille he wolde say to him that came to seke remedye in their language : *Prega dio te la*

(1) In orig and in Singer this is printed as prose, according to the usual practice. The same is the case with the line below.

mandi bona. That is to saye : Praye God to sende the a good one.

By this tale ye may se, that miserable is their state whiche fortune muste helpe and nat reason. Suche a phisitian on a tyme sayde to Pausanias : Thou aylest nothinge. No, sayde he, I haue nat had to do with thy phisicke. And an other tyme a frende of his sayde : Syr, ye ought not to blame that phisitian : for his phisicke dyd you neuer hurte. Thou sayest trouthe, quod he : for, if I hadde proued his phisicke, I shulde nat nowe haue been alyue. And ageyne to an other that sayde : Syr, ye be an olde man, he answered : yea, thou were nat my phisitian. Such maner [of] checkes are to lyttell for the leude foles, that wyll practise phisicke, before they knowe what [be]longeth to theyr name.

¶ *Of hym that wolde confesse hym by writinge.* xxxix.

¶ THER was a yonge man on a tyme, which wrote a longe lybell[1] of his synnes ; whether he did hit for hypocrisy, folysshenesse, or oblyuion I can not say : and whan he shulde confesse him, he gaue hit to the confessour to rede : whiché confessor,

(1) Narrative or account. In its original signification, libel merely implied *libellus*, a little book or volume, a pamphlet, but not necessarily one of an offensive kind.

beinge well lerned and experte in that busynes, parceyued hit wolde requyre a longe tyme to rede ouer: wherfore after a fewe wordes he sayde: I assoyle the frome all the synnes conteyned in this lybell. Yea, but what shall my penaunce be, quod the yonge man? Nothinge els, sayde the confessour, but that thou shalte the space of a moneth rede this lybell ouer euery daye vii tymes. And all thoughe he sayde it was impossyble for him to do, yet the confessour wolde nat chaunge his sentence. By which mery subtyle answere he confuted the breble brable[1] of the folysshe felowe.

By this tale ye may perceyue that he that occupyeth this office, that is to saye, a confessour, ought to be discrete, prudent, and well lernedde. This confessour knewe well the ordinaunce of holye churche: whiche wylleth confession to be made with the mouthe, and nat by wrytynge.

¶ *Of the hermite of Padowe.* xl.

¶ AN hermite of Padow,[2] that was reputed for an holy man, vnder the semblaunce of confession,

(1) Silly and licentious talk. Taylor the Water-Poet, at the end of his *Wit and Mirth*, 1622 (*Works*, 1630, folio I. p. 200), uses the expression *Ribble-rabble of Gossips*, which seems to be a phrase of very similar import.
(2) Padua.

entyced many of the notablest wyues of the towne vnto folye and lewednes. So at last, whan his offence was dyuulgate and knowen (for hypocrisy can nat longe be hid) he was taken by the prouost, and brought before the prince of Padowe, duke Francis the vii of that name, whiche for his disporte sent for his secretarye, to wryte the womens names, that the hermit had layen by. Whan the hermyte had rehersed manye of the dukes seruantes wyues, and the secretarye merely laughenge had writen them, he semed as he had al said. Be there any mo, sayde the duke? No forsothe, said the hermite. Tel vs trouth, quod the secretarie, who be mo, or els thou shalte be sharply punisshed. Than the hermyte sighinge said: Go to, write in thin owne wife amonge the nomber of the other; which saienge so sore greued the secretarye, that the penne felle out of his hande and the duke laughed right hartily, and sayde it was well done: that he that with so great pleasure harde the fautes of other mennes wyues, shulde come in the same nombre.

By this ieste we may lerne, that one ought nat to reioyce at an others grefe or hurte: For lytell woteth a man what hangeth ouer his owne heed.

¶ *Of the Uplandysshe man, that sawe the
kynge.* xli.

¶ AN vplandysshe man, nourysshed in the woddes, came on a tyme to the citie, whanne all the stretes were full of people, and the common voyce amonge them was : The kynge cometh. This rurall manne, moued with noueltie of that voyce, had great desyre to se, what that multitude houed[1] to beholde. Sodaynly the kynge, with many nobuls and states before hym, came rydynge royally. Than the people all about stedfastly behelde the kynge and cryed aloude : God saue the kynge : God saue the kynge. This villayne[2] herynge them crye so, sayde : O where is the kynge, where is the kynge? Than one, shewynge hym the kynge, sayde : yonder is he, that rydeth upon the goodly whyte horse. Is that the kyng, quod the villayne? what, thou mockest me, quod he; me thinke that is a man in a peynted garment.

By this tale ye may perceyue (as Lycurgus proued by experience) that nourysshynge, good bryngynge vp and exercyse ben more apte to leade folke to

(1) Hovered. This form of the word is used by Gower and Spenser. See Nares (ed. 1859), voce *Hove.*
(2) Rustic.

humanite and the doynge of honest thynges than Nature her selfe. They for the mooste part are noble, free, and vertuous, whiche in their youthe bene well nourysshed vp, and vertuously endoctryned.

¶ *Of the courtier that bad the boy holde his horse.* xlii.

¶ A COURTIER on a tyme that alyghted of his horse at an Inde[1] gate sayde to a boye that stode therby : Ho, syr boye, holde my horse. The boye, as he had ben aferde, answered : O maister, this a fierce horse ; is one able to holde him ? Yes, quod the courtier, one may holde hym well inough. Well, quod the boye, if one be able inough, than I pray you holde hym your owne selfe.[2]

¶ *Of the deceytfull scriuener.* xliii.

¶ A CERTAYNE scriuener, whiche hadde but a bare lyuynge by his crafte, imagyned howe he myght gette money. So he came to a yonge man, and asked hym if he were payde x li. whiche a certayne man, that was deade, borowed and ought to paye his father in tyme paste. The yonge manne sayde

(1) Inn.   (2) See *Introduction* vi.

there was no such duetye[1] owynge in his father's name, that he knewe of. It is of trouthe, quod the scriuener: for here is the oblygacyon therof, whiche I made my selfe. He prouoked the yonge manne so moche, that he gaue hym money for the oblygation, and before the mayre he required the duetie. His sonne, that was named to be dettour, sayde playnely, that his father neuer borowed money: for if he had, it wolde appere by his bokes, after the marchantes' maner. And forth with he went to the scriuener and sayde to hym, that he was a false man to write a thing that neuer was done. Sonne, sayde the scriuener, thou wotteste nat what was done that tyme: whan thy father borowed that somme of money, thou were nat borne: but he payde it agayne within thre monthes after, I made the quittance therof my selfe: wherby thy father is discharged. So the yonge man was faine to gyue hym money for the quittaunce. And whan he had shewed the quittaunce he was discharged of that greuance. Thus by his faire fraude he scraped money from them bothe.

By this tale ye may se, that the children in this our tyme be very prudent to get money.

(1) Debt.

¶ *Of hym that saide he beleued his wyfe better than other, that she was chaste.* xliiii.

¶ A CERTAYNE man, whose wyfe (as the voyce wente) was nat very chaste of her bodye, was warned of his frendes to loke better to the matter. The man wente home and sharpely rebuked his wyfe, and told her betwene them bothe, what his frendes had sayde. She, knowynge that periurye was no greatter offence than aduoutry,[1] with wepynge and swerynge defended her honestie: and bare her husbande on hande, that they feyned those tales for enuye that they hadde to se them lyue so quietly. With those wordes her husbande was content and pleased. So yet an other tyme agayne, his frendes warned him of his wyfe, and badde hym rebuke and chastice her. To whome he sayd: I pray you trouble me no more with suche wordes. Telle me, whether knoweth better my wiue's fautes, you or she? They sayde: She. And she (quod he), whom I beleue better than you all, sayth playnly, that ye lye. This was well and

(1) Adultery. The word occurs in Bacon's Essays. In his *Essay of Empire*, the writer says:—"This kind of danger is then to be feared chiefly when the wives have plots for the raising of their own children, or else that they be *advoutresses*." Sir Simonds D'Ewes, in his account of the murder of Sir Thomas Overbury, in 1613, describes the Countess of Essex as "Somerset's *advoutress*" (*Autobiography and Correspondence of Sir Simonds D'Ewes*, ed. Halliwell, I. 74).

wysely done : For one ought nat to gyue light credence to those thinges, wherin resteth perpetuall grefe of mynde.

¶ *Of hym that payde his dette with crienge bea.* xlv.

¶ THERE was a man on a tyme, which toke as moche ware of a marchaunt, as drewe to fyftie li. and riottously playde and spente the same awaye within shorte space. So whanne the day of payemente came, he hadde nother [1] moneye nor ware to paye : wherfore he was arrested, and muste come before the Justyce ; whan he sawe there was none other remedye, but that he shulde be constrayned eyther to pay the dette, or else to go to prison. Wherfore he went to a subtyle man of lawe, and shewed to hym his matter, and desyred of hym [2] his counsayle and helpe. What wylt thou gyue me (quod the man of lawe), if I rydde the of this dette ? By my faythe, sayde the dettour, v marke : and lo, here it is redy ; as sone as I am quitte, ye shall haue hit. Good inough, quod the man of lawe ; but thou muste be ruled by my counsaile, and thus do. Whan thou comest before the Justice, what som euer be saye [3] vnto the, loke that

(1) An old form of *neither*. (2) In orig. *desired him of.*
(3) Orig. reads *sayd.*

Quicke Answeres. 61

thou answere to nothing, but cry bea styl: and lette me alone with the reste. Content, quod he.

So, whan they were com before the Justice, he said to the dettour : doste thou owe this marchant this somme of money or no? Bea! quod he. What beste! (quod the Justice) answere to thy plaint, orels thou wilte be condemned. Bea! quod he agayne. Than his man of lawe stode forth, and sayd : Sir, this man is but an ideot. Who wolde beleue that this marchaunt, whiche is both wyse and subtyle, wolde truste this ideot, that can speke neuer a redy worde, of xl peny worth of ware? and so with suche reasons he perswaded the Justyce to caste the marchaunt in his owne action. So whan the sentence was gyuen, the man of lawe drewe the dettour asyde, and said: Lo, howe sayst thou nowe? Haue not I done well for the? Thou arte clere quitte of the dette that was demanded of the : wherfore giue me my money, and God be with the. Bea! quod he. What, quod the laweer, thou nedest not to crie bea no longer; thy matter is dispatched; all is at a poynt, there resteth nothynge but to gyue me my wages, that thou promysyddest. Bea! quod he agayne. I saye, quod the man of lawe, crie bea no longer nowe, but gyue me my money. Bea! quod he. Thus the man of lawe, neyther for fayre nor foule, coulde gette any other thinge of his client but Bea : wherfore all angerly he departed, and went his waye.

By this tale ye may perceyue, that they whiche be the inuenters and diuisers of fraude and disceit, ben often times therby deceyued them selfe. And he, that hath hyd a snare to attrap an other with, hath hym selfe ben taken therin.

¶ *Of the woman that appeled fro kyng Philip to kynge Philippe.* xlvi.

¶ A WOMAN, whiche [was] gyltlesse, on a tyme was condempned by kynge Philippe of Macedone, whan he was not sobre : wherfore she sayde : I appele. Whether[1], quod the kynge? To kynge Philippe, quod she ; but that is whan he is more sobre and better aduysed ; whiche sayenge caused the kynge to loke better on the matter, and to do her ryght.

This wryteth Val. Maximus. But Plutarche sayth, it was a man, and kynge Philip was halfe a slepe, whan he gaue sentence.

(1) Whither.

¶ *Of the olde woman, that prayde for the welfare of the tyrant Denise.* xlvii.

¶ WHAT tyme Denyse[1] the tyranne raygned, for his cruelte and intollerable dealynge he was hated of all the[2] cite of Syracuse, and euery body wysshed his dethe, saue one olde woman, the whiche euery mornyng praid God to saue him in good life and helth. Whan he vnderstode that she so dyd, he meruailed greatly at her vndeserued beniuolence: wherfore he sente for her, and asked, why and howe he had deserued, that she prayde for hym? She answered and sayd: I do it nat with out a cause. For, whan I was a mayde, we had a tyran raignynge ouer us, whose death I greatly desyred; whan he was slayne, there succided an other yet more cruell than he, out of whose gouernance to be also deliuered I thought it a hygh benifyte. The thyrde is thy selfe, that haste begon to raygne ouer vs more importunately[3] than either of the other two. Thus, fearynge leest, whan thou arte gone, a worse shuld succede and reigne ouer vs, I praye God dayly to preserue the in helthe.

(1) Dionysius. (2) Orig. reads *che*.
(3) *Importunate* seems to be used here in the sense of *oppressive* or *overbearing*.

¶ *Of the phisitian Eumonus.* xlviii.

¶ A PHISITIAN called Eumonus tolde a sicke man, that laye in great payne, that he coulde nat scape, but he muste nedes dye of that disese. This sicke man within a whyle after, nat by the phisitians helpe, but by the wille of God, guerysshed[1] and was holle of his disease: howe be hit, he was verye lowe and bare[2] broughte. And as he walked forth on a daye, he met the same phisytian, whiche, doubtynge whether hit were the same sycke man or nat, sayd: Arte nat thou Gaius? yes, truelye, quod he. Arte thou alyue or deed, sayde the phisitian? I am deed, quod he. What doste thou here than, said the phisitian? Bycause, quod he, that I haue experience of many thinges, God hath commanded me that I shulde come and take vp all the phisitians that I can get, to him. Whiche sayenge made Eumonus as pale as asshes for fere. Than Gaius sayd to him: drede thou nat, Eumonus, thoughe I sayd all phisitians: for there is no man that hath wytte, that wylle take the for one.

(1) Fr. "guerir," to heal. (2) Poor, or, perhaps, poorly.

¶ *Of Socrates and his scoldinge wyfe.* xlix.

¶ LAERTIUS wryteth, that the wyse man Socrates had a coursed scoldinge wyfe, called Xantippe, the whiche on a daye after she hadde alto[1] chydde him powred a * * * * * potte on his heed. He, takynge all paciently, sayde: dyd nat I tell you that, whan I herde Xantippe thonder so fast, that it wolde rayne anone after?

Wherby ye maye se, that the wyser a man is, the more pacience he taketh. The wyse poet Virgil sayth : all fortune by suffrance must be ouercome.

¶ *Of the phisitian that bare his paciente on honde, he had eaten an asse.* l.

¶ A PHISITIAN, which had but smalle lerning, vsed whan he came to viset his pacientes to touche the pulce ; and if any appayred, he wolde lay the blame on the paciente, and beare him on hande,[2] that he did eate fygges, apples, or some other thinge that he forbade : and bicause the pacientes other whyle confessed the same, they thought he

---

(1) Orig. reads *all to*. We take the true reading to be *alto*, as above, *i.e.* in a loud key.

(2) Delude him with the false notion. *To bear on hande*, I presume to be synonymous with *To bear in hande*, of the use of which among old authors several examples are furnished by Nares (edit. 1859).

had ben a very connynge man. His seruante hadde great maruayle, howe he parceyued that, and desyred his mayster to telle hym, whether he knewe hit by touching of the pulce, orels by some other hygher knowlege. Than sayde his mayster: for the good seruice that thou haste done me, I wyll open to the this secrete point. Whan I come in to the pacientes chamber, I loke al a bout : and, if I spye in the flore shales,[1] parynge of chese, of aples, or of peares, or any other scrappes, anone I coniecte,[2] that the paciente hoth eaten thereof. And so to th' ende I wold be blameles, I lay the faute on theyr mysdiettynge.

Nat longe after, the same seruaunte toke on hym to practise physike, whyche in lyke maner blamed his pacientes, and sayde, that they kepte nat the diete that he gaue them ; and he bare them on hande that they yete some what, wherof he sawe the scrappes in the flore. On a tyme he cam to a poure man of the countre, and promysed to make him hole, if he wolde be gouerned after him, and sa gaue him to drinke I wote nat what, and went his waye tyll on[3] the morowe. Whan he came agayne, he founde the man sicker than euer he was. The rude fole, nat knowinge the cause, behelde here and there aboute, and whan he coude

(1) Shells.   (2) Conjecture.   (3) Orig. and Singer read *an*.

se no skrappes nor parynges, he was sore troubled in his mynde. So at the last he espied a saddel vnder the bed. Than said he all a loude, that he hadde at length parceyued, howe the sicke man enpayred : he hath so excessiuely passed diete (quod he), that I wonder he is nat deed. How so, quod they? Marye, quod he, ye haue made him to eate an holle asse! Lo, where the saddell lyethe yet vnder the bedde. For he thoughte the saddell had be lefte of the asse, as bones are of· fleshe. For which folysshnes he was well laughed to skorne and mocked.

Thus as a good faythfull phisitian is worthy of greate honour: for truely of hym dependethe the greattest parte of mans helthe, so lyke wyse a folysshe and an vnlerned, that thynkethe to cure with wordes, that he ought to do with herbes, is nat onely worthy to be deryded and mocked, but also punysshed : for nothynge is more perillous.

¶ *Of the inholders wyfe and her ii louers.* li.

¶ NERE vnto Florence dwelled an inholder, whos wyfe was nat very dangerous of her tayle. Vpon a nyghte as she was a bed with one of her louers, there came a nother to haue lyen with her. Whan

(1) Innkeeper.   (2) Jealous, careful.

she herde him come vp the ladder, she met him, and bade hym go thence, for she hadde no tyme than to fulfylle his pleasure. But for all her wordes he wolde nat go a waye, but stylle preaced[1] to come in. So longe they stode chydinge, that the good man came vpon them, and asked them why they brauled so. The woman, nat vnprouyded of a disceytefull answere, sayde : Syr, this man wolde come in per force to slee or myschiefe an other, that is fled in to our house for succoure, and hitherto I haue kepte him backe. Whan he, that was within, herde her saye so, he beganne to plucke vp his harte and say, he wold be a wreked[2] on him withoute. And he that was withoute made a face, as he wolde kylle him that was within. The folysshe man, her husbande, enquered the cause of theyr debate, and toke vpon him to sette them at one.[3] And so the good sely man spake and made the pese betwene them both ; yea, and farther he gaue them a gallon of wyne, addynge to his wiues aduoutry the losse of his wine.

¶ *Of hym that healed franticke men.* lii.

¶ THERE dwelled a man in Italy, whiche vsed to heale men, that were franticke, on this maner.

(1) Pressed.   (2) Wreaked, revenged.   (3) Reconcile them.

Quicke Answeres. 69

He had within his house a gutter, or a ditche, full of water, wherin he wold put them, some to the middell legge, some to the knee, and some dypper, as they were madde.[1] So one that wsa well amended, and wente aboute the house to do one thinge and other for his meate, as he stode on a tyme at the gate, lokinge in to the strete, he sawe a gentyll man ryde by with a great sorte[2] of haukes and houndes; the which he called to him and said: you gentyll man, whither go ye? On huntynge, quod the gentyll man. What do you with all those kytes and dogges, quod he? They be haukes and houndes, quod the gentyll man. Wherfore kepe you them, quod the other? For my pleasure, quod the gentyl man. What costeth it you a yere to kepe them, quod the other? XL duckettes, quod the gentyll man. And what do they profytte you, quod he? Foure duckettes, quod the gentyll man. Gette the lyghtlye hense, quod the madde man: for, if my mayster come and fynde the here, he wyll put the in to the gutter vp to the throte.

This tale toucheth suche young gentyll menne, that dispende ouer moche good[3] on haukes, houndes, and other trifils.

(1) *i. e.* according to their degree of madness. See *Introduction*, viii. ix.
(2) Assortment.   (3) Goods.

¶ *Of hym that sayde he was not worthy to open the gate to the kynge.* liii.

¶ As a kynge of Englande hunted on a tyme in the countie of Kent, he hapte to come rydynge to a great gate, wherby stode a husbande man of the countrey, to whom the kynge sayde : good felowe, putte open the gate. The man perceyuynge it was the kynge, sayde : no, and please your grace, I am nat worthy ; but I wyll go fetche Mayster Couper, that dwelleth nat past ij myles hense, and he shal open to you the gate.

¶ *Of mayster Uauasour and Turpin his man.* liiii.

¶ MAYSTER Vauasour,[1] sometyme a iudge of Englande, hadde a seruaunt with hym called Turpin, whiche had done hym seruyce many yeres ; wherfore he came vnto his mayster on a tyme, and sayde to hym on this wyse : syr, I haue done you seruice longe ; wherfore I pray you gyue me somwhat to helpe me in myn old age. Turpin,

---

(1) This old Yorkshire family produced several persons eminent in the legal profession from the time of Henry I. downward ; but the one here intended was, in all probability, John Vavasour, who became Recorder of York, 1 Henry VII., and was made a justice of the Common Pleas in August, 1490. See Foss's *Judges of England*, v. 78, 79.

quod he, thou sayst trouthe, and hereon I haue thought many a tyme; I wyll tell the, what thou shalt do. Nowe shortly I must ride vp to London; and, if thou wilt beare my costis thether, I wyll surely gyue the suche a thing, that shall be worth to the an hundred pounde. I am contente, quod Turpin. So all the waye as he rode Turpin payd his costis, tyll they came to theyr last lodginge: and there after souper he cam to his mayster and sayde: sir, I haue born your costes hitherto, as ye badde me; nowe, I pray you let me se, what thynge hit is, that shulde be worthe an hundred pounde to me. Dyd I promise the suche a thynge, quod his maister? ye, forsoth, quod Turpin. Shewe me thy wrytinge, quod maister Vauasour. I haue none, sayde Turpin. Than thou arte lyke to haue nothinge, sayde his maister. And lerne this at me.[1] Whan so euer thou makest a bargayne with a man, loke that thou take sure wrytynge, and be well ware howe thou makest a writynge to any man. This poynte hath vayled[2] me an hundred pounde in my dayes: and so hit may the. Whan Turpin sawe there was none other remedy, he helde him selfe contente. On the morowe Turpin taryed a lytelle behynde his mayster to reken with the hostes, where they laye, and of her he borowed so

(1) Of me.   (2) *i. e.* availed, has been worth £100 to me.

moche money on his maysters skarlet cloke, as drewe to[1] all the costes that they spente by the waye. Mayster Vauasour had nat ryden past ii myle but that it began to rayne; wherfore he calledde for his cloke.—His other seruauntes saide, Turpin was behinde, and had hit with him. So they houedde[2] vnder a tre, tylle Turpin ouer toke them. Whan he was come, Mayster Vauasour all angerly sayde : thou knaue, why comest thou nat aweye with my cloke? Syr, and please you, quod Turpin, I haue layde hit to gage[3] for your costes al the waye. Why, knaue, quod his mayster, diddiste thou nat promyse to beare my charges to London? Dyd I, quod Turpin? ye, quod his mayster, that thou diddest. Let se, shew me your wriytinge therof, quod Turpin; wherto his mayster, I thinke, answered but lytell.

¶ *Of hym that sought his wyfe agaynst the streme.* lv.

¶ A MAN the[re] was whose wyfe, as she came ouer a bridg, fell in to the ryuer and was drowned ; wherfore he wente and sought for her vpward against the stream, wherat his neighboures, that

---
(1) *i. e. came* to, or amounted to, covered.
(2) Hovered, *i. e.* halted for shelter.   (3) Laid it in pledge.

wente with hym, maruayled, and sayde he dyd nought, he shulde go seke her downeward with the streme. Naye, quod he, I am sure I shall neuer fynde her that waye: for she was so waywarde and so contrary to euery thynge, while she lyuedde, that I knowe very well nowe she is deed, she wyll go a gaynste the stream.

¶ *Of hym that at a skyrmyshe defended him with his feet.* lvi.

¶ A LUSTYE yonge gentyll man of France, that on a tyme was at a skyrmysshe, and defended him selfe valyantly with his feet, came in to the courte, in to a chambre amonge ladies, with a goodly ringe vpon his fynger, to whom a fayre lady sayde : syr, why weare ye that rynge vpon your fynger ? Wherfore aske you, madame, quod he ? Bycause (sayde she) your feet dyd you better seruice than your handes at the last skyrmysshe that ye were at.

By this tale yonge men may lerne to beare them well and valyantly for drede of reproche. Better it is with worshyp to dye than with shame to lyue, albe hit that Demosthenes sayde : he that fleethe cometh agayne to batayle.

¶ *Of hym that wolde gyue a songe for his dyner.* lvii.

¶ THERE came a felowe on a tyme in to a tauerne, and called for meate. So, whan he had well dyned, the tauerner came to reken and to haue his money, to whom the felowe sayde, he had no money, but I wyll, quod he, contente you with songes. Naye, quod the tauerner, I nede no songes, I must haue money. Whye, quod the felowe, if I synge a songe to your pleasure, will ye nat than be contente? yes, quod the tauerner. So he began, and songe thre or foure balades, and asked if he were pleased? No, sayde the tauerner. Than he opened his pourse, and beganne to synge thus :

> Whan you haue dyned make no delaye
> But paye your oste, and go your waye.

Dothe this songe please you, quod he? Yes, marye, sayd the tauerner, this pleaseth me well. Than, as couenant was (quod the felowe), ye be paide for your vitaile. And so he departed, and wente his waye.

This tale sheweth, that a man may be to hastye in makynge of a bargayne and couenantynge; and therfore a man ought to take good hede, what he sayth : for one worde may bynde a man to great inconuenience, if the matter be weighty.

¶ *Of the foole that thought hym selfe deed.* lviii.

¶ THERE was a felowe dwellynge at Florence, called Nigniaca, whiche was nat verye wyse, nor all a foole, but merye and iocunde. A sorte[1] of yonge men, for to laughe and pastyme, appoynted to gether to make hym beleue that he was sycke. So, whan they were agreed howe they wolde do, one of them mette hym in the mornynge, as he came out of his house, and bad him good morowe, and than asked him, if he were nat yl at ease? No, quod the foole, I ayle nothynge, I thanke God. By my faith, ye haue a sickely pale colour, quod the other, and wente his waye.

Anone after, an other of them mette hym, and asked hym if he had nat an ague : for your face and colour (quod he) sheweth that ye be very sycke. Than the foole beganne a lyttel to doubt, whether he were sycke or no : for he halfe beleued that they sayd trouth. Whan he had gone a lytel farther, the thyrde man mette hym, and sayde : Jesu! manne, what do you out of your bed? ye

(1) Knot, party.

loke as ye wolde nat lyue an houre to an ende.
Nowe he doubted greatly, and thought verily in
his mynde, that he had hadde some sharpe ague;
wherfore he stode styll and wolde go no further;
and, as he stode, the fourth man came and sayde:
Jesu! man, what dost thou here, and arte so sycke?
Gette the home to thy bedde: for I parceyue thou
canste nat lyue an houre to an ende. Than the
foles harte beganne to feynte,[1] and [he] prayde
this laste man that came to hym to helpe hym
home. Yes, quod he, I wyll do as moche for the
as for myn owne brother. So home he brought
hym, and layde hym in his bed, and than he fared
with hym selfe, as thoughe he wolde gyue vp the
gooste. Forth with came the other felowes, and
saide he hadde well done to lay hym in his bedde.
Anone after, came one whiche toke on hym to be
a phisitian; whiche, touchynge the pulse, sayde the
malady was so vehement, that he coulde nat lyue
an houre. So they, standynge aboute the bedde,
sayde one to an other: nowe he gothe his waye:
for his speche and syght fayle him; by and by he
wyll yelde vp the goste. Therfore lette vs close his
eyes, and laye his hands a crosse, and cary hym forth
to be buryed. And than they sayde lamentynge

(1) To grow faint.

Quicke Answeres.

one to an other: O! what a losse haue we of this good felowe, our frende?

The foole laye stylle, as one [that] were deade; yea, and thought in his mynde, that he was deade in dede. So they layde hym on a bere, and caryed hym through the cite. And whan any body asked them what they caryed, they sayd the corps of Nigniaca to his graue. And euer as they went, people drew about them. Among the prece[1] ther was a tauerners boy, the whiche, whan he herde that it was the cors of Nigniaca, he said to them: O! what a vile bestly knaue, and what a stronge thefe is deed! by the masse, he was well worthy to haue ben hanged longe ago. Whan the fole harde those wordes, he put out his heed and sayd: I wys, horeson, if I were alyue nowe, as I am deed, I wolde proue the a false lyer to thy face. They, that caryed him, began to laugh so hartilye, that they sette downe the bere, and wente theyr waye.

By this tale ye maye se, what the perswasion of many doth. Certaynly he is very wyse, that is nat inclined to foly, if he be stered therevnto by a multitude. Yet sapience is founde in fewe persones: and they be lyghtly[2] olde sobre men.[3]

(1) Crowd.　　(2) Usually. See Nares, edit. 1859, *in voce*.

(3) This story is to be found in Poggius, who calls it *Mortuus Loquens*, and from Poggius it was transferred by Grazzini to his collection of Tales, not published till after his death ;

¶ *Of the olde man and his sonne that brought his asse to the towne to sylle.* lix.

¶ AN olde man on a tyme and a lyttell boye his sonne droue a litel asse before them, whiche he purposed to sylle at the markette towne, that they went to. And bicause he so dyd, the folkes that wrought by the way syde, blamed hym; wherfore he set vp his sonne, and went hym selfe on fote. Other, that sawe that, called hym foole, by cause he lette the yonge boye ryde, and he, beynge so aged, to goo a foote. Than he toke downe the boye, and lepte vp and rode hym selfe. Whanne he hadde rydden a lyttell waye, he harde other that blamed hym, bycause he made the lyttell yonge boye ronne after as a seruaunte, and he his father to ryde. Than he sette vppe the boye behynde hym, and so rode forthe.

Anone he mette with other, that asked hym if the asse were his owne, by whiche wordes he coniected, that he did nat wel so to ouercharge the lyttell sely asse, that vnethe[1] was able to beare one. Thus he, troubled with their dyuers and manyfolde opinions; whiche, neither with his asse vacant, nor he alone, nor his sonne alone, nor

(1) Scarcely.

bothe to gether rydyng at ones on the asse, coulde passe forth with out detraction and blame. Wherfore at last he bounde the asse[s] feet to gether, and put through a staffe ; and so he and his sonne began to beare the asse betwene them on their shulders to the towne. The nouelte of whiche syght caused euery body to laughe and blame the folysshenes of them both. The sely olde man was so sore agreued that, as he sat and rested hym on a ryuers syde, he thréwe his asse in to the water ; and so whan he had drowned his asse he tourned home agayne. Thus the good man, desyrynge to please euerye bodye, contentynge none at all, loste his asse.

By this tale appereth playnelyè, that they, whiche commyt them selfe to the opinion of the common people, ben oppressed with great myserye and seruage : for how is it possible to please all, whan euerye man hath a dyuers opinion, and dyuerslye iudgeth ? and that was well knowen to the poet, whan he sayde :

Scinditur incertum studia in contraria vulgus.

And as Cicero, Persius, and Flaccus say : as many men so many myndes : as many heedes so many wyttes. That, that pleaseth one, displeaseth an other : Fewe alowe that that they loue nat : and that that a man aloweth, he thynketh good. Therfore the beste is, that euery man lyue well, as a good Christen man shulde, and care nat for the vayne wordes and ianglynge of the people. For bablynge (as Plutarchus sayth) is a greuous disease, and harde to be remedied. For that that shulde heale it (which is wordes of wisdome) cureth them that harkneth there vnto; but pratlers wille here none but them selfe.

¶ *Of him that sought his asse and rode on his backe.* lx.

¶ THERE was in the countrey of Florence an husbande man, that vsed to carye corne to the market vpon many lytell asses. On a time as he came home warde, bycause he was somewhat werye, to ease him selfe, he rode on one the strongest of them. And as he rode, dryuinge his asses before him, he counted them, and forgot the asse that he rode on; wherfore he thought still that he lacked one. Thus sore troubled in his mynde, he bad his wyfe set vp his asses, and hastily rode agayne backe to the towne vii myles of, to seke the asse that he rode on. He asked euery body that he met, if they sawe an asse straye alone. Whan he herde euery bodye saye they sawe none suche, makynge great sorowe, he retourned home agayne. At laste, whan he was alyghted his wyfe parceyued and shewedde hym playnlye, that the asse, that he rode on, was the same that he soughte, and made suche sorowe fore.

This ieste may be well applied vnto suche as note the defautes, that they lyghtly[1] spy in other, and take none hede, nor can nat se, what ils they haue or[2] bene spotted with them selfe.

¶ *The answere of Fabius to Liuius.* lxi.

¶ WHAN Anniball, the capitayne of Cartage, had conquered Tarent (a towne perteinyng to the Romayns), all saue the castell, and had lefte a garnison to kepe it, whan the worthy Romayne Fabius had knowelege therof, he pryuely conducted an armye thether, and got the towne agayne, and pylled[3] it. Than M. Liuius that kepte the castell with a garnison, sayde bostynge him selfe, that Fabius had gotte the towne through him and

(1) Readily. A story very like this occurs in *A Sackful of Newes*, 1673. It was originally related by Poggius in his Facetiæ, where it is entitled *Asinus Perditus*, and it has been imitated by La Fontaine in the fable of " Le Villageois qui cherche son veau." It is also the 12th tale of *Les Cent Nouvelles Nouvelles*.

(2) Before. (3) Pillaged.

his helpe. You saye trouth, quod Fabius: for if you had nat loste the towne, I shulde néuer haue gotte hit.[1]

¶ *The answere of Poltis, the kynge of Thrace, to the Troyan embassadors.*[2] lxii.

¶ PLUTARCHE lyke wyse reherseth that, durynge the warre of Troy, the Grekes and also the Troians sente ambassadours to a kynge of Thrace calledde Poltis, whiche kynge answered th ambassadours and bade, that Alexandre shulde delyuer agayne Helayne (for she was the cause of the warre), and he wolde gyue him ii fayre wyues for her.

(1) "Now there was one *Marcus Livius*, a ROMAINE that was Gouernour of TARENTUM at that time when *Hanniball* tooke it, and neverthelesse kept the castell still out of *Hannibals* hands, and so held it untill the city came againe into the hands of the ROMAINES. This *Livius* spited to see such honour done to *Fabius*, so that one day in open Senate, being drowned with enuy and ambition, he burst out and said, that it was himselfe, not *Fabius*, that was cause of taking of the city of TARENTUM again. *Fabius*, smiling to hear him, answered him opely: 'Indeed, thou saiest true, for if thou hadst not lost it, I had neuer won it again.'"—Plutarch's *Lives*, transl. by Sir T. North, ed. 1603, fol. 192.

(2) Πόλτυς, ὁ Θρακῶν βασιλεὺς ἐν τῷ Τρωϊκῷ πολέμῳ πρεσβευσαμένων πρὸς αὐτὸν ἅμα τῶν Τρώων καὶ τῶν Ἀχαιῶν, ἐκέλευσε τὸν Ἀλέξανδρον ἀποδόντα τὴν Ἑλένην, δύο παρ' αὐτοῦ λαβεῖν καλὰς γυναῖκας. —Plutarchi *Apothegmata* (Opera Moralia et Philosophica, vol. vi. p. 665, edit. Lipsiæ, 1777).

Quicke Answeres. 83

¶ *The wyse answere of Hanibal to kynge Antiochus, concerninge his ryche armye.* lxiii.

¶ WHAN kynge Antiochus had prepared to make warre to the Romayns, he caused his armye to mustre before Anniball. So they shewed and mustred, both horse men and fote men; of whose ryche and sumptuous armour and apparaile al the felde glistred and shone. How saye you, quod the kynge to Hanibal, is nat this armye sufficient ynough for the Romayns? Yes, quod Haniball, and though they were the moste couetous of all the worlde. The kynge mente one thing, and he answerd an other.[1]

¶ *The wordes of Popilius the Romayn embassadour to Antiochus the kynge.* lxiiii.

¶ ONE C. Popilius was sente vp[o]n a tyme by the Senatours of Rome with letters to Antiochus the kynge of Syrye, wherin the kyng was commaunded to calle his armye backe agayne oute of Aegipte. and that he shulde suffer the chyldren of Ptolome and theyr realme in peace. As th embassadour

(1) See the 21st Novel of the 1st tome of the *Palace of Pleasure* (Haslewood's edit. i. 74).

came by the kynges tentes and pauylyons, Antiochus a good waye of saluted him, but he did nat salute the kynge agayne, but delyuered to him his letters. Whan the kynge hadde redde the letters, he sayde, that he muste take counsayle, before he made him an answere. Popilius, with a rod that he had in his hande, made a compace aboute the kynge, and sayde : euen here standinge, take counsayle, and make me an answere. Euery man hadde meruayle at the grauite and stout stomacke of the man ; and whan Antyochus was contente to do as the Romayns wolde haue hym, than Popilius both saluted and embraced him.[1]

¶ *Of him that loued the marchants wyfe.* lxv.

¶ THER was a yonge lusty gentyll man vpon a tyme that was ryght amorous, and loued a certayne marchauntes wyfe oute of all measure, in so moch that he folowed her to the churche and other places, but he durste neuer speake. At the laste he, with two or thre of his felowes, folowed her to

---

(1) "Quibus perlectis, quum se consideraturum, adhibitis amicis, quid faciendum sibi esset, dixisset, Popilius, pro cetera asperitate animi, virgâ, quam in manu gerebat, circumscripsit regem : ac, 'Priusquam hoc circulo excedas,' inquit, 'redde responsum, senatui quod referam.' Obstupefactus tam violento imperio parumper quum hæsitasset, ' Faciam,' inquit 'quod censet Senatus.' Tum demum Popilius dextram regi, tanquam socio atque amico, porrexit."—Livy, lib. xlv. c. 12, edit. Twiss.

a fryers, where he hadde tyme and place conueniente to speake thre or four wordes to her, that he before had deuysed. So one of his felowes sayde: go nowe, speake to her. But he stode styll all astonied. They egged[1] and prouoked him so moche, that at last he wente vnto her, and, clene forgettynge those wordes that he had thoughte to haue spoken, he said to her on this wise: maistres, I am your owne lytel seruante; wherat she smyled and sayd: syr, I nede nat your seruyce: for I haue seruantes inow at home, that can brusshe, sponge, wasshe and do all my other busines. The whiche answere and folysshe basshemente of the gentyl man caused his felowes to laugh hartelye. This maner of folye was well knowen to the poet, whan he sayde:

Incipit affari, mediaque in voce resistit.

Folysshe loue maketh folkes astonied
And eke to raue without remembrance
Whan they shulde speake, they bene abasshed
And of theyr wordes can make none vtterance
Nor be so hardye them selfe to auance
What tyme they se of her the swete face
Of whom the loue theyr hartes doth enbrace.

(1) Edged.

¶ *Of the woman that couerd her heed and shewed her taile.* lxvi.

¶ As a woman, that for a certayne impedimente had shaued her heed, sat in her house bare heed, one of her neighbours called her forth hastely into the strete, and for haste she forgotte to putte on her kerchefe. When her neighbour sawe her so, she blamed her for cominge abrode bare heed : wherfore she whypte vp her clothes ouer her heed. And so to couer her hed she shewed her ***. They, that stode by, beganne to laugh at her folysshenes, whiche to hyde a lytell faute shewed a greatter.[1]

This tale touchethe them, that wolde couer a smalle offence with a greatter wyckednesse ; and as the prouerbe saythe : Stomble at a strawe, and leape ouer a blocke.

¶ *Howe Alexander was monysshed to slee the fyrste that he mette.* lxvii.

¶ WHAN great Alexander wolde entre in to Perse lande with his armye, he counsayled with Apollo of his good spede :[2] and by lotte[3] he was warned, that he shulde commaunde to slee the fyrst that

(1) "Mal est caché a qui lon void le dos."—Leigh's *Select French Proverbs*, 1664.   (2) Good fortune.   (3) Casting of lots.

Quicke Answeres. 87

he mette, whan he issued out at a gate. Perchaunce, the fyrste that he mette was a man dryuynge an asse before hym. Incontinent the kyng commaunded to take and put hym to dethe. Whan the poore man sawe, that they wolde slee him, he said: what haue I done? Shall I that am an innocent [man] be putte to deathe? Alexander, to excuse his dede, sayde, he was warned by diuine monition to commaunde to slee the fyrste, that he mette comynge out at that gate. If it be so, myghty kyng (quod the man), than the lotte dyuine hath ordeyned an other to suffre this deth and not me: for the lytel asse, that I droue before me, mette you fyrste.

Whiche subtyle sayenge greatly pleased Alexander: for elles he had done amysse; and so he caused the beaste to be slayne.

By this tale one may note, that it is better sometyme to be laste than fyrste.

¶ *Howe the cite of Lamsac was saued from destruction.* lxviii.

¶ As great Alexander on a tyme was fully purposed to haue vtterly distroyed a great cite, called Lamsac,[1] he sawe his mayster Anaximenes[2] come to-

(1) Lampsacus.
2 Anaximenes, the historian, who wrote an account of the Life of

warde him withoute the walles: and bicause the kynge perceyued manifestlye, that he came to entreate hym for the cite, he sware a great othe, that he wolde nat do that that he came to desyre hym fore. Than Anaximenes sayde: sir, I desyre your grace, that this same cite Lampsac may be vtterly distroyed. Through which sage and subtile sayeng the noble auncient citie was saued from ruyne and destruction.

¶ *Howe Demosthenes defended a mayde.* lxix.

¶ THERE were two men on a time, the whiche lefte a great somme of money in kepyng with a maiden on this condition, that she shulde nat delyuer hit agayne, excepte they came bothe to gether for hit. Nat lang after, one of them cam to hir mornyngly arayde, and sayde that his felowe was deed, and so required the money, and she delyuered it to hym. Shortly after came the tother man, and required to haue the moneye that was lefte with her in kepyng, The maiden was than so sorowfull, both for lacke of the money, and for one to defende her cause, that she thought to hange her selfe. But Demosthenes,

---

Alexander the Great. He was a native of Lampsacus, and the nephew of the orator of the same name.

Quicke Answeres. 89

that excellent oratour, spake for her and sayd : sir, this mayden is redy to quite her fidelite,[1] and to deliuer agayne the money that was lefte with her in kepynge, so that thou wylt brynge thy felowe with the to resceyue it. But that he coude nat do.

¶ *Of him that desired to be made a gentilman.* lxx.

¶ THERE was a rude clubbysshe[2] felowe, that longe had serued the duke of Orliance; wherfore he cam on a tyme to the duke, and desired to be made a gentyll man. To whom the duke answered : in good feyth, I may well make the ryche, but as for gentyl man I can neuer make the.[3]

(1) *i.e.* Discharge, or acquit herself of, her trust.

(2) Uncouth. "If thou shuldest refuse to do any of these thynges, and woldest assaye to do some thing of more sadnes and prudence, they wyll esteme and count the vnmanerly, *cloubbysshe*, frowarde, and clene contrarye to all mennes myndes."—Erasmus *De Contemptu Mundi*, transl. by Thomas Paynel, 1533, fol. 42. " Rusticitie may seem to be an ignorance of honesty and comelinesse. A Clowne or rude fellow is he, who will goe into a crowd or presse, when he hath taken a purge : and hee that sayth, that Garlicke is as sweet as a gilliflower : that weares shooes much larger then his foot : that speakes alwaies very loud : " &c. *Theophrastus His Characters* translated by John Healey, 1616, pp. 15, 16. It is a generally received opinion that this work has come down to us in a corrupt shape.

(3) Times were altered when the curious ballad "These Knights will hack," printed by Mr. Halliwell from Addit. MS. 5832, in one of the Shakespeare Society's publications, (*Marriage of Wit and Wisdom*, &c. p. 144), was directed against the mushroom-knights of James I. :—

By which wordes appereth, that goodes and riches do not make a gentyl·man, but noble and vertuous conditions do.

¶ *Of the gentyll man and his shrewde wyfe.* lxxi.

¶ THERE was a certayne gentyll man, that had a cursed chydynge wyfe, that wente euery day, and complayned on hym to a religious man, the whiche religious man toke vpon hym by weye of confession to reconcile and accorde them to gether: and the gentyll man was very well contente, that he so shulde do, and came to him therfore. Whan the gentyll man was come, the religious man badde hym shewe his offences and trespaces. No, quod the gentyll man, that nedeth nat: for I knowe verye well my wyfe hath shewed vnto you all the offences that euer I dyd, and moche more.

> "Come all you farmers out of the countrey,
>   Carters, plowmen, hedgers, and all,
> Tom, Dick, and Will, Ralph, Roger, and Humphrey,
>   Leave of your gestures rusticall.
> Bidde all your home-sponne russets adue,
> And sute yourselves in fashions new:
> Honour invits you to delights;
> Come all to court, and be made knights.
> He that hath fortie pounds per annum
>   Shalbe promoted from the plow:
> His wife shall take the wall of her grannam,
>   Honour is sould so dog-cheap now," &c.

¶ Of the two yonge men that rode to Walsyngham.[1] lxxii.

¶ ONE John Roynoldes[2] rode oute of London vpon a tyme towarde Walsyngham, in company of a yonge man of the same cite, that hadde

(1) Consult the new edition of Nares' Glossary, voce *Walsingham*. "This is an Image of oure Ladye. Ergo it is oure Ladye, and here she wyll worke wounders more than in an other place, as she dyd at Walsingham, at Boston, at Lincoln, at Ipswiche, and I cannot tell where."—Wilson's *Rule of Reason*, 1551, 8vo. sign S ii *verso*. In Percy's *Reliques*, ii. 91, is the ballad "As I went to Walsingham." "Have with you to Walsingham" is mentioned as a musical composition in Ward's *Lives of the Professors of Gresham College*. See also Burney's *Hist. of Music*, iii. p. 111. When people employed this form of adjuration, as was formerly very common, they were said, for brevity's sake, "to swear Walsingham." In the play of *The Weakest Goeth to the Wall*, 1600, 4to. Barnaby Bunch the Botcher sings:
"King Richard's gone to Walsingham,
To the Holy Land!"
with what are intended for comic interlocutions. In March, 1502—3, Elizabeth of York, consort of Henry VII. made an oblation of six shillings and eightpence to "oure lady of Walsingham" (*Privy Purse Expenses of Elizabeth of York*, edited by Nicolas, p. 3). This offering may not appear very large, but it was thought a considerable sum to devote to the purpose in those days; for in the *Northumberland Household Book*, ed. 1827, p. 337, we find that the yearly offering of the Earl of Northumberland (Henry Algernon Percy, 5th Earl, b. 1478, d. 1527) to the same shrine was fourpence. There is a fuller account of the Shrine of Walsingham &c. in Chappell's *Popular Music of the Olden Time*, 121, et seqq.

(2) It is just possible that this individual may be identical with the "John Reynolde" mentioned in the subjoined extract from the *Privy Purse Expenses of Elizabeth of York*, under date of December, 1502:—
"Itm̄ the xvth day of Decembre, to John Reynolde for money by him payed to a man that broke a yong hors of the Quenes at Mortymer by the space of v wekes, every weke ii$s$. sm̄^{n}, xs.

nat moche ben accustomed to ryde. So they came to an Inne, where a[1] great companye was lodged. And in the mornynge whan euery man made hym redy to ryde, and some were on horsebacke setting forwarde, John Roynoldes founde his companion, syttynge in a browne study at the Inne gate, to whom he sayd : for shame, man, how syttest thou? Why doste thou nat make the redy to horsebacke, that we myght sette forwarde with companye? I tary (quod he) for a good cause. For what cause, quod Roynoldes? Marye (quod he), here be so many horses, that I can nat telle whiche is myne owne amonge the other, and I knowe well, whan euery man is riden and gone, the horse that remaineth behynde must nedes be myn.

¶ *Of the yonge man of Bruges, and his spouse.*
lxxiii.

¶ A YONGE man of Bruges, that was betrouthed to a fayre mayden, came on a tyme, whan her mother was out of the way, and had to do with her. Whan her mother was come in, anone she perceyued by her doughters chere, what she had done; wherfore she was so sore displesed, that she

(1) Orig. reads *as*.

Quicke Answeres. 93

sewed a diuorse, and wolde in no wyse suffre that the yonge man shulde marye her daughter.

Nat longe after, the same yonge man was maryed to an other mayden of the same parysshe : and as he and his wyfe satte talkynge on a tyme of the forsayde dammusell, to whome he was betrouthed, he fell in a nyce[1] laughyng. Whereat laugh ye, quod his wyfe? It chaunced on a tyme (quod he), that she and I dydde suche a thyng to gether, and she tolde hit to her mother. Therin (quod his wyfe) she playde the foole : a seruante of my fathers playde that game with me an hundred tymes, and yet I neuer tolde my mother. Whan he herde her saye so, he lefte his nyce laughynge.

¶ *Of hym that made as he hadde ben a chaste lyuer.* lxxiiii.

¶ A FELOWE, that toke vpon him, as he had ben the moste chaste and beste disposed man lyuinge, was by one of his felowes on a tyme taken in aduoutry,[2] and sharpely rebuked for it, bycause he prated so moche of chastite, and yet was taken in

---

(1) Foolish. Used in this sense by Chaucer and Shakespeare. See the last edit. of Nares *in voce.*

(2) I have already explained this word to signify adultery. The latter form appears to have been little used by old writers (though it occurs in the *Rule of Reason,* 1551, 8vo. by Thomas Wilson). Thus in Payne's

the same faute. To whome he answerde againe: O fool, doste thou thinke that I did it for bodely pleasure? No! no! I dyd it but onely to subdue my flesshe, and to purge my reynes.

Wherby ye may perceyue, that of all other dissemblynge hipocrytes are the worste.

¶ *Of hym that the olde roode fell on.* lxxv.

¶ As a man kneled vpon a tyme prayenge before an olde rode, the rode felle downe on him and brak his hede; wherfore he wolde come no more in the churche halfe a yere after. At lengthe, by the prouocation of his nighbours, he cam to the churche agayne; and bycause he sawe his nighbours knele before the same rode, he kneled downe lyke wyse and sayde thus: well, I may cappe and knele to the; but thou shalte neuer haue myn harte agayne, as long as I lyue.

By which tale appereth, that by gentyll and courteyse entreatinge mens myndes ben obteyned.[1] For though the people cappe and knele to one in highe authorite, yet lyttell whoteth he, what they thynke.

translation of Erasmus *De Contemptu Mundi*, 1533, fol. 16, we find—
" Richesse engendre and brynge forth inceste and advoutry."
"*Hobs.* Mass, they say King Henry is a very *advowtry man*.
King. A devout man? And what King Edward?"—
            Heywood's *Edward IV*. Part I. 1600.
(1) Orig. and Singer read *opteyned*.

¶ *Of the wydow that wolde nat wedde for bodily pleasure.* lxxvi.

¶ THERE was a ryche wydowe, whiche desyredde a gossyp of hers, that she wold get her an husband: nat for the nyce playe, quod she, but to th'entente he may kepe my goodes to gether, whiche is an harde thinge for me to do, beynge a lone woman. Her gossyp, whiche vnderstode her conceyte, promysed her so to do. Aboute iii or iiii dayes after, she came to her agayne, and sayde: gossyp, I haue founde an husbande for you, that is a prudente, a ware, and a worldlye[1] wyse man, but he lacketh his priuey members, wherof ye force nat. Go to the dyuell with that husbande (quod the wydowe): for though that I desyre nat the nyce playe: yet I wylle that myne husbande shall haue that, where with we may be reconciled, if we falle at variance.

¶ *Of the couetous ambassodour, that wolde here no musike.* lxxvii.

¶ WHAN a couetous man on a time was come vnto a certain cite, whither he was sent as ambassadour for his contrey, anon the mynstrels of the cite came to him to fil his eares with swete din, to th' intente he shuld fyl their purses with money. But

(1) Orig. and Singer read *wordlye*.

he, perceyunge that, bad one of his seruauntes go and telle them, that he coulde nat than intende[1] to here their musicke, but he muste demene great sorow, for his mother was deed. So the minstrels, disapointed of theyr purpose, all sadlye went theyr waye. And whan a worshipfull man of the cite, that was his frende, herd tell of his mourning, he came to visete and comforte him; and so in talkynge together he asked, howe longe a go it was that his mother deceased? Truelye (quod he), hit is xl yere ago. Than his frende, vnderstandinge his subtilte, beganne to laughe hartely.

This tale is aplyed to the couetous men, whiche by al crafte and meanes study to kepe and encreace theyr money and substance; agaynst whiche vyce many thinges ben wryten. As farre (sayth one) is that frome a couetous man that he hath, as that he hath nat.[2] And Diogenes calleth couetousnes the

(1) Give attention.

(2) The covetous man is servaunt and nat mayster vnto riches: and the waster will nat longe be mayster therof. The one is possessed and doth nat possesse; and the other within a shorte whyle leueth the possession of riches."—Erasmus *De Contemptu Mundi*, 1533, fol. 17 (Paynel's translation). So also, in the *Rule of Reason*, 1551, 8vo. Wilson says:—"Is a covetous man poore or not? I may thus reason with my self. Why should a couetous man be called poore, what affinitie is betwixt theim twoo? Marie, in this poynct thei bothe agree, that like as the poore man ever lacketh and desireth to have: so the covetous manne ever lacketh, wantyng the use of that whiche he hath, and desireth stil to have." "To a covetous mā he (Pythagoras) sayde:— "O fole, thy ryches are lost upon the, and are very pouertie."—Baldwin's *Treatise of Morall Phylosophie*, 1547.

heed of all yuels, and saynt Hieronyme calleth couetousnes the rote of all yuels. And for an example, the tale folowinge shall be of couetousnes.

¶ *How Denise the tirant serued a couetous man.*
lxxix.

¶ IT was shewed to Denise the tyran, that a couetous man of the cite had hyd a great some of money in the grounde, and lyued moste wretchedly : wherfore he sente for the man, and commaunded him to go dyg vp the money, and so to deliuer it vnto him. The man obeyed, and delyuered vnto the tyran all the golde and treasure that he hadde, saue a small some, that he priuelye kept a syde : where with he wente in to an other cite, and forsoke Syracuse : and there bought a lytell lande, where vpon he lyued. Whan the tyran vnderstode that he hadde so done, he sent for him agayne; and whan he was come, the tyran sayde to him : syth thou haste lerned nowe to vse well thy goodes, and nat to kepe them vnprofytably, I wyll restore them all to the agayne. And so he dyd.

¶ *Of the olde man, that quengered*[1] *the boy oute of the apletree with stones.* lxxx.

¶ As an olde man walked on a tyme in his orcherd he loked vp, and sawe a boye sytte in a tree, stealynge his apples; whom he entreated with fayre wordes to come downe, and let his apples alone. And whan the olde man sawe, that the boye cared nat for him, by cause of his age, and set noughte by his wordes, he sayde : I haue harde saye, that nat onlye in wordes, but also in herbes, shulde be greatte vertue. Wherfore he plucked vp herbes, and beganne to throwe them at the boye, wherat the boye laughed hartelye, and thought that the olde man hadde ben mad, to thynke to driue him out of the tree with casting of herbes. Than the olde man sayde : well, seynge that nother wordes nor herbes haue no vertue agaynste the stealer of my goodes, I wylle proue what stones wylle do, in whiche, I haue harde men saye, is great vertue; and so he gathered his lappe full of stones, and threwe them at the boye, and compelled hym to come downe, and renne awaye.

This tale sheweth, that they, that bene wyse, proue many wayes, before they arme them.

(1) Conjured.

¶ *Of the ryche man that wolde not haue a glyster.*
lxxxi.

¶ THERE was a certayn riche man on a tyme, whiche felle sycke, to the whose curynge came many phisitians (for flyes by heapes flee to honye). Amonge them all there was one that sayde, that he muste nedes take a glyster, if he wolde be holle. Whan the sicke man, that was nat envred with that medicine, harde hym saye so, he sayde in a great furye : out a dores with those phisitians ! they be madde : for, where as my payne is in my heed, they wolde heale me in myne ****.

This fable sheweth that holsom thynges to them, that lacke knowlege and experyence, seme hurtfull.

¶ *Of hym that feyned hym selfe deed to proue what his wyfe wolde do.* lxxxii.

¶ A YONGE married man on a time, to proue, to here and to se what his wyfe wolde do, if he were deed, came in to his house, whyle his wyfe was forthe wasshynge of clothes, and layd him downe in the floore, as he had ben deed. Whan his wyfe came in, and sawe him lye so, she thought he had ben deed in dede; wherfore she stode euen stylle, and deuysed with her selfe whether was better to bewayle his dethe forth with, or els to dyne fyrste: for she had eate of no meate[1] all the day. All other thinges consydered, she determined to dyne fyrste. So she cut a coloppe of baken, and broyled it on the coles, and began to eate theron a pace; she was so hungrye, that she toke no hede of drynke. At laste, the saltenes of the meate made her to thyrste so sore, that she muste nedes drynke. So, as she toke the potte in her hande, and was goyng downe into her seller to drawe drynke, sodaynely came one of her neyghbours for a cole o' fyre.[2] Wherfore she stepped backe quickely, and though she was right thyrsty, yet she sette the potte a syde; and as [if] her husbande had than fallen downe deed, she beganne to wepe, and with many lamentable wordes to bewayle his dethe; which wepynge and walyng and sodaine dethe of her husbande caused all the neyghbours to come thyther. The man laye stylle in the floore, and so helde his brethe, and closed his eies, that he semed for certayne to be deade. At laste, whanne he thought he had made pastyme inough, and herynge his wyfe saye thus: alas! dere husbande, what shall I do nowe? he loked vp and sayde: full yll, my swete wyfe, excepte ye go quyckely and drynke;

(1) Orig. reads *no meat of*.   (2) Orig. reads *a fire*.

wherwith they al from wepyng tourned to laughynge, specially whan they vnderstode the matter and the cause of her thyrste.

Wherby ye may se, that nat without a good skyl the poete sayde :

Ut flerent oculos erudiere suos.

¶ *Of the poure man, into whose house theues brake by nyghte.*[1] lxxxiii.

¶ THERE was a poore man on a tyme, the whiche vnto theues, that brake into his house on nyght, he sayde on this wyse : syrs, I maruayle, that ye thynke to fynde any thyng here by nyght : for I ensure you I can fynd nothing, whan it is brode day.

By this tale appereth playnly
That pouerte is a welthy mysery.

¶ *Of hym that shulde haue ben hanged for his scoffynge.* lxxxiiii.

¶ THERE was a mery felowe in hygh Almayn, the whiche, with his scoffynge and iestynge, had so moche displeased a great lorde of the countreye, that he thretned to hange hym, if euer he coude take hym in his countrey. Nat longe after, this

(1) This tale, which is a very old one, is also found in *Jests to Make You Merie*, by T[homas] D[ekker] and George Wilkins, Lond. 1607, 4to. and in the *Philosophers Banquet*, 1614, 8vo.

lordes seruauntes toke hym, and hanged he shulde be. Whanne he sawe there was no remedy but that he shulde dye, he sayde : my lorde, I muste nedes suffre dethe, whiche I knowe I haue wel deserued. But yet I beseke you graunte me one peticion for my soule[s] helthe. The lorde, at the instaunce of the people that stode aboute, so it dydde not concerne his lyfe, was contente to graunte it hym. Than the felowe sayde : I desyre you, my lorde, that after I am hanged, to come iii mornynges, fresshe and fastynge, and kysse me on the bare ✱ ✱ ✱ ✱. Where vnto the lorde answered : the deuyll kysse thyne ✱ ✱ ✱ ✱ : and so let hym go.

¶ *Of hym that had his goose stole.* lxxxv.

¶ A MAN, that had a goose stoole from hym, went and complayned to the curate, and desyred hym to do so moche as helpe, that he had his goose again. The curate sayde he wolde. So on Sonday the curate, as though he wolde curse, wente vp in to the pulpit, and bade euery body syt downe. So, whan they were set, he said : why sit ye nat downe ? We be set all redy, quod they. Naye (quod the curate) he that dyd stele the goose sitteth nat. Yes, that I do, quod he. Sayste thou that, quod the curate ? I charge the, on peyne of cursing, to bryng the goose home ageyn.

¶ Of the begger that sayd he was kyn to kyng Philip of Macedone. lxxxvi.

¶ THERE came a begger to kyng Philip of Macedone on a tyme, and prayde the kyng to gyue hym some what; and farther he sayde he was his kynse man. And whan the kyng asked hym which way, he answered and sayde howe they came bothe of Adam. Than the kynge commanded to gyue hym an almes. Whan the begger sawe it was but a small pece of moneye, he sayde, that was nat a semely gyfte for a kynge. The kynge answered: if I shuld gyue euery manne so moche, that is my kynse manne lyke as thou arte, I shulde leaue nothynge for my selfe.[1]

¶ Of Dantes answere to the iester. lxxxvii.

¶ DANTES the poete dwelled a whyle with Can, the Prince de la Scale,[2] with whome also dwelled an

(1) In *Chevræana*, première partie, Paris, 1697, 8vo. p. 119, this story is altered to suit the Emperor Maximilian I.

(2) See Balbo, *Vita di Dante*, edit. 1853. Can de la Scala, mentioned in the text, was one of the sons of Alberto de la Scala, Lord of Verona, and was born in 1292. Some account of Alberto de la Scala may be found in my *Venetian History*.

The anecdote related here probably refers to the earlier period of Dantes acquaintance with the prince, about A.D. 1318-20. Balbo does not seem to have thought this story worthy of notice, though he furnishes one or two other examples of the poet's powers of retort. See also Cinthio's *Hecatommithi, Deca Settima, Novella settima*, edit. 1608.

other Florentyne, that hadde neyther lernynge nor prudence, and was a man mete for nothynge but to scoffe and ieste; but yet with his mery toyes, he so moued the sayd Can, that he dydde greatly enryche hym. And, bycause Dantes dispised his foolysshenes, this scoffer sayd to hym: how cometh it, Dantes, that thou art helde[1] so wyse and so well lerned, and yet arte poore and nedy? I am an vnlerned man and am an ignorant fole, and yet I am farre richer than thou art. To whom Dantes answered: if I may fynde a lord lyke and conformable to my maners, as thou hast founde to thyn, he wyll lyke wyse make me ryche.

¶ *Of hym that had sore eyes.*[2] lxxxviii.

¶ ONE, that had sore eies, was warned of the phisitian, that he shulde in any wyse forbeare drinking or els lose his eies: to whom he sayd: it is more pleasure for me to lose myne eies with drinkynge, than to kepe them for wormes to eate them oute.

(1) Orig. reads *holde*.
(2)   "*On Sore Eyes.*

    Fuscus was councell'd if he would preserve
    His eyes in perfect sight, drinking to swerve;
    But he reply'd, 'tis better that I shu'd
    Loose the, then keep them for the worms as food."
              Wits Recreations, 1640 (p. 35 of reprint 1817)

By this tale ye may perceyue, that it auayleth nat to warne some for theyr owne profytte.

¶ *Of the olde woman that had sore eyes.* lxxxix.

¶ THERE was an olde woman, the whiche bargayned with a surgean to heale her sore eyes; and whanne he hadde made her eies hole, and that she sawe better, she couenaunted that he shulde be payde his moneye, and not before. So he layde a medycyne to her eyes, that shulde not be taken awaye the space of v dayes, in whiche tyme she myghte nat loke vppe. Euery daye, whan he came to dresse her, he bare awaye some what of her householde stouffe, table clothes, candelstickes and disshes. He lefte no thinge, that he coulde carye clene. So whan her eies were hole, she loked vp, and sawe that her householde stouffe was caryede awaye. She sayde to the surgian, that came and required his money for his labour : syr, my promise was to pay you, whan ye made me se better than I did before. That is trouth, quod he. Mary, quod she, but I se worse nowe than I did. Before ye layde medicins to myn eies, I saw moche fayre stouffe in myn house, and now I se nothinge at all.

¶ *Of hym that had the custodi of a warde.* xc.

¶ A CERTAYN man, that had the custody of a ward and his goodes, and in shorte space had spente all awaye, was by the gouernour of the cite commanded to bring in his bookes of *Introitus et exitus*, that is to saye, of entraunce and layenge oute, and to gyue accompte of the orphlins[1] goodes. So whan he came, he shewed fyrste his mouthe, and sayde, here it wente in : and after he shewed vp his ****, and sayde : here hit wente out, and other bookes of *Introitus et exitus* I haue none.

¶ *Of the excellent paynter, that had foule children.* xci.

¶ THERE was a peinter in Rome that was an excellent counnynge man, and bycause he had foule children, one sayde to him : by my feyth, I maruayle that you paynte so goodelye, and gette so foule chyldren. Yea, quod the peynter, I make my chyldren in the darke, and I peynte those fygures by daye lyght.[2]

---

(1) See the new edition of Nares *in voce*. *Orphlin* is merely a contraction of the French *orphelin*.
(2)   "A Skilfull Painter such rare pictures drew,
       That every man his workemanship admir'd :

¶ *Of the scoffer that made a man a south sayer.*
xcii.

¶ THERE was a mery scoffynge felowe on a tyme, the whiche toke on him to teach a man to be a south sayer. Whan they were agreedde, what he shuld haue for his labour, the scoffer sayde to the man : holde ! eate this rounde pellet, and I warant thou shalte be a south sayer. The man toke and put it in his mouth, and began to champe theron, but hit sauered so ill, that he spyt it out forth with, and said : phy ! this pellet, that thou gyueste me to eate, sauereth all of a ***** : Thou sayst trouth (quod the scoffer), nowe thou arte a south sayer; and therefore paye me my money.[1]

¶ *Of the marchaunt of Florence called Charles.*
xciii.

¶ A MARCHAUNT of Florence, called Charles, came frome Auignone to Rome ; and as he sate at souper

> So neere the life in beautie, forme and hew,
> As if dead Art 'gainst Nature had conspir'd.
> Painter, sayes one, thy wife's a pretty woman,
> I muse such ill-shapt children thou hast got,
> Yet mak'st such pictures as their likes makes no man,
> I prethee tell the cause of this thy lot ?
> Quoth he, I paint by day when it is light,
> And get my children in the darke at night."—
> Taylor's *Sculler*, 1612 (*Works*, 1630, iii. 22).

(1) See *Scoggin's Jests*, p. 28 (edit. 1796).

with a great company, one asked him how the
Florentins at Auignone fared? He sayde they
were merye and gladde : for they that dwelle there
a yere (quod he) be as men that were franticke and
out of theyr myndes. Than an other, that sate at
souper with them, asked this Charles, how longe
he had dwelled there. He answerde : vi monethes.
Charles (quod he that asked him the question),
thou haste a great wytte : for hit, that other be
about xii monethes, thou hast fulfylled in halfe a
yere.

¶ *Of the chesshire man called Eulyn.* xciiii.

¶ THER dwelled a man in Chesshyre called Eulyn,
whiche vsed to go to the towne many tymes;
and there he wolde sytte drynkyng tyl xii of the
clocke at nyghte, and than go home. So on a
tyme he caryed a lyttell boye his sonne on his
shulder with him, and whan the chylde fell a slepe
about ix of the clocke, the ale wyfe brought him to
bed with her chyldren. At mydnyghte Eulyn wente
home, and thought no more on his chylde. As
sone as he came home, his wyfe asked for her
chyld. Whan she spake of the chylde, he loked
on his shulder ; and whan he sawe he was not
ther, he said he wist nat where he was. Out vpon

the, horson (quod she), thou hast let mi child fal in to the water (for he passed ouer the water of Dee at a brige). Thou list,[1] hore (quod he) : for if he had fallen into the water, I shuld haue hard him plump.

¶ *Of him that desired to be set vpon the pillori.*

xcv.

¶ THERE were iii loytteringe felowes fell in companye on a tyme, the whiche wente so longe to gether tylle all theyr money was spente. Whan their money was gone, one of them sayd : what shal we do now? By my faith (quod an other), if I might come where preace of people were, I coulde get moneye inough for vs. And I (quod the iii) can assemble people to gether lyghtly. So whan they came in to a lyttelle towne, where a newe pillory was sette vp, he, that sayde he coude lyghtly assemble people to gether, went to the bayly of the towne whiche was a boucher, and desyred him, that he wolde gyue him leaue to haue the 1..aidenheed of the pyllory. Whiche requeste at the fyrste abasshed the bayllye : for he wyst not what he mente therby ; wherfore he toke counsayle of his neighbours, what was best to do, and they

(1) Liest.

bade him set vp the knaue, and spare nat. So whan he was on the pillorye, he loked aboute, and sawe his ii felowes busy in the holes of the bouchers aprons, where thei vsed to put theyr money. Than he said : ther now, go to a pace. The people gaped vp styll and laughed ; and whan he saw that his felowes had sped their maters, and were going away, he said to the peple : now turne the pilori ones about, and than I wyl com downe. So they laughing hartily did. Whan the felow was com downe from the pyllory, the baylie sayde to hym : by my faythe, thou arte a good felowe, and by cause thou haste made vs so good sporte, holde I wyll gyue the a grote to drynke, and so putte his hande in the hole of his apron. But there he founde neuer a penye. Cockes[1] armes! (quod the

(1) (?) God's alms. Browne calls this a *dunghill* oath :—

"With that the *Miller* laughing brush'd his cloathes,
Then swore by Cocke and other dung-hill oathes."
Britannias Pastorals, lib. i. p. 100 (ed. 1625).

It is very commonly found in the early dramatists, and long before the statute of James the First, *By cock* and similar phrases were used, in order to evade the charge of profaning the name of the Deity. It is of particularly frequent occurrence in Skelton's *Magnyfycence* :—

" *Cr* [afty] *Con*[veyance]. Cockes armes, thou shalt kepe the brew-
house boule.
Fol [ye]. But may I drynke thereof whylest that I stare?"
Magnyfycence (Skelton's Works, ed. Dyce, i. 268).

But this writer seems to have employed it rather fantastically than from any desire to soften the oath; for elsewhere in the same piece we find

Quicke Answeres. 111

bayllye) my pourse is pycked, and my moneye is gone. Syr (quod the felowe), I truste ye wyll beare me recorde, that I haue hit nat. No, by the masse, quod he, thou were on the pyllorie the whyle. Than, no force, quod the felow, and wente his waye.

¶ *Of the wydowes daughter that was sent to the abbot with a couple of capons.* xcvi.

¶ THERE was an abbot that had a wydowe to his tenant, which wydow on a tyme sent her doughter with a couple of capons to the abbotte. And whan the mayden came with her present, she founde the abbot syttyng at dyner, to whom she sayd: moch good dutte[1] the, my lorde! Ha! welcome, mayden, quod he. My lorde (quod she), my mother hath sent the here a couple of capons.

By G !, Goddes fote, &c. The practice of swearing had grown to such a pitch in the time of Taylor the Water-Poet, that that writer says (*Against Cursing and Swearing*, Works, 1630, i. 50):—"If the penalty of twelve pence for every oath had been duly paid (as the statute hath in that case provided) I doe verily beleeve that all the coyned money in England would have been forfeited that way." Whitford, in his *Werke for Housholders*, first printed about 1528 (edit. 1533, sign. c. ii et seqq.), relates several remarkable judgments as having fallen, within his personal knowledge, on profane swearers, who were as plentiful and as reckless in the time of Henry VIII. as they were a century later.

(1) Do it.

God a mercy,[1] mayden, quod he. And so he made her to be sette downe atte his owne table to eate some meate. Amonge other meates, the abbotte had than a grene goose with sorell sauce, wherof he dyd eate. So one, that sat at the abbottes tables, gaue the rompe of the goose to the mayde to picke theron. She toke the rompe in her hande, and bycause she sawe the abbot ånd other wete their meate in the sorell sauce, she sayde: my lorde, I pray the gyue me leue to wete myn rompe in thy grene sauce.

¶ *Of the two men, that dranke a pynte of whyte wyne to gether.* xcvii.

¶ THERE came two homely men of the countreye in to a tauerne on a tyme to drinke a pynte of wine. So they satte stylle, and wyste not what wyne to calle for. At last, herynge euerye man call for white wyne as clere as water of the rocke, they bad the drawer brynge them a pynte of whyte wyne as clere as water of the rocke. The drawer, seyng and perceyuyng by their wordes that they were but blont felowes, he brought them a pinte of clere water. The one of them fylled the cuppe, and dranke to his felow, and

(1) God thank you.

Quicke Answeres. 113

sayd : holde, neighbour, by masse, chadde[1] as lefe drynke water, saue only for the name of wyne.[2]

(1) *i.e.* I had.

(2) The beverage of which these persons are here supposed to partake, was probably what, in Charles the First's time, was called *white wine;* which, if diluted, as was no doubt very commonly done, would present a very watery aspect. A very curious account of the wines in vogue during the reigns of Elizabeth and James I. is given by Taylor the Water-Poet in his *Praise of Hempseed.* Cartwright, in his *Ordinary*, has the following passage, describing the various sorts of wine used in his day :—

"*Hearsay.* Thou hast forgotten Wine, Lieutenant, wine.
Slicer.   Then to avoid the grosse absurdity
   Of a dry Battel, 'cause there must some bloud
   Be spilt (on th' enemies side, I mean) you may
   Have there a Rundlet of brisk Claret, and
   As much of Aligant, the same quantitie
   Of Tent would not be wanting, 'tis a wine
   Most like to bloud.   Some shall bleed fainter colours,
   As Sack, and white wine.   Some that have the itch
   (As there are Taylors still in every Army)
   Shall run with Renish, that hath Brimstone in't."

Aligant mentioned in this extract was the wine grown in Alicante, a province of the ancient Kingdom of Valencia. Sometimes it was spelled Aligaunt or Aligaunte :—

   "*Pseud.* In Ganges Iles I thirty rivers saw
      Fill'd with sweet nectar.
   Lach.   O dainty lyer !
   Pseud. Thirty rivers more
      With Aligaunte."
            Timon, a Play, p. 39.

In the *Privy Purse Expenses of Henry VIII.*, under date of Feb. 16, 1530, occurs the following item :—" Paied to the S'geant of the Sello' for iii tonne of white wyne of galiake (Gaillac in Languedoc)." See also *the Northumberland House-Hold Book,* ed. 1827, p. 414; and Taylor's *Penniless Pilgrimage,* 1618 (*Works*, 1630, i. 136).

¶ *Of the doctour that went with the fouler to catche byrdes.* xcviii.

¶ THERE was a doctour on a tyme, whiche desired a fouler, that went to catche byrdes with an owle, that he might go with hym. The byrder was content, and dressed hym with bowes, and set hym by his oule, and bad hym say nothynge. Whan he saw the byrdes alyght a pace, he sayde : there be many byrdes alyghted, drawe thy nettes ; where with the byrdes flewe awaye. The byrder was very angry, and blamed him greatly for his speakyng. Than he promysed to holde his peace. Whan the byrder was in agayn, and many byrdes were alyghted, mayster doctour said in latyn : *aves permultæ adsunt;* wherwith the byrdes flewe away. The byrder came out ryghte angrye and sore displeased, and sayde, that by his bablynge he had twyse loste his pray.[1] Why, thynkest thou, foole (quod the doctour), that the birdes do vnderstand latin? This doctour thought that the vnderstandynge, and nat the noyse, hadde feared awaye the byrdes.

(1) "He that will take the bird, must not skare it"—Herbert's *Outlandish Proverbs*, 1640, No. 41.

¶ *Of hym that vndertoke to teache an asse to rede.* xcix.

¶ There was a certayne tyran,[1] the which, to pylle one of his subiectes of his goodes, commaunded hym to teache an asse to spelle and rede. He sayd it was impossible, except he might haue space inough therto. And whan the tyran bade hym aske what tyme he wolde, he desyred x yeres respite. But yet, bycause he vndertoke a thynge impossible, euerye bodye laughed hym to scorne. He tourned towarde his frendes and sayde : I am nothynge affrayde : for in that space, either I, the asse, or elles my lorde may dye.

By whiche tale appereth, that it is holsome to take leyser inough aboute a thynge that is harde to do, specially whanne a man can nat chose to take hit on hande.[2]

(1) This word, which frequently occurs in the course of the present work, must be understood to be merely equivalent to the Greek τύραννος, a prince whose authority is unlimited by constitutional restraints. There seems to be some ground for the supposition that τύραννος is nothing more than the Doric form of κοίρανος. It may be mentioned that in middle-Greek the word *despota* (δεσπότης) bore no harsher meaning than that of a *petty prince*, acting independently, but acknowledging a suzerain. It is to be found in this sense, I think, almost in all the Byzantine historians.

(2) *i.e.* when the undertaking is no matter of choice.

Tales and

¶ *Of the fryer that confessed the woman.*[1] c.

¶ As a fayre yong woman of the towne of Amilie confessed her to a friere, he beganne to burne so in concupiscence of the flesshe, that he entyced her to consente to his wylle. And they agreed, that she shulde feyne her selfe sycke, and sende

(1) This is a very favourite tale with the early Italian novelists. In Dunlop's *History of Fiction*, ii. 364-5 (Second Edition), the incident is said to have been founded on a real adventure of a French priest. In the following extract from a highly curious pamphlet, it appears in a different form :—

"There was a rich Burgess of Antwerp, a Mercer by his trade, who was a Bawd to his own Wife (though it was against his will or knowledge), but I blame him not, for I doubt hee hath many more fellowes as innocent and ignorant as himselfe, but this was the case, his wife wearing corke shooes, was somewhat light-heel'd, and like a foul player at Irish, sometimes she would beare a man too many, and now and then make a wrong Entrance. The summe was, that shee lov'd a Doctor of Physicke well, and to attaine his company shee knew no better or safer way, than to faine her selfe sicke, that hee under the colour of visitation might feele her pulses, and apply such cordiall Remedies as might either ease or cure her.

In briefe, the Doctor being sent for, comes and finds the Mercer her husband walking in his shop with a neighbour of his, where after a leash of *Congees*, and a brace of *Baza los manus*, the Mercer told him that his Wife is a languishing sicke woman, and withall entreats him to take the paines to walke up the staires, and minister some comfort unto her: Master Doctor, who knew her disease by the Symptomes, ascends up into the Chamber to his longing patient, staying an houre with her, applying such directions and refections, that her health was upon the sudden almost halfe recovered ; so taking his leave of her (with promise of often visitation) he comes downe into the shoppe, where the guiltlesse *Bawd* her husband was, who demanding of the Doctor how all did above, truely quoth hee, much better than when I came, but since I went up, your wife hath had two such strange violent fits upon her, that it would have grieved your very heart to have seene but part of one of them."— Taylor's *Bawd* (Works, 1630, ii. 94).

for hym to shryue her. Within iij dayes after, she feyned her selfe sycke, and laye downe in her bedde, and sente for the same fryere to shryue her. Whan the friere was come, and euery body voided out of the chambre, he went to bedde to the woman, and there laye a longe space with her. Her husbande, suspectyng so longe a confession, came in to the chaumbre; whose sodayne comynge so sore abasshed the fryer, that he went his way and lefte his breche behynde him lyenge on the bedde. Whan her husbande sawe the breche, he sayd a loude, this was nat a frier, but an aduouterer; and for great abbomination of the dede he called all his householde to se hit. And forthe with he went and complayned to the warden of that couent, and thretned to slee hym that had done the dede. The wardyen, to appease his anger, sayde, that suche publysshynge was to the shame of hym and his householde. The man said, the breche was so openly founde, that he coude nat hyde it. The warden to remedy the matter sayde, it was saynt Fraunces' breche, an holy relyke that his brother caryed thither for the womans helth, and that he and his couent wolde come and fetche hit home with procession. With those wordes the man was contente. Anone the warden and his frieres, with the crosse before them, and arayed in hólye vestementes, went to the house and toke vppe the breche; and two of them, on a clothe of sylke, bare it solemlye on hyghe betwene theyr handes, and euerye bodye that mette them kneled downe and kyssed it. So, with great ceremony and songe, they brought it home to their couente. But after, whanne this was knowen, ambassadoures of the same citie wente and complayned therof before the Holy See Apostolyke.

¶ *Howe a chaplen of Louen deceyued an vsurer.* ci.

¶ IN the towne of Louen[1] was a chaplayne called Antonye, of whose merye sayenges and doynges is moche talkynge. As he mette on a daye one or two of his acqueyntaunce, he desyred them home with him to dyner: but meate had he none, nor money. There was no remedy but to make a shefte. Forth he goth, and in to an vserers kytchynne, with whome he was famylier; and priueilye vnder his gowne he caryed oute the potte with meate, that was sod[2] for the vsurers dyner. Whan he came home, he putte oute the meate, and made the pot to be scoured bryght, and sente a boye with the same pot to the vserer to borowe ii grotes theron, and bade the boye take a bylle of his hande, that suche a brasse potte he delyuered hym. The boy

(1) Louvaine   (2) Cooked.

did as he was bydde; and with the money that he hadde of the vsurer, he bought wine for theyr dyner. Whan the vsurer shulde go to dyner, the potte and meate was gone, wherfore he alto chydde his mayde. She said there came no bodye of all the daye, but syr Antony.[1] They asked him, and he sayde he had none. At length, they sayde in erneste, he and no man els had the pot. By my fayth (quod he), I borowed suche a potte vpon a tyme, but I sente hit home agayne; and so called witnes to them, and sayde: lo, howe peryllous it is to deale with men nowe a dayes withoute wrytynge. They wolde lay thefte to my charge, an' if I had no wrytinge of the vsurers hande; and so he shewed oute the wrytinge. And whan they vnderstode the disceyte, there was good laughynge.

¶ *Of the same chaplen and one that spited him.* cii.

¶ THE same Antony dyned on a tyme with a sorte of merye felowes, amonge whome there was one

(1) It is scarcely necessary to mention that formerly all priests were styled Sir. One of John Heywood's interludes is called: *A Play between Johan the Husband, Tyb the Wife, and Sir Johan the Prest.* In an old ballad in the Ashmole Collection, beginning, "Adew I my pretty pussy," there is this passage:—
"But the gyrld ys gon, syr,
With a chokynge bon, syr,
For she hath got Syr John, syr,
And ys oure vyckars wyff."

that greatly spited[1] him in his scoffes and merye iestes. And as they sate laughynge and sporting, one asked whiche was the most reuerent part of mans bodye? One sayd the eie, an other the nose; but Antony, bycause he knew his enuyer wolde name the clene contrarye, sayde the mouth was the most reuerent parte. Naye, quod his enuyer, the parte that we sytte on is the moste reuerent; and bicause they meruayled whye, he made this reason, that he was moste honourable amonge the common people, that was fyrst sette; and the parte that he named was fyrste sette. Whiche sayenge contented them, and they laughed merelye. He was nat a littell proude of his sayenge, and that he hadde ouer come Antonye. This past forth. Four or fyue dayes after, they were bothe bydde to dyner in a nother place. Whan Antony cam in, he found his enuier, that sat talkynge with other, whyle the diner was makynge redy. Antony tourned his backe to him and lette a great ***** agaynst his face. His enuyer, greatlye disdayninge, sayde: walke knaue with a myschiefe, where hast thou ben nourtered? Why and dysdaynest thou, quod Antony? if I had saluted the with my mouthe, thou woldest haue saluted me agayne; and nowe I grete the with that parte of my body, that by

(1) Thwarted, crosse l.

thyn owne sayenge is moste honourable, thou callest me knaue.

Thus he got agayne his praise, that he hadde loste before.

¶ *Of the olde man that put him selfe in his sonnes handes.* ciii.

¶ THERE was a certayne olde man, whiche let his sonne to mary, and to brynge his wyfe and his chyldren to dwelle within him, and to take all the house in to his owne hande and gydinge. So a certeyne tyme the olde man was sette and kepte the vpper ende of the table; afterwarde they sette him lower, aboute the myddes of the table; thyrdely they set him at the nether ende of the table; fourthly he was set amonge the seruantes; fyfthly they made him a couche behynde the halle dore, and cast on him an olde sacke clothe. Nat longe after, the olde man died. Whan he was deed, the yonge mans sonne came to him and sayde: father, I prey you gyue me this olde sacke cloth, that was wonte to couer my graundfather. What woldest thou do with it, sayde his father? forsoth, sayd the chylde, it shall serue to couer you whan ye be olde, lyke as it did my grandfather;—at whiche wordes of the chylde this man ought to haue ben ashamed and sory. For it is wryten: sonne, reuerence and helpe thy father in his olde age, and make him not thoughtfull and heuy in his lyfe, and though he dote, forgyue it him. He that honoreth his father, shall lyue the longer, and shall reioyce in his owne chyldren.[1]

¶ *Of hym that had a flye peynted in his shilde.*
ciiii.

¶ A YONGE man, that on a tyme went a warfare, caused a flye to be peynted in his shylde, euen of the very greatnes of a flye; wherfore some laughed at him and sayde: ye do well, because ye wyll not be knowen. Yes, quod he, I do it because I wyll be knowen and spoken of. For I wyll approch so nere our enemys, that they shall well decerne what armes I beare.

Thus it, that was layde to him for a blame of cowardise, was by his sharpe wytte turned to a shewe of manlynes; and the noble and valiaunt Archidamus sayde: shotte of crossebowes, slynges, and suche lyke ingins of warre are no proffe of manhode; but whan they come and fyghte hande to hande, appereth who be men and who be not.

(1) The original of this is the Fabliau of *La Houce Partie*, in Barbazan's Collection. The Story has been used by Lando, in his *Varii Componimenti*, 1552, 8vo.

¶ *Of th emperour Augustus and the olde men.* cv.

¶ As the noble emperour Augustus on a time cam in to a bayne,[1] he behelde an olde man, that hadde done good seruice in the warres, frotte[2] him selfe a gaynste a marble pyller for lacke of one to helpe to wasshe him. Th emperour, moued with pite, gaue an annuite to fynde hym and a seruaunt to wayte vpon him. Whan this was knowen, a great sorte of olde men drewe them to gether, and stode where as the emperour shulde passe forth by, euerye one of them rubbynge his owne backe with a marble stone. The emperour demaunded why they dyd so? Bycause, noble emperour, sayd they, we be not able to kepe seruantes to do it. Why, quod the emperour, one of you maye clawe and frote an others backe well inough.

¶ *Phocions oration to the Athen[ian]s.*[3] cvi.

¶ PHOCION on a daye, treatynge a longe oration to the people of Athenes, plesed them very wel; and whan he sawe, that they all to gether allowed his wordes, he tourned to his frendes and sayd:

(1) Bath. (2) Rub, from the French, *frotter*.
(3) Phocion, the celebrated Athenian patriot, b. 402 B.C. d. 317 B.C. Full particulars about him may be found in Mr. Grote's *History of Greece*, and in Dr. Smith's *Dictionary of Classical Biography*.

haue I vnwarely spoken any hurte? So moche he perswaded hym selfe, that nothyng coude plese them that was well and truely spoken.

¶ *Of Demosthenes and Phocion.* cvii.

¶ DEMOSTHENES sayde to Phocion: if the Atheniens falle ones in a madnes, they woll slee the. To whom he answered: ye, surely, if they waxe madde they woll slee me; but an' they waxe ones wyse, they wyll slee thee. For Demosthenes spake moche to the peoples pleasure, and spake thynges rather delytable than holsome.

¶ *Of Phocion that refused Alexanders gyfte.* cviii.

¶ WHAT tyme Alexander, kynge of Macedone, sent an hundred besauntes of golde for a gyfte to Phocion, he asked them that brought the money, how it came that Alexander sent it to hym alone, seyng there were many other men in Athenes beside him. They answered: bycause he iugeth you alone to be an honest and a good man. Therfore, quod he, let hym suffre me to be taken to be suche one styll.[1]

Who wolde not wonder at the cleane and vncorrupt courage of this Phocion? He was but a

(1) Orig. reads unnecessarily, *and to be such one styll.*

poore man, and yet the greatnes of the gyft coude nothinge moue hym. Besyde also he shewed, that they the whiche, while they mynistre the common welthe, absteyne not from takyng of gyftes, neyther be nor ought not to be taken for good men.

¶ *Of Denyse the tyranne and his sonne.* cix.

¶ WHAT tyme Denyse the tyranne vnderstode that his sonne, that shulde reigne after hym, had commytted aduoutry with a worshypfull mans wyfe, angerly he sayde to hym: dyd I, thy father, euer suche a dede? The yonge man answered: no, ye had not a kynge to your father. Nor thou, sayde Denyse, art not lyke to haue a sonne a kynge, excepte thou leaue commyttynge of suche wyckedde dedes.

¶ *Of Pomponius the Romayne, that was brought before Mithridates.* cx.

¶ POMPONIUS, a noble man of Rome sore hurte and wounded, was taken and brought before Mithridates, whiche asked hym this questyon: if I cure and heale thy woundes, wylte thou than be my frende? He answered hym agayne thus: if thou wylte be a frende to the Romaynes, thou shalt than haue me thy frende.

This was a noble stomacke, that preferred the welth of his countrey before his owne helth.

¶ *Of Titus and the iester.* cxi.

¶ SUETONIUS sheweth that Titus the father prouoked a scoffer, that stode iesting with euery body, that he shulde lyke wyse saye somewhat to hym. I woll, sayde the scoffer, after ye haue done youre easement. He iested at the emperours countinance; he loked alway as one that streyned hym selfe.

On suche a visaged man writeth Martiall.

> *Utere lactucis, ac mollibus utere maluis.*
> *Nam faciem durum Phebe cacantis habes.*

¶ *Of Scipio Nasica and Ennius the poete.*[1] cxii.

¶ WHAN Scipio Nasica came on a tyme to speake with Ennius the Poete, he asked his mayde at the dore, if he were within; and she sayde, he was not at home. But Nasica perceyued, that her mayster badde her say so, and that he was within; but, for that tyme dissemblynge the matter, he wente his waye. Within a fewe dayes after, Ennius came

(1) The celebrated Latin poet. "Quintus Ennius," Gellius tells us (*N. A.* lib. xvii. cap. 17), "said he had three hearts, because he understood the Greek, Oscan, and Latin languages."

to Nasica, and knockynge at the dore, asked if he were within. Nasica hym selfe spake oute a loude and sayd, he was not at home. Than sayde Ennius: what, manne, thynke you that I knowe not your voyce? Wherevnto Nasica aunsweredde and sayde: what a dishoneste man be you? Whan I sought you, I beleued your mayde, that sayde ye were not at home, and ye wyll not beleue me myn owne selfe.

¶ *Of Fabius Minutius and his sonne.* cxiii.

¶ FABIUS Minutius was of his sonne exhorted on a tyme to gette and conquere a place that was mete for them, and to theyr great auauntage, the whiche thynge he sayde, they myght do with the losse of a fewe men. Wyll ye be one of those fewe, sayde Fabius to his sonne?

Therby shewynge, that it is a poynt of a good capiteyne to care for the lest of his souldiours, and to saue them as nere as he can.[1]

Th' emperour Antoni[n]us Pius loued moche this sentence of Scipio, whiche wolde ofte saye: I hadde leauer saue one citezen, thanne slee a thousande ennemyes.

(1) Orig. reads *coude*.

¶ *Of Aurelian, that was displeased, bycause the cite Tyna was closed agaynst hym.* cxiiii.

¶ WHAT tyme the emperour Aurelian came to the cytie Tyana, he founde hit closed agaynste hym; wherfore all angerly he sayde: I woll not leaue a dogge a lyue in this towne;—whiche wordes reioyced moche his menne of warre, by cause of the great praye and botye that they thoughte to wynne there. One of the citezins, called Heradamon, for feare lest he shuld be slayne amonge the other, betrayed the cyte. Whan Aurelian had taken the cite, the fyrste thinge he dyd, he slewe Heradamon the traytour to his contrey; and to his souldiors that came to hym and desyred, that they myght accordynge to his promyse, ouerren and spoile the cyte, he answered: go to, I sayde, I wolde nat leaue a dogge a lyue; spare nat, kyll al the dogges in the towne.

By this meane the gentyl prince rewarded the traytoure accordinge to his deseruinge, and dispointed the couetise of his souldyours.[1]

(1) So far extends Berthelet's edition, of which the colophon is: Imprinted at London in Flete Strete in the house of Thomas Berthelet nere to the Cundite, at the sygne of Lucrece. ¶ Cum priuilegio. The remaining 26 tales are from the Ed. of 1567.

¶ *Of the Nunne forced that durst not crie.* CXV.

¶ A CERTAYNE Nunne with swellyng of hir bealie was bewrayed to haue companied with a man. And beyng called before the couente, was right sharpely rebuked of the Abbesse, for puttinge of their house to so great a shame. She, to excuse hir-selfe, sayde, she was forced by a yonge man, that came into hir bedde chaumbre, agaynst whom (beynge stronger than she) it was in vain for hir to striue, and force coulde not be imputed to hir for a cryme. Then sayde the Abbesse : thou moughtest haue bene helde excused, if thou haddest cryed. The Nunne sayed : so woulde I haue doone, had it not beene in our Dortour[1] where to crye is contrary to our Religion.

¶ *Of him that sayde he was the Diuelles man.* CXVI.

¶ IN the ciuile seditious time of Edwarde the fourth and Henry the syxte,[2] one chaunced to mete with a company, that quickly asked him : whose man art

(1) Dormitory.
(2) During the Wars of the Roses. In *The First Part of Edward IV.*, by Thomas Heywood, 1600 (Shakesp. Soc. repr. p. 41), Hobs, the Tanner of Tamworth, says :—
"By my troth, I know not, when I speak treason, when I do not. There's such halting betwixt two kings, that a man cannot go upright, but he shall offend t'one of them. I would God had them both, for me.'

thou? Kinge Edwardes, quoth he. Art thou so (quoth they)? and all [set] to beate him : For they were of Henrie's syde. Wherefore to the nexte company that mette him and demaunded whose man he was, he answered : kyng Henries. Art thou so (quoth they), and likewyse all [set] to bete him. For they were on Edwardes parte. The Felow, thus sore beaten, went foorth, and met with another route, who asked him : whose man art thou? He, beynge at his wittes ende what to saye, aunswered : the Dyuelles man. Than the dyuell goe[1] with thee (saide they). Amen (quoth he) : For it is the best maister that I [have] serued this daie.

By this tale ye maye perceiue, how greuouse and perillous all ciuyle sedicions be, so doubtfull may it stand, that a man can not tel on which side to holde. For he that now is stronger another tyme is weaker, as Fortune list to turne hir wheele.

¶ *Of the vplandishe[2] priest, that preached of Charitie.* cxvii.

¶ A PRIEST in the countrey, not the wysest nor the best learned, preached to his parisheners of charitie so vehemently, that he sayed plainely, that it was

---

(1) This word is in the original text printed twice by an oversight. I have struck out the duplicate.

(2) *i. e.* a person dwelling in the uplands or mountainous districts

impossible for anye man to be saued or to come to heauen without charitie, except onely the kynges grace, God saue hym.

¶ *Another sayinge of the same preest.* cxviii.

¶ BEFORE the kynges Maiestyes commissioners sent[1] downe intoo the realme in visytacyon, it chaunced the forsayd preest among other to appere : to whom one of the vysytours (guessyng quickly what docter he was) sayde : Mayster parsone, howe spende you youre tyme ? what rede you ? Forsoothe, syr (sayd the preest), I occupy my selfe in readyng the New Testament. That is very well done (sayd the commissioner). But sir, I pray you, who made the newe Testament? That dyd (said the preest) kynge Henry the eyghte, God haue mercye vpon hys soule ![2]

where the learning of the cities had not very deeply penetrated. Hence the word became synonymous with ignorant and uninformed. Alexander Barclay's fifth eclogue is "Of the Citizen and Uplandish Man." The poem of *Jack Upland* is printed in the old editions of Chaucer and in Wright's *Political Poems and Songs*, 1861, ii. 16. Mr. Wright assigns to it the date of 1401.

"He hath perus'd all the impressions
Of Sonnets, since the fall of Lucifer,
And made some scurvy quaint collections
Of fustian phrases, and *uplandish* words.
Heywood's *Fair Maid of the Exchange*, 1600.

(1) Perhaps *went* is the true reading.

(2) "What must he (the king) do then? He must be a student. He must write God's booke himselfe, not thinking because he is a king [but

¶ *Of the fryer that praysed sainct Frauncis.* cxix.

¶ A FRYER, preachyng to the people, extolled saynct Frauncis aboue confessors, doctours, vyrgins, martyrs, prophetes, yea, and aboue one more than prophetes, John the Baptist, and finially aboue the Seraphicall order of angels; and stil he sayd: yet let vs goe higher. So whan he could goe no further, excepte he shoulde put Christe out of hys place, whiche the good man was halfe afrayed to do, hee sayd aloude: and yet we haue founde no fit place for hym. And staying a lyttell whyle, hee cryed out at laste, sayinge: Where shall we place this holy father? A frowarde felowe, standyng among the audeynce, saide: if thou canst find none other, than set hym here in my place: for I am weary. And so went his way.

¶ *Of hym that warned his wife of wasshynge her face in foule puddell water.* cxx.

¶ A MAN dwellyng in the countrey, takynge his iourney, bad hys wife in his absence playe the good husewyfe, that he at his home comyng[1] might finde

he hath licence to do what he will, as these worldly flatterers are wont to say."—Latimer's *Second Sermon before King Edward VI.* 1549.

(1) *i.e.* coming home.

all thynges well. Swete husbande (quoth she), commaunde what ye wyll, and you shall fynde me obedyense in al thynges. Dere heart (sayd he), I wil you no more but this one thynge, whiche is easye ynough to do. What is that (quoth she)? That you wasshe not your face wyth this water, shewing hir a puddell in a donghill, foule blacke, and stinkynge. As oft as she in his absence went by that puddell, hir mynde was meruallously moued, for what cause hir husebande so diligently warned hir of that thynge onely. Nor shee coulde not perswade hir selfe, but that there was some great thynge in it. To be brefe, it tempted hir so, that she wasshed, that is, she defiled hir face. She loked in the glasse, and was greatly displeased with hir self. Yea, and it was foure or fyue daies after, er shee coulde wasshe out the stynke and steinyng. Whan the good manne came home, hee found his wyfe very pensife and loking angerly. What is the matter (quoth he)? Shee at laste coulde not forbeare, but blamed him for warnyng hir to wasshe in that water, and shewed hym what had chaunced. Why wasshed you in it (quoth he)? I gaue you warnynge, that you shoulde not wasshe therein, to the intente this harme shoulde haue not happned.

By thys tale ye may perceyue, that the more yee

forbydde some women a thynge, the greater desyre they haue to do it.

¶ *Of the husbandman that caused the iudge to geue sentence agaynst him selfe.* cxxi.

¶ AN husbandman in Zeland came before the chiefe ruler of the countrey (whose bull had kyld the poore mans cow) and after he had leaue to speake, hee sayde : my bull leapyng ouer the dyche hath kyld your cow; what is the law? The ruler, mistrustyng no deceit, answered : thou muste paie for hir. Than with licence the poore man sayd : Sir, I failled in my tale : your bull hath kyld my cow. The ruler, beyng a little amoued, sayde : this is another matter. The poore man sayd : Verely it is all one thyng : and you haue truely iudged.

By this tale ye perceyue, that a wyse iudge wyll first know the cause well, and yet will not be hasty to geue sentence. The prouerbe biddeth thus : Iudge righteously the cause of the pore and needy.

¶ *Of the Italian friar that shoulde preach before the B. of Rome and his cardinals.* cxxii.

¶ A FAMOUS frier in Italye, called Robert Liciens,[1] appoincted to preache before the bishop of Rome

(1) Better known as Roberto Caraccioli-Caraccioli. He was born n 1425 at Licio, in the Neapolitan territory, and was thence often called Robertus

and his cardynals beinge in the pulpit, and beholdyng the bishop and his cardinals, enter into the churche with so great pompe, noise, and rufflyng, that no king vse[d] the lyke, and seyng the bishop borne by vi men, and beynge at great leysure set downe, and harkenyng what he would saye, he sayd nought elles but this: Phy on S. Peter! phy on S. Paule! and with rauyng he spit now on the ryght side, and nowe on the left syde: and so, without more ado, shouyng through the preace,[1] gat hym awaie, leauyng them all astonied : some thynkyng hym to bee fallen into a furie : other supposyng him to bee fallen into some heresy, Iewishe or Paganise belefe, that he so burst out intoo suche blasphemies. And whan it was consulted to laie hym in prison, a cardinall, who knewe his wytte, and loued hym, perswaded, that he shoulde fyrste be called before the bishop and certayne cardinals, to here what he would saye. And so beyng inquired, why hee burste out into so horrible blasphemies,

Liciensis. Watt (*Bibliotheca Britannica*, voce *Licio*) mentions only his sermons : but he published several other tracts.

(1) Usually spelt *prease* or *prese*. The word signifies *crowd*. It occurs in this sense in Edwardes' *Damon and Pythias*, composed about 1564.

"Yet shall there no restraynt
Cause me to cese,
Among this prese,
For to encrese
Youre goodly name."
　　　Skelton's *Garlande of Laurell*.

he answered, that he had appointed a farre other argument : and in fewe woordes declared the whole summe of hys sermon. But whan I (sayde he) sawe you lyue so pompously, and in so great delites and pleasures : and on th'other side consydered, howe homely, howe peyneful, and how harde a lyfe the Apostles ledde, whose places you supplie, I gathered, that eyther they were mad, that by so sharpe a waye contended to come to heauen, or els that you holde [1] the streight way to hell. But of you that beare the keyes of heauen, I could not perswade my self to deeme euill. Than what els could I do, but detest theyr foolyshnes whiche, whan thei might after this facion haue liued gloriously in all welth and pleasure, wold rather all their life turment them selfes with watchynges, fastynges and other peynfull labours?

¶ *Of the doctour that sayd, in Erasmus workes were heresies.* cxxiii.

¶ A NOTABLE doctour, preachyng in a solemne audience, sayd, that in Erasmus workes were certayne heresies. Who, beyng come out of the pulpit, was desired of a learned man to shewe foorthe some place hereticall. Hee aunswered, that he had

---

(1) Orig. and Singer read *or els you to holde*.

neuer red Erasmus bookes: hee began once to reade the woorke intitled *Moria*,[1] but by reason it was so high a stile, he feared to fal into some heresy.

¶ *Of the frier that preached at Paules crosse agaynst Erasmus.* cxxiv.

¶ A GREAT clerke, noseld [2] vp in scoole doctours, not well vnderstanding the latin stile and phrase, that than began to florishe apase, and hauynge smale acquaintaunce with the noble authours of the latyne tongue, saide, that Erasmus, with his rhetorike and eloquence went about to corrupte the Byble. For this (quoth he) I dare be bolde to say: that the holy scripture ought not to be mingled with the eloquence of Tully, nor yet of Cicero.[3]

(1) The celebrated *Moriæ Encomium*, of which an English version appeared in 1549.

(2) *Nosled* or *nousled* is the same as *nursled*, brought up. See Todd's Johnson, 1827, in voce *nosled;* and Richardson's Dict. *ibid.* The word is not in Webster or Nares.

(3) The allusion in the text is probably to the paraphrastic version of the New Testament by Erasmus, which had then recently appeared in two volumes, folio (1516). The work did not appear in an English dress til 1548.

¶ *Of an other frier that taxed Erasmus for writyng Germana theologia.* cxxv.

¶ A FRYER, that preached on a tyme too the people, inueighed greatly agaynste Erasmus, because he, in his booke called *Enchiridion*,[1] preysyng the Apostles doctryne, sayde, that theirs was *Germana theologia*, that is to saye in Englishe, the very ryght diuinitee. Lo (sayeth this dotishe fryer), here may ye see, what a man Erasmus is: he sayeth, there is no diuinite but in Germonie, where heretikes are specially fauored and maintayned.

¶ *Of an other that inueighed agaynst the same Erasmus.* cxxvi.

¶ BECAUSE Erasmus wrote, that it wer better for the monke of the charterhouse to eate fleshe than to suffer his brother *Venire in capitis discrimen*, that is to saye, than his brother should stand in ieoperdie of his life: this dotishe doctour interpretat his wordes thus: The charterhouse monke wer better eate fleshe, than his head shoulde a littell ake.[2]

---

(1) *Enchiridion Militis Christiani.* An English translation of this work appeared in 1533, in which Enchiridion is rendered *The Handsome Weapon.*

(2) These pleasantries at the expense of the preachers in the time of

Quicke Answeres. 139

By these tales we may se, what peuysshe preachers haue been in this world: And be thei neuer so foolishe: yet the ignorant people, lacking lerninge to iudge suche matters, thinke them selues well taught, when they be cleane misledde.,

¶ *Of kyng Richarde the iii, and the Northern man.*[1] cxxvii.

¶ AFTER kyng Richard the iii had vsurped the crowne of England, he to staye and stablishe the people, that sore murmured against his dooynges, sent for fyue thousand men out of the North partes vp to London: and as he was mustryng of them in Thickettes feelde, one of the souldiers, cam, and clappynge the kyng on the shoulder, said: Diccon, Diccon, by the mis, ays blith that thaust kyng![2]

Henry VIII. bear perhaps a little hard upon the fraternity. The rendering of Latin authors was not much improved a century or two later.

(1) The Northern men seem to have been formerly favourite subjects for story-tellers and ballad-writers. Martin Parker published a poem called "The King and a Poore Northern man," and there is a ballad entitled "The King and the Northern man." Neither has anything to do with the present tale. No. 95 of the *C. Mery Talys*, of which only a small fragment is at present known to exist, is entitled, "Of the northern man that was all harte."

(2) "Richard, Richard, by the mass I am glad that thou art king!"

¶ *Of the Canon and his man.* cxxviii.

¶ A CANON in Hereforde, that kepte a good house, toke into his seruice a gentilmans sonne, to trane and bryng hym vp, to wayte and serue at the table.[1] So on a day the sayde canon, hauynge many strangers at his bourd, made a signe to his man, that there wanted some thyng. He, nought perceuyng, cam to his maister and sayde : Sir, what lacke you? Seest not, man (quoth he), they haue no bread on the table? Sir, saide his man, there was enough euen now, if they woulde haue let it alone.

¶ *Of the same Canon and his sayd man.* cxxix.

¶ THE same Canon, an other tyme, bad his sayd seruant after supper, go downe and draw a cuppe of wyne, to make his guestes drinke at theyr departing, whom he had before taught, how he shuld take of the couer. So the yong man, bringyng the candell in one hand, and the cup of wine couered in the

---

(1) A very usual practice in those days. At p. 254 of the *Northumberland House-hold Book* (ed. 1827) we find :—

"Two Gentlemen waiters for the Bordes Ende and a servaunt betwixt theim iii—Hannsmen and Yonge Gentlemen at their Fryndes fynding v (as to say Hanshmen [Henchmen] iii and yong Gentlemen iii)."

Orig. and Singer, for *traue* read *trade.*

other, offred it vnto them. His mayster, seyng that, made a token to hym. He, not knowyng wherfore, sayd: Sir, what woulde you haue? Take of the couer (quoth his mayster). Than holde you the candell (saide the seruaunt).

¶ *Of the gentilman that checked hys seruant for talke of ryngyng.* cxxx.

¶ A GENTILMAN, brought vp at London in an In of court, was maryed, and kepte an house in the countrey: and as he sate at supper with his neyghbours aboute hym, vpon an alhalow-daie at night, amonge other communication, he talked of the solemne ringyng of the belles (as was the vsage than). His man, that waited on the table, sayd to his maister: sir, he that were this nyghte in London, shoulde here wonderfull ryngyng, and so began a tale. Hys mayster, not content with his talke, said: Hold thy peace, foole, wilt thou tel me of ringing in London? I know it (I trow) a lyttell better than thou. For I haue beene there an C alhalow nyghtes.

¶ *Of the blynde man and his boye.* cxxxi.

¶ A CERTAYNE poore blynde man[1] in the countrey was ledde by a curst boy to an house where a weddyng was: so the honest folkes gaue him meate, and at last one gaue hym a legge of a good fatte goose: whiche the boy receyuyng kept a syde, and did eate it vp hym selfe. Anon the blynde man saide: Iacke, where is the leg of the goose? What goose (quod the boy)? I haue none. Thou liest (quoth the blinde man), I dyd smell it. And so they wente forth chidyng together, tyll the shrewde boye led the poore man against a post: where hittyng his brow a great blow, he cryed out: A hoorson boy, what hast thou done? Why (quod the boy) could you not smell the post, that was so nere, as wel as the goose that was so farre from your nose?

¶ *Of him that sold two lodes of hey.* cxxxii.

¶ IN London dwelled a mery pleasant man (whiche for [t]his tyme we may call Makeshift[2]) who, beyng

(1) Tricks upon blind persons naturally form a feature in the jest books. The eighty-third adventure of Tyl Owlglass is a practical joke on a blind man, and in *Scoggin's Jests*, 1626, there are one or two examples.

(2) A cheat or rogue. See Rowlands' *Knave of Clubbs*, 1600 (Percy

Quicke Answeres. 143

arrayed somewhat haruest lyke, with a pytcheforke on his necke, went forth in a mornyng and mette with twoo lode of hey comeyng to the citieward, for the whiche he bargayned with the owners to paye xxx shillynges. Whyther shall we bring them, quoth thei? To the Swan in Longe Lane[1]

Soc. ed. p. 18). The word *Shifter* is employed by Rowlands in the *Knave of Harts*, 1613, and by others of our elder writers in the same sense. In the following passage, shift is used to signify a piece of knavery:—
   "*Ferd.* Brother, you lie; you got her with a *shift.*
   Frank. I was the first that lov'd her."
Heywood's *Fair Maid of the Exchange*, 1607 (Shakesp. Soc. ed. p. 87).
   See also Taylor's *Works*, 1630, ii. 144. In his *Sculler*, 1612, the last-mentioned writer introduces a sharper into one of his epigrams under the name of *Mounsieur Shift*, "cozen-german to Sir Cuthert *Theft*" (*Works*, iii. 25).
   (1) Antiently, no doubt, Long Lane ran between hedges into Smithfield; but it appears that even in the early part of Elizabeth's reign building had commenced in this locality. Stow (*Survey of London*, edit. 1720, lib. iii. p. 122) says:—"*Long Lane*, so called from its length, coming out of *Aldersgate Street* against *Barbican*, and falleth into *West Smithfield.* A Place also of Note for the Sale of Apparel, Linnen, and Upholsters Goods, both Secondhand and New, but chiefly for old, for which it is of note." See also p. 284 of the same book, and Cunningham's *Hand Book of London*, edit. 1848, *in voce*, with the authorities and illustrations there given. Rowlands, in his *Letting of Humors Blood in the Head Vein*, 1611, Sign. C, 2, *verso*, celebrates this spot as one of the principal haunts of the pawnbrokers. In *Wits Recreations*, 1640 (edit. 1817, p. 109), there is the following epigram:—
   " He which for 's wife a widow doth obtain,
      Doth like to those that buy clothes in *Long Lane*,
      One coat's not fit, another's too too old,
      Their faults I know not, but th' are manifold."
Day, in the *Parliament of Bees*, 1641, 4º, Sign. G, speaks very disrespectfully of the population of Long Lane in his time. See *Maroccus Extaticus*, 1595 (Percy, Soc. ed. p. 16), Dekker's *Knights' Conjuring*, 1607, ed. Rimbault, p. 54. Webster's Works, by Hazlitt, i. 94, and

by Smithfeeld (quoth he), and soo left them, and sped him thether the next [1] waye. Whan he came to the good man of the Swanne, he asked, if he would bye two good lodes of hey? Yes marie, sayde he. Where be thei? Euen here they come (quoth Makshyft). What shall I paye? sayde the inholder. Foure nobles (quoth hee): but at length they agreed for xx shilling. Whan the hey was come, Makshyft bad them vnlode. While they were doyng so,[2] he came to the inholder,[3] and said: sir, I prai you let me haue my monei: for, while my men be vnloding, I wil goe into the citee to buy a littell stuffe to haue home with me. The good man was content, and gaue it hym. And so he went his way. Whan the men had vnloded the hey, they came and demanded their money. To whom the inholder saide: I haue paid your maister. What master (quoth they)? Mary, quod he, the same man that made you bring the hey hether. We know hym not, quod they. No more doe I (quod he); that same man bargayned with me for the hey, and hym haue I payed: I neyther

Taylor's Works, 1630, Sign. Ggg4. The *Swan* Inn has disappeared, but whether it has merged in the *Barley Mow*, or the *Old Red Cow*, I do not know.

(1) Nearest.

(2) The original reading is, *so while they were doying*.

(3) Innkeeper. This form of the word continued to be used by English writers even in the later half of the seventeenth century.

Quicke Answeres. 145

bought nor sold with you. That is not enough for vs, quod they; and thus thei stroue together. But what ende thei made, I know not. For I thynke Makeshift came not againe to agree them.

¶ *How a mery man deuised to cal people to a playe.* cxxxiii.

¶ A MERY man, called Qualitees,[1] on a tyme sette vp billes vpon postes aboute London, that who so euer woulde come to Northumberlande Place,[2] should here suche an antycke plaie[3] that, both for the mattier and handelyng, the lyke was neuer heard before. For all they that shoulde playe therin were gentilmen.

Those bylles moued the people (whan the daye came) to come thyther thycke and threfolde. Now he had hyred two men to stande at the gate with a boxe (as the facion is), who toke of euery persone that came in a peny, or an halfe peny at the least. So whan he thought the market was at the best, he came to the gate, and toke from the men[4] the

(1) Perhaps this, like Make-shift, was merely intended as a phrase to disguise the real name of the person intended.
(2) Northumberland *Alley* was in Fenchurch Street, and was notorious for bowling-greens, gaming-houses, &c. Probably this is the locality intended. See Cunningham's *Handbook to London*, 596, edit. 1848.
(3) *i. e.* a burlesque play.
(4) Orig. and Singer read *man*.

boxe with money, and geuynge theym their duitie, bade them go into the hall, and see the rome kepte : for hee shoulde gooe and fetche in the plaiers. They went in, and he went out, and lockt the gate faste, and toke the key with hym : and gat hym on hys geldynge, whiche stode ready saddilled without Aldryshegate [1] at an In,[2] and towarde Barnet he roade apace. The people taryed from twoo a clocke tyll three, from three to foure, styll askyng and criyng : Whan shall the plaie begyn ? How long shall we tarye? Whan the clocke stroke foure, all the people murmured and sayed : Wherefore tarye we any longer? Here shall be no playe. Where is the knaue, that hath beguyled vs hyther? It were almes to [3] thruste a dagger throughe hys

(1) Aldersgate. In the *Ordinary*, by W. Cartwright, Moth the Antiquary says :—

"Yclose by *Aldersgate* there dwelleth one
Wights clypen *Robert Moth;* now *Aldersgate*
Is hotten so from one that *Aldrich* hight ;
Or else of Elders, that is, ancient men ;
Or else of Aldern trees which growden there ;
Or else, as Heralds say, from *Aluredus.*"

(2) Inns were not so plentiful at this time as they afterward became. Perhaps the establishment here referred to was the celebrated *Bell* Inn, which was still standing in the time of James the First, and which is mentioned by Taylor the Water-Poet in his *Penniless Pilgrimage*, 1618 (*Works*, 1630, i. 122) :—

" At last I took my latest leave, thus late
    At the Bell Inn, that's *extra* Aldersgate."

(3) *i. e.* it were a charity to thruste, &c. The original and Singer have, "it were almes *it* thruste."

chekes, sayeth one. It were well done to cutte of hys eares, sayeth an other. Haue hym to Newgat! sayeth one : nay, haue hym to Tyburne! sayed an other. Shall wee loose our money thus, saieth he? Shall wee bee thus beguiled, sayeth this man? shulde this be suffered, saieth that man? And so muttrynge and chydyng, they came to the gate to goe oute; but they coulde not. For it was faste lockt, and Qualitees had the key away with him. Now begynne they a freshe to fret and fume: nowe they swere and stare : now they stampe and threaten : for the locking in greeued them more than all the losse and mockery before : but all auayle not. For there muste they abide, till wayes may be founde to open the gate, that they maye goe out. The maidens that shoulde haue dressed theyr maisters suppers, they wepe and crye; boyes and prentises sorow and lament; they wote not what to say, whan thei come home.

> For al this foule araye,
> For al this great frai,
> Qualites is mery ridyng on his waie.(1)

(1) In the original this is printed as prose, perhaps to economize space. *Array*, or *araye*, as it is here spelled, signifies obviously disturbance or clamour. So in the *History of King Arthur*, 1634, Part iii. cap. 134 :—" So in this rumour came in Sir Launcelot, and found them all at a great aray;" and the next chapter commences with, "Aha! what aray is this? said Sir Launcelot."

¶ *How the image of the dyuell was lost and sought.*
cxxxiiii.

¶ IN the Goldesmithes hall, amonge theyr other plate, they had a fair standyng cuppe, with an image of S. Dunstane on the couer, whiche image hadde an image of the dyuell at his foote.[1] So it chaunced at a banket that the sayed image of the dyuell was lost and gone. On the morow after, the bedyll of the company was sent about to serche amonge the goldesmythes, if any suche came to be sold. And lyke as of other[2] he enquired of one, if any man had brought to hym to be solde the foole that sate at sainct Dunstanes foote vpon the couer of the cuppe? What foole meane you? quoth he. Mary, the diuell, sayde the bedill. Why, quoth the other, call ye the diuell a foole; ye shal find him a shrewd foole, if ye haue ought to do with hym? And why seke you for him here amonge vs? Where shoulde I els seke for hym?

(1) Probably the cup bequeathed by Sir Martin Bowes to the Gold smiths' Company, and still preserved, is here meant. See Cunningham's *Handbook of London*, art. *Goldsmiths' Hall*, and for some account of the Bowes family, which intermarried with that of D'Ewes, see *Autobiography and Correspondence of Sir Simonds D'Ewes*, ii. 17, 18. It seems to have been a rather common practice formerly to engrave figures of Saints, representations of the Passion, &c. on the bottom of drinking cups.—See Rowlands' *Knave of Clubbs*, 1600. (Percy Soc. repr. p. 64.)

(2) In the same manner that he inquired of others, &c.

(sayde the bedill). Mary in hell, quoth he, for there ye shall be sure to fynde the dyuell.

¶ *Of Tachas, kyng of Aegypt, and Agesilaus.*
CXXXV.

¶ WHAT tyme Agesilaus, king of the Lacedemonians, was come to Tachas the kyng of Egipt, to aide him in his wars: Tachas beholdyng Agesilaus to bee a man of so litel stature and smal personage tauntyng hym with this scoffe, sayde: The mountayne hath trauayled, Iupiter forbode, but yet hee hathe broughte forth a mouse.[1] Agesilaus beynge offended wyth hys saying, answered: and yet the tyme wyl come, that I shall seeme to the a Lyon. And not longe after, it chaunced through a sedycion that arose amonge the Aegypcyans, whan Agesilaus was gone from him, the king was constreyned to flee to the Persians.

(1) This is related differently in Plutarch. "Now *Agesilaus* being arrived in ÆGYPT, all the chiefe Captaines and Governors of King *Tachos* came to the seashore, and honourably received him: and not they onely, but infinite numbers of Ægyptians of all sorts . . . came thither from all parts to see what manner of man he was. But when they saw no stately traine about him, but an olde gray-beard layed on the grasse by the sea side, a litle man that looked simply of the matter, and but meanely apparelled in an ill-favored thread-bare gowne: they fell a-laughing at him, remembring the merry tale, that a mountaine," &c.— North's *Plutarch*, edit. 1603, fol. 629-30.

¶ *Of Corar the Rhetorician, and Tisias hys scoler.*
cxxxvi.

¶ A CERTAYNE man called Corar, determyned hym selfe for mede[1] to teache the arte of Rhetorycke, with whom a yong man, named Tisias, couenanted on this wyse that he wold pay him his wages, whan he had perfectly learned the scyence. So whan he had lerned the art, he made no haste to paye his teacher, wherfore hys mayster sued hym. Whan they came before the iudges, the yonge man demaunded of hys mayster, what was the effecte of the scyence? He aunswered: In reasonyng to perswade.[2] Than go to, if I perswade these honourable iudges, that I owe you nothing, I wil pay you nothyng: for you are cast in your action. And yf I can not perswade them, than wil I pay you nothing, because I haue not yet perfectly learned the art. Corar wrestyng[3] the yonge mans owne argumente agaynst hym selfe, said: If thou perswade them, that thou oughteste[4] me nothynge, than (accordynge to the couenaunt) thou must nedes pay mee my wages: for thou haste the art perfectly.

(1) Remuneration. (2) To persuade by reasoning.
(3) Turning by force of ingenuity. (4) Owed.

Now yf thou canst not perswade them : yet shalt thou pay mee my wages, because thou arte condemned by the Iudges' sentence to be my detour.

¶ *Of Augustus and Athenodorus the Phylosopher.*
cxxxvii.

¶ WHAT tyme Athenodorus the Phylosopher had (by reason of hys greate age) obteyned lycence of Auguste to depart home, he admonysshed him, that beyng angry, he should neyth saye nor dooe any thyng, before he had by hym selfe rehearsed ouer the xxiiii Greeke letters. Whych saying whan the prince heard, he sayed: he had yet nede of him to teache hym the arte to keepe sylence, by coloure whereof he retayned the olde man about hym a whole yere longer.

By this tale we maie perceyue, that of al things a prince, a ruler, a iudge ought specyally to eschewe wrathe. For the morall booke sayeth : Anger troubleth the mynde, that it can not discerne the truth. And Seneca wryteth, that slowe tarryinge doeth profite in nothyng but in wrathe.

¶ *Of the frenche kyng and the brome seller.*[1]
cxxxviii.

¶ As a Frenche kyng on a tyme was in huntyng, he hapned to lose his companie, and comyng through a brome heath, he herde a poore man and his wife piteously complayne on fortune. The kyng, after he had wel heard the long lamentacion of theyr poore and miserable state, came vnto them, and after a few words he questioned with them howe they liued. They shewed him, how they came daily to that heath, and all the brome, that thei and their asse coud cary home, was lyttell enough to finde theim and their poor children meat. Well (quoth the kyng), loke that you bryng to morow early to the court gate as many bromes as you and your asse can carye, and see that you sell them well. For I warrant you thei shalbe bought apase. They thanked hym, and so he departed from them. Anon came the lordes, knightes, and gentilmen to the kinge, and home they rode. After supper the kyng called them all before hym, and gaue them in commaundement that neither lord, knyght, nor gentilman, should on the morow come into the courte wythout a new brome in his hande.

(1) See Lane's *Arabian Tales and Anecdotes*, 1845, p. 73, for a story similar to this.

Quicke Answeres. 153

For he had a thyng to doe, whiche they shoulde know afterwarde. So on the morowe, whan they come to the court gate, there found they the poore man, his wife and the asse loded with bromes, whiche hee solde to the galauntes of the court, euen as he wolde him selfe. Wherby the sayd poore man was made riche for euer and they lyttell the woorse. Thus whan the kynge sawe the states and gentilmen of his court come in so wel furnished with grene bromes, and consydring the cause wherfore it was, he laughed merilye.

¶ *An other tale of the same frenche kyng.*[1] cxxxix.

¶ THERE chaunced, in a certaine part of the realme, an offyce to fal into the kings handes by the deth of a man which was worth a cccc crounes by the yere. An honest witty gentilman, dwelling therby, trustyng to obteyne the sayde offyce, made as good speede to the courte as hee could, and as soone as he might come to the kynges presence, he kneled downe, and in most humble wise desired his grace to geue vnto hym that offyce, declaring what it was. The king perceiuing how good an

(1) This story is applied by Richard Johnson, editor of the *Pleasant Conceits of Old Hobson the Merry Londoner*, 1607, 4to, to his own purposes. Johnson was an unscrupulous appropriator.

office it was, and thinking therwith to rewarde
some suche one of hys seruauntes, that had well
deserued it, answered quickely, and sayd : My
frend, be content ; you get it not. The gentilman,
heryng those wordes, sayd : I most hertely thancke
your grace ; both I and myne are mooste bounden
to praye for your hyghnesse ;—and so, makynge
lowe obeysaunce, wente his waye. Whan he had
gone a lyttell waye, the kyng commaunded to call
hym againe. Whan he was come backe, the kyng
asked him if he dyd well vnderstand, what answere
he gaue hym. Yes, truely, sayd the gentilman.
What sayd I, quoth the kynge ? Marye, your grace
bad me bee contente, for I shoulde not haue the
offyce. Why dyd you than (quoth the kyng) geue
me so great thankes ? Because, sayde the gentylman, your grace gaue me so sone an answere
without longer suite and losse of tyme, whiche
would haue bene to me a very muche hyndraunce.
For I haue at home a great householde, vnto the
which it behoueth me to loke dylygently, or els
it wyl be wrong wyth me. The kynge, markynge
well the wysedom and dexterytee of the gentylman,
and conceyuyng a fauoure towarde hym, sayd :
Wel, nowe shal you thanke me twyse : for you
shall haue the offyce that you sewe for : and than,
castynge hys eyes vpon hys Chauncelloure, com-

maunded hym, that all suche wrytynges as concerned [t]hys sayd offyce, shoulde wyth al speede bee made oute, that he were at home agayne to ouerloke hys famyly.

¶ *What an Italyan fryer dyd in his preachyng.* cxl.

¶ ROBERT Lyciense, a fryer of Italye (of whome we spake before), preachyng on a tyme with great vehemencye of wordes and gesture, exhorted the prynces and people to make warre agaynste the Turkes and other the enemies of chrystendome: and whan he came to the very effect, and [was] moste hotte and earnest in his tale, he began to wepe, that there were none, that wold to so godly a purpose offer them selfe to be capitains. If this be the let[1] of the mattier, beholde me here, whiche will be nothynge abasshed to cast aside this grey friers coate, and to take vpon mee to be a souldiour, or your capitaine. And euen with that woorde he caste of his vpper coate; and vnderneth he was a playne souldiour, arraied in a skarlet cloke, and a long rapier hangeyng by his side. And in this warlyke apparell, in the personage of a Capitan, he stode and preached halfe an houre.

(1) The obstacle to the matter.

Being sente for of the Cardinals with whom he was familiar, hee was asked what was the pretence of that new example. He answered, that he did it for his wenches pleasure, who familiarly confessed that nothynge in the sayd Robert displeased hir, saue his friers coate. Then saide he to hir: In what apparell shal I best plese you? In a man of warres quoth shee? Than se that you be at my sermon to morow, quoth he.[1]

---

[1] This tale is followed by the colophon, which is: Imprinted at London in Fletestrete, by Henry Wykes. Cum priuilegio ad imprimendum solum.

ADDITIONAL NOTES AND ILLUSTRATIONS.

MERY TALES AND QUICK ANSWERES.

P. 16. *Of him that preched on Saynt Christophers day.*
In *A Booke of Meery Riddles*, 1617 (repr. of ed. 1629, p. 73 of Mr. Halliwell's *Literature of the xvith and xviith centuries Illustrated, &c.* 1851), we have the following:—
     The xvii Riddle
"Who bare the best burthen that ever was borne
At any time since, or at any time befor[n]e
Solution.—It was the asse that bare both Our Lady and her Sonne out of Egypt."

P. 21. *Of the yonge woman that sorowed so greatly her husbondes deth.*
"There was a poor young Woman who had brought herself even to Death's Door with grief for her sick Husband, but the good Man her Father did all he could to comfort her. *Come, Child,* said he, *we are all mortal. Pluck up a good heart, my Child: for let the worst come to the worst, I have a better Husband in store for thee. Alas, Sir,* says she, *what d'ye talk of another Husband for? Why, you had as good have stuck a Dagger to my Heart. No, no; if ever I think of another Husband, may——!* Without any more ado, the Man dies and the Woman, immediately, breaks into such Transports of tearing her Hair, and beating her Breast, that everybody thought she'd have run stark-mad upon it. But, upon second Thoughts, she wipes her Eyes, lifts them up, and cries, *Heaven's will be done!* and turning to her Father, *Pray, Sir,* says she, *about t'other Husband you were speaking of, is he here in the House"—Complete London Jester,* 1771, p. 49.
This story was appropriated by the Editor of *Pasquil's Jests, mixed with Mother Bunch's Merriments,* of which there were several editions, the first appearing in 1604. In Pasquil's Jests, the tale is told of a "young woman of Barnet."
She rowned her father in the eare.
Gower (*Confessio Amantis,* ed. Pauli, Vol. 1. p. 161) has a precisely similar expression :—
    "But whan they rounen in her ere,
    Than groweth all my moste fere."

P. 21. *Of him that kissed the mayde with the longe nose.*

"'Good Sir William, let it rest,' quoth shee, 'I know you will not beleeue it when I haue reuealed it, neither is it a thing that you can helpe : and yet such is my foolishnesse, had it not beene for that, I thinke, verily I had granted your suite ere now. But seeing you vrge me so much to know what it is, I will tell you : it is, sir, your ill-fauoured great nose, that hangs sagging so lothsomely to your lips, *that I cannot finde in my heart so much as to kisse you.*'"—*Pleasant History of Thomas of Reading*, by T. D. circa 1597, p. 73 (ed. Thoms).

P. 26. *Of the Marchaunt that lost his bodgette betwene Ware and Lon[don].*

In *Pasquil's Jests*, 1604, occurs an account substantially similar to the present, of "how a merchant lost his purse between *Waltam* and London."

P. 28. *Of the fatte woman that solde frute.*

" Being thus dispatcht he layes downe Jacke
A peny for the shot :
' Sir, what shall this doe ?' said the boy.
' Why, rogue, discharge my pot !
So much I cald for, but the rest
By me shall nere be paid :
For victualls thou didst offer me ;
Doe and thou woot, I said.'"

The Knave of Clubbs, by S. Rowlands, 1600 (Percy Soc. ed. p. 10).

P. 31.—Wilson introduces the "notable historie" of Papirius Pretextatus into his *Rule of Reason*, 1551, 8°, and it had previously been related in Caxton's *Game and Playe of the Chesse*, 1474.

P. 33. *Of the corrupte man of law.*

" An arch Barber at a certain Borough in the West, where there are but few Electors, had Art enough to suspend his Promise till the Voters, by means of *Bribery*, the *old Balsam*, were so divided, that the casting Vote lay in himself. One of the Candidates, who was sensible of it, came into his little dirty Shop to be shaved, and when the operation was finish'd, threw into the Bason *Twenty Guineas*. The next Day came the other Candidate, who was shaved also, and left *Thirty*. Some Days after this, the first return'd to solicit the Barber's Vote, who told him very coldly, *That he could not promise. Not promise !* says the Gentleman ;

why I thought I had been shaved here! 'Tis true, says the Barber, *you was, but another Gentleman has been trimm'd* since that; however, if you please, I'll trim you again, and then tell you my mind."—*Complete London Jester*, ed. 1771, p. 99.

P. 35. *Conon peaked into the court.*—So in Skelton's *Colin Clout* (Works by Dyce, i, 312), we have:—

"He cryeth and he creketh,
He pryeth and he peketh.
He chides and he chatters," &c.

In the *Posthume Poems of Richard Lovelace, Esq.* 1659, 8o, p. 60, the word is employed in a different sense:—

"Have you not marked their Cœlestial play,
And no more peek'd the gayties of day?"

To peak, however, in the sense in which it is used by Skelton, and in the *Merie Tales*, &c. is of rather frequent occurrence in *Scoggin's Jests*, 1626 (but first printed before 1565); and Gascoigne employs the word in the same manner in the *Steel Glas*, n. d. (1576), 4°. The passage in Gascoigne, which I perused long ago, was brought back to my recollection by a note by the Rev. A. Dyce to Skelton's *Colin Clout*.

P. 38.—See Diogenes Laertius, transl. by Yonge, p. 226. Diogenes the Cynic evidently had Thales in his mind when he said "that mathematicians kept their eyes fixed on the sun and moon, and overlooked what was under their feet."

P. 40. *Of him that dreamed he fonde golde.*
In *Pasquil's Jests*, we are told "how drunken Mullins of Stratford dreamed he found golde." It is the same story.

P. 52. *Gelidus jacet anguis in herba.*—Whoever edited this collection of stories seems to have had a great fancy for quotations. Throughout the *C. Mery Talys*, on the contrary, there is not a single instance of this passion for extracts. Sir Thomas Overbury, in his *Characters* (if at least they were written by him), ed. 1632, sign. K4, describes "An Innes of Court man" as talking "*ends of Latine*, though it be false, with as great confidence as ever *Cicero* could pronounce an oration." I suspect that the *Mery Tales and Quicke Answeres* were collected by some person more or less versed in the classics and in foreign authors, which was probably not the case with the *C. Mery Talys*, which do not smell so much of the inkhorn, as Gascoigne would have said.

P. 54. *Breble-brable.*
In *Twelfth Night*, act iv. sc. 2, Shakespeare makes the Clown use *bibble-babble* in a similar sense; but afterwards in the same drama, act v. sc. 1, *brabble* is put for "a brawl."
This word is no doubt the same as the "pribbles and prabbles" which Sir Hugh uses more than once in the *Merry Wives of Windsor.* See act v. sc. 5.

P. 60. *Of hym that payde his dette with crienge bea.*—Compare the story of "the subtility of Kindlewall the lawyer repayed with the like craft," printed in *Pasquil's Jests*, ed. Gilbertson, n. d. 4°.

P. 65. *All to.*—I fear that I too hastily adopted the self-suggested notion that the former words might be read more properly as one word and in the sense which I indicated. Perhaps as *all to* or *al to* is not uncommonly used by early writers in this way, though the meaning in the present case is not particularly clear, it may be better to restore the original reading.

P. 67. *Of the Inholders wyfe and her ii lovers.* — See Rowlands' *Knave of Clubbs*, 1600, ed. Rimbault, p. 25.

P. 67. *Daungerous of her tayle.* So in the *Schole-house of Women*, 1542, the author says:—
"Plant them round with many a pin,
Ringed for routing of pure golde,
Faire without, and foule within,
And of their tailes have slipper holde."

P. 70. *Of Mayster Vavasour and Turpin his man.*
"A Lawyer and his Clerk riding on the Road, the Clerk desired to know what was the chief Point of the Law. His Master said, if he would promise to pay for their Suppers that Night, he would tell him; which was agreed to. Why then, said the Master, good Witnesses are the chief Point in the Law. When they came to the Inn, the Master bespoke a couple of Fowls for Supper; and when they had supped, told the Clerk to pay for them according to Agreement. O *Sir*, says he, where's your witness."—*Complete London Jester*, ed. 1771, p. 102.

P. 72. One of *Pasquil's Jests* is "how mad Coomes, when his wife was drowned, sought her against the stream." It is merely a new application of the present anecdote.

P. 75. *Of the foole that thought hym selfe deed.*—A story of a similar character occurs in *The Meeting of Gallants at an Ordinarie, or, the Walkes in Powles,* 1604, (repr. 1841 p. 19), where " mine Host" gives an account of "how a yong fellow was even bespoke and jested to death by harlots."

P. 93. *He fell to a nyce laughyng.*

Nice, in the sense of *foolish,* is also used by Gower, who likewise employs the substantive *nicete* in a similar way :—

"But than it were a *nicete*
To telle you, how that I fare !"
Confessio Amantis, lib. vi.

Chaucer employs the word in a similar sense very frequently. In the *Cuckoo and the Nightingale,* is the following passage :—

" To telle his might my wit may not suffice,
For he can make of wise folks ful nice."

P. 103. Crakers.—See the last edition of Nares, voce *Crake* and *Craker.* But an earlier example of the use of the word than any given in the glossary occurs in Lupset's *Works,* 1546, 12mo (*A Compendious Treatise teachying the waie of dying well,* fol. 34 *verso ;* this treatise was first printed separately in 1541). In a reprint of the *C. Mery Talys,* which appeared in 1845, the Editor, not knowing what to make of *crake* and *craker,* altered them, wherever they occurred, to *crack* and *cracker* respectively !

P. 113. Ch' adde.—In *Wits Interpreter, The English Parnassus,* by J. Cotgrave, 1655, ed. 1662, p. 247, is "the Devonshire Ditty," from which the following is an extract :—

"Cockbodikins, chil work no more,
Dost think chi labour to be poor?
No, no, ich chave a do—" &c.

But this phraseology is not peculiar to Devonshire.

P. 113. note 2.—Some additional particulars of interest, relative to ancient wines, may be found in *Morte Arthure,* ed. 1847, pp. 18, 20 ; and in the *Squyer of Low Degre* (Ritson's *Ancient Engl. Met. Ranancees,* iii).

P. 121. *Of the Courtear that ete the hot costerde.*

"An arch Boy being at Table where there was a piping hot Applepye, putting a Bit into his Mouth, burnt it so that the Tears ran down his Cheeks. A Gentleman that sate by, ask'd him, Why he wept? Only, said he, because it is just come into my Remembrance, that my poor Grandmother died this Day Twelvemonth. Phoo! says the other, is that all? So whipping a large Piece into his Mouth, he quickly sympathized with the Boy; who seeing his Eyes brim-full, with a malicious Sneer ask'd him, Why he wept? A Pox on you, said he, because you were not hanged, you young Dog, the same Day your Grandmother died."—*Complete London Jester*, ed. 1771, p. 53.

P. 140.—*Of the Canon and his man. note.*
"When King James came into England, coming to Boughton, hee was feasted by Sir Edward Montague, and his six sonnes brought upp the six first dishes; three of them after were lords, and three more knights, Sir Walter Montague, Sir Sydney, and Sir Charles, whose daughter Lady Hatton is."—*Ward's Diary*, ed. Severn, p. 170–1.

P. 143. *For al this foul araye.*—So, in the *Child of Bristow*, an early metrical legend, we read:—
"When the burges the child gan se,
He seid then, "benedicite,
Sone, what *araye* is this?"
Some later writers thought it necessary to use this word with a qualifying adjective, as *shrewd array*, &c. thus, in fact, reducing it to something like its ordinary and modern signification.

P. 148, *note* 1. See Pepys' *Diary*, 6th ed. I. 29. "They brought me a draft of their drink in a brown bowl, tipt with silver, which I drank off, and at the bottom was a picture of the Virgin with the child in her arms, done in silver."—27th Feb. 1659–60. See also Brydges' *British Bibliographer*, vol. ii. p. 109.

THE END.

www.ingramcontent.com/pod-product-compliance
Lightning Source LLC
Chambersburg PA
CBHW022116230426
43672CB00008B/1403